BEST OF

Tokyo

Wendy Yanagihara

Best of Tokyo
2nd edition – June 2005
First published – February 2002

Published by Lonely Planet Publications Pty Ltd
ABN 36 005 607 983

Australia	Head Office, Locked Bag 1, Footscray, Vic 3011
	☎ 03 8379 8000 fax 03 8379 8111
	🖳 talk2us@lonelyplanet.com.au
USA	150 Linden St, Oakland, CA 94607
	☎ 510 893 8555 toll free 800 275 8555
	fax 510 893 8572
	🖳 info@lonelyplanet.com
UK	72–82 Rosebery Avenue, London EC1R 4RW
	☎ 020 7841 9000 fax 020 7841 9001
	🖳 go@lonelyplanet.co.uk

This title was commissioned in Lonely Planet's
Melbourne office and produced by: **Commissioning
Editor** Rebecca Chau **Coordinating Editor** Lou McGregor
Coordinating Cartographer Kusnandar **Layout
Designer** Adam Bextream **Editors** Andrea Dobbin &
Gabbi Wilson **Cartographers** Corey Hutchison & Tadhgh
Knaggs **Managing Editor** Darren O'Connell **Managing
Cartographer** Corie Waddell **Cover Designer** Radek
Wojcik **Cover Artwork** Jim Hsu **Project Manager** Rachel
Imeson **Mapping Development** Paul Piaia **Thanks to**
Adriana Mammarella & Kate McDonald

Photographs by Lonely Planet Images and Greg Elms
except for the following: p6 Judy Bellah, p11 John
Ashburne, p11 Martin Moos, p17 Frank Carter, p20
Richard l'Anson, p21 Richard l'Anson, p23 Oliver Strewe,
p24 John Ashburne, p25 John Ashburne, p25 Frederic
Silva, p32 Martin Moos, p35 David Ryan, p36 Mason
Florence, p39 Dominic Bonuccelli, p39 Martin Moos,
p42 Adina Tovy Amsel, p47 Adina Tovy Amsel, p48 Chris
Mellor, p49 Bob Charlton, p50 Chris Mellor, p100 Michael
Taylor. **Cover photograph** Shinjuku, Tokyo, Japan,
Stefano Cellai/Photolibrary.com. All images are copyright
of the photographers unless otherwise indicated. Many of
the images in this guide are available for licensing from
Lonely Planet Images: 🖳 www.lonelyplanetimages.com.

ISBN 1 74104 176 7

Printed by Markono Print Media Pte Ltd, Singapore

Acknowledgements Tokyo Metro map © Tokyo Metro 2002

HOW TO USE THIS BOOK

Colour-Coding & Maps

Each chapter has a colour code along the
banner at the top of the page which is also
used for text and symbols on maps (eg all
venues reviewed in the Highlights chapter
are orange on the maps). The fold-out
maps inside the front and back covers are
numbered from 1 to 12. All sights and venues
in the text have map references; eg (3, B2)
means Map 3, grid reference B2. See p128
for map symbols.

Prices

Multiple prices listed with reviews (eg
¥1000/500) usually indicate adult/child
admission to a venue. Exceptions to this rule
are spelt out in practicality lines. Meal cost and
room rate categories are listed at the start of
the Eating and Sleeping chapters, respectively.

Text Symbols

☎	telephone
✉	address
🖳	email/website address
$	admission
☽	opening hours
ℹ	information
Ⓢ	subway
Ⓡ	train
Ⓟ	parking available
♿	wheelchair access
✗	on site/nearby eatery
♣	child-friendly venue
Ⓥ	good vegetarian selection

Contents

INTRODUCING TOKYO 5

NEIGHBOURHOODS 6

ITINERARIES 7

HIGHLIGHTS 8
Tokyo National Museum 8
Meiji-jingū 9
Tsukiji Market 10
Edo-Tokyo Museum 11
Sensō-ji 12
Harajuku & Omote-sandō 14
Mori Art Museum 15
Ginza 16
Kabuki-za 17
Ueno-kōen 18
Sumō Wrestling 20
Sumida-gawa Cruise 22
Yebisu Garden Place 23
Ōedo-onsen Monogatari 24
Akihabara 25
Shibuya 26

SIGHTS & ACTIVITIES 27
Architecture 27
Galleries 28
Museums 30
Parks & Gardens 34
Public Baths & Hot Springs 35
Quirky Tokyo 37
Temples & Shrines 38
Tokyo for Children 40

OUT & ABOUT 43
Walking Tours 43
Day Trips 47
Organised Tours 51

SHOPPING 52
Department Stores & Malls 53
Markets 54
Art & Antiques 55
Music & Books 56
Cameras & Electronics 57
Clothing 58
Food & Drink 60
Homewares 61

Kids' Stuff 61
Jewellery & Accessories 62
Paper & Stationery 63
Specialist Stores 63

EATING 64
Akasaka, Nagata-chō & Toranomon 65
Akihabara & Kanda 66
Asakusa 66
Ebisu & Daikanyama 68
Ginza, Nihonbashi, Tsukiji
  & Yūrakuchō 69
Harajuku & Aoyama 71
Ikebukuro 72
Ōdaiba 73
Roppongi & Nishi-azabu 74
Shibuya 76
Shinjuku 77
Ueno 79

ENTERTAINMENT 80
Bars & Pubs 82
Dance Clubs 86
Cinemas 88
Live Music Venues 89
Contemporary Dance & Theatre 91
Traditional Arts 93
Gay & Lesbian Tokyo 94
Spectator Sports 95

SLEEPING 96
Deluxe 97
Top End 97
Mid-Range 98
Budget 102

ABOUT TOKYO 103
History 103
Government & Politics 105
Economy 106
Environment 106
Society & Culture 107
Arts 108

DIRECTORY 111

INDEX 123

MAP LEGEND 128

From the Publisher

AUTHOR

Wendy Yanagihara

Wendy first toured Tokyo perched on her mother's hip at the age of two. Between and beyond childhood summers spent in Japan, she has travelled through Mexico, Central America, Europe and Southeast Asia and spent stints as a psychology and art student, bread peddler, espresso puller, jewellery pusher, graphic designer and, more recently, co-author on LP's Southeast Asia on a Shoestring, Mexico and Vietnam. She had long dreamed of going back to live in Japan to revive her language skills and reconnect with family and so jumped at the chance to spend a sweltering, quaking, typhoon-lashed (and utterly sublime) season reacquainting herself with Tokyo.

Thank you to Mom, Dad, Jason and the Yamamoto, Maekawa and Giichi families, all of whom are inseparable from my wonderful memories in Japan. Many thanks also to Anazawa Kenichi, Kisaburo Minato and Aaron Held for their insights and our illuminating conversations, and to the countless Tokyoites who acted as expert informants on their complicated city. Thanks to John Ashburne for writing such a solid, knowledgeable and insightful previous edition of this book. To Sarah, Lana, Anja and Enrique, dōmo dōmo for perspective and playtime in Tokyo. And to Eric, tack så mycket for everything. Big thanks to Paul Wellman for shooting the author photo.

The 1st edition of this book was written by John Ashburne.

PHOTOGRAPHER

Greg Elms

Lured by magazine images of exotic locales, Greg has always dreamed of becoming a travel photographer. He completed a Bachelor of Arts in Photography at the Royal Melbourne Institute of Technology, then embarked on a travel odyssey across Australia, Southeast Asia, India, Africa, Europe and the Middle East. He has been photographer for numerous award-winning books, and has worked from Melbourne for 12 years, for a variety of magazines, ad agencies, designers and, of course, book publishers such as Lonely Planet. This Tokyo guide is Greg's seventh Lonely Planet commission.

SEND US YOUR FEEDBACK

We love to hear from travellers – your comments keep us on our toes and help make our books better. Our well-travelled team reads every word on what you loved or loathed about this book. Although we cannot reply individually to postal submissions, we always guarantee that your feedback goes straight to the appropriate authors, in time for the next edition – and the most useful submissions are rewarded with a free book. To send us your updates – and find out about Lonely Planet events, newsletters and travel news – visit our award-winning website: 🖳 **www.lonelyplanet.com/feedback.**

Note: We may edit, reproduce and incorporate your comments in Lonely Planet products such as guidebooks, websites and digital products, so let us know if you don't want your comments reproduced or your name acknowledged. For a copy of our privacy policy visit 🖳 www.lonelyplanet.com/privacy.

Introducing Tokyo

Everyone knows something about Tokyo – if nothing else, that the city is idiosyncrasy incarnate. This is a dizzyingly dynamic, postwar-reinvented megalopolis, where the input of international culture is transformed into output that is uniquely Japanese. From hip-hop to *haute couture*, fusion cuisine to funky technology, Tokyo is synthesis central, its creative denizens mixing sashimi with tahini, or turntables with traditional koto (13-stringed zither) music. What results is the wonderful, weird and decidedly worldly culture of modern Tokyo.

But there are also strong ties to tradition: the kaleidoscopic elegance of a *kaiseki ryōri* (artfully presented multicourse traditional meal), the celebration of cherry blossoms in spring, the clean fragrance of tatami floors in a Japanese inn. Stray a bit beyond – and below – the skyscrapers and buzzing neon and you'll find pockets of tile-roofed houses, old red temple gates hidden within angular alleys, and an attention to design that honours simplicity – and a sense of fun. Traditions such as summer *matsuri* (festivals) and the tea ceremony continue as they have for centuries, forming a part of Tokyo's identity as Japanese, even as it exists as an island of modernity all on its own.

As such an island, Tokyo is naturally an engaging, bizarre, manic and totally fascinating maze-like cosmopolis full of immaculately clad and spectacularly odd citizens. They're fixed on their *keitai* (cellphones), trendy on tomorrow's terms, and cranking the wheels of this city's unpredictable path. Welcome to Tokyo; now go get lost!

Votive figure painted on the ceiling at Sensō-ji, Asakusa (pp12-13)

Neighbourhoods

Hop on the merry-go-round – more commonly known as the JR Yamanote line – going round Tokyo and get to know some of the city's most vibrant quarters. The serene **Imperial Palace** near **Tokyo Station**, in central Tokyo, is a short stroll northwest from the shopping mecca **Ginza** and the flying fish at **Tsukiji Produce & Fish Market**. Northward on the JR line are museums in **Ueno**; westward are department stores in **Ikebukuro**; and lying south are boutiques and bistros around **Ebisu** and **Daikanyama**.

Looping off the JR line are subway lines travelling through old-town **Asakusa** to the northeast or foreigner-friendly clubland **Roppongi** in the south. Must-visit neighbourhoods for those pressed for time include **Shibuya** and **Harajuku**, in the southwest, to rate your coolness quotient against Tokyo's hipster kids; and **Shinjuku** to the west, with its bling-bling of neon and skyscrapers. And lest you forget that Tokyo's a coastal city, trek out to **Ōdaiba** on Tokyo Bay for sea breezes and, of course, shopping.

Off the Beaten Track

When the city drives you mad, escape to the **Nature Study Garden** (p34), the serene green of **Meiji-jingū** (p9) or the walking paths down in **Ōdaiba** (p46). Or curl up with coffee in too-cool-for-school **Daikanyama** (p68).

Irises in full bloom at Meiji-jingū-gyoen (p9)

Elusive Addresses

In Tokyo, finding a place by address alone is challenging at best, even for locals. Apart from *dōri* (main roads), very few streets have names – so, addresses work by narrowing down the location of a building to a number within an area of a few blocks. Note that, in this book, addresses are organised as such: subarea number, block number and building number, followed by subarea and ward. For example, 1-11-2 Ginza, Chūō-ku.

The best strategy is to do as the taxi drivers do and ask directions. Businesses often include a small map in their advertisements and on their business cards and websites to show their locations. Major landmarks are also a boon for navigating Tokyo's maze-like streets.

Kore wa nan to iu dōro desu ka? (What street is this?) Somewhere in Asakusa perhaps?

Itineraries

You may need to take your Tokyo in a concentrated dose, so we've concocted some short and sweet themed itineraries for travellers with only a day or three to sightsee. Sample a fusion of Tokyo's old and new, or feed your soul and senses with art and culture. Either way, you're sure to get a balanced taste of Tokyo elixir.

Tokyo Fusion

For a blend of both old and new: start early (around daybreak, ideally) at **Tsukiji Produce & Fish Market** (p10). After dodging fish scales and entrails, stroll by the striking **Kabuki-za** (p17) to **Ginza** (p16) for a look at Chanel's latest fashion designs. Lunch in **Tokyo International Forum**'s (p27) plaza, then take in the impressive collection of centuries-old pottery and paintings at **Idemitsu Art Museum** (p30). Finish with *yakitori* (grilled chicken) under the tracks of Yūraku-chō.

> ### Lowlights
> - Overblown Roppongi club cover charges
> - Arse-to-armpit crammed rush-hour trains
> - Subway stations requiring GPS to navigate
> - Personal space? What's that?

What's the rush? Ueno station, Ginza line

Spend a morning visiting **Sensō-ji** (p12) and Asakusa, enjoy a local lunch, and then head for Roppongi Hills, where the **Mori Art Museum** (p15) exhibits excellent contemporary art. Dine in Roppongi, then follow the multicultural crowd to the dance floor.

Get a feel for traditional times at **Shitamachi History Museum** (p33); then take immersion to the next level at **Ōedo-Onsen Monogatari** (p24), a modern *onsen* (hot spring) modelled on old Edo.

Museums & Temples

First stop: **Tokyo National Museum** (p8) in Ueno-kōen. Study the map at the park entrance to plan a morning museum crawl. Take lunch in old Asakusa and explore Tokyo's slower side at **Sensō-ji** (p12). Consider taking a rickshaw tour of Asakusa.

Next morning, head for gorgeous **Meiji-jingū** (p9). Afterwards, admire wood-block prints at **Ota Memorial Art Museum** (p32) and follow with a local café lunch. Window-shop down Omotesandō ending at **Nezu Institute of Fine Arts** (p32) to view pan-Asian Buddhist artworks.

Not yet arted out? Find contemporary installations at **Mori Art Museum** (p15) and lunch at one of the gazillion restaurants at Roppongi Hills. View ancient treasures at **Ōkura Shūkokan** (p32) and detour to **Hie-jinja** (p39).

Highlights

TOKYO NATIONAL MUSEUM (10, B1)

Magnificent and unmissable, the **Tokyo National Museum** (Tokyo Kokuritsu Hakubutsukan) is by far the city's best rainy-day option. It's Japan's largest museum, with an awe-inspiring collection of 89,000 examples of Japanese and Asian art, variously donated (and plundered from) across the region. Only a portion of the museum's huge collection is displayed at any time.

INFORMATION

- ☎ 3822 1111
- 🖳 www.tnm.jp
- ✉ 13-9 Ueno-kōen, Taitō-ku
- 💲 ¥420/130
- 🕥 9.30am-5pm Tue-Sun, 9.30am-8pm Fri Apr-Sep
- 🚉 Yamanote line to Ueno (Park exit)
- ♿ excellent
- 🍽 2 restaurants on site

The museum is a five-gallery compound in the eastern section of **Ueno-kōen** (p18). The most important gallery is the **Honkan** (Main Hall). Straight ahead as you enter, its impressive collection includes swords, sculpture, masks, wood-block prints, gorgeous lacquerware and *byōbu* (antique folding screens).

To the right of the ticket booth is the **Tōyōkan** (Gallery of Eastern Antiquities), housing a collection of art and archaeological finds from all of Asia east of Egypt. The majority is from China and Korea, with some pieces dating back to the Bronze Age.

The cupola-capped **Hyōkeikan** displays visiting exhibits and a superb collection of ancient-Japanese art and archaeological finds dating back to the Jōmon period (before 7000 BC).

Most impressive of all is the **Hōryū-ji Hōmotsukan** (Gallery of Hōryū-ji Treasures), featuring 300 priceless Buddhist antiquities once belonging to Hōryū Temple in Nara. As some of the exhibits are more than a thousand years old, this building remains closed during humid or wet weather.

Finally, there's the **Heiseikan** at the back of the complex, featuring Japanese archaeology on the first floor and regularly rotating special exhibitions in its upper galleries.

Arrive early to beat the crowds, and avoid visiting on national holidays and weekends. Entry is free on the second Saturday of each month. End your museum tour with a stroll in the **Tokugawa Shōgun Cemetery**, behind the museum.

DON'T MISS

- Ainu artefacts from Hokkaidō's indigenous people, in the Honkan and Hyōkeikan
- The bronze seated Buddhas in the Hōryū-ji Hōmotsukan
- A spiralling Asian art stroll through the Tōyōkan

The priceless Hōryū-ji Hōmotsukan

MEIJI-JINGŪ

(3, A5)

Meiji-jingū is without a doubt Tokyo's, if not Japan's, most splendid Shintō shrine. Completed in 1920, Meiji-jingū was constructed in honour of Emperor Meiji and Empress Shōken, under whose rule Japan ended its long isolation from the outside world. Unfortunately, like much of Tokyo, it was obliterated by WWII incendiary bombing. Up it sprang again in 1958, next door to Yoyogi-kōen. It might be a reconstruction of the original, but unlike so many of Japan's postwar reconstructions, it was rebuilt with all the features

INFORMATION
- 🖳 www.meijijingu.or.jp
- ✉ 1-1 Yoyogi Kamizono-chō, Shibuya-ku
- 💲 free; garden & museum ¥500
- 🕑 dawn to dusk; garden & museum 9am-4.30pm
- 🚃 Yamanote line to Harajuku (Omote-sandō exit)
- ♿ good
- 🍴 Fujimamas (p71), Home (p71)

DON'T MISS
- Weekend Cos-play-zoku kids vamping on Jingū-bashi (p14)
- Taking a meditative walk through Meiji-jingū-gyoen
- Elaborate displays of traditional archery in January, October and November

of a Shintō shrine preserved: the main building with Japanese cypress, and the huge *torii* (shrine gate) with cypress from Ali Shan in Taiwan.

In the grounds of the shrine (on the left, before the second *torii*) is **Meiji-jingū-gyoen**, a tranquil, shaded park that was formerly an imperial garden. It has some very peaceful walks and is almost deserted on weekdays. Simply stepping into the garden may lower your blood pressure and heighten your sense of spirituality. It's particularly beautiful in June, when the irises burst into bloom.

Meiji-jingū is also a popular spot for weddings, and the subsequent photo sessions, on weekends and public holidays, are a lovely sight (some couples come bedecked in distinguished traditional wedding dress). On New Year's Eve the shrine is the focus, for young and old alike, of Shintō celebrations in the city.

TSUKIJI MARKET   (12, D5)

After it's been fished out of the sea and before it turns up on your sashimi platter, most of Tokyo's seafood transits through Tsukiji Produce & Fish Market. This gigantic pulsating heart at the centre of Tokyo's gastronomic system pumps at an incredible, frenetic, fish-fuelled pace. Workers yell, slice blocks of ice, haul gigantic bluefin tuna, spit, stop for a smoke, laugh, bone an eel, yell some more. Watching the rough-and-ready, hardworking market men and women of Tsukiji,

DON'T MISS
- Namiyoke-jinja, where market wholesalers give thanks for a good day's business
- Sampling wares at their freshest with a sushi breakfast in the market's side streets
- Watching catches being unloaded from the boats at dawn

INFORMATION
- ☎ 3541 2640
- 🖥 www.tsukiji-market .or.jp
- ✉ 5-2 Tsukiji, Chūō-ku
- 💲 free
- 🕐 24hr
- 🚇 Hibiya line to Tsukiji (exit 1)
- ♿ fair
- 🍴 restaurants around the market

Hauling frozen tuna, brrrrr

you can imagine the massive creative communal energy that allowed Tokyo to rise, in less than 200 years, from riverside swamp to one of the world's greatest cities.

Tsukiji keeps market hours, with the pre-dawn arrival of fish and its wholesale auctioning. Though the wholesale market isn't open to the public, there's plenty of seafood-slinging to see if you get there early. Around 7am the market is at its best, but if you get there by 9am you'll catch some of the action. Wear old shoes – there's a lot of muck and water on the floor – and watch out for the electric carts that hurtle along the narrow aisles.

After poking around the fish market, move out into the nearby streets to **Tsukishijō-gaishijō** (external market), northwest of the wholesale market, where hundreds of little stalls sell pottery, cooking equipment, food supplies, baskets, cutlery and packaged foods for a fraction of the prices charged by department stores. This is great souvenir-hunting territory, and terrific photo opportunities abound.

EDO-TOKYO MUSEUM (3, F4)

The oddly modern exterior of the Edo-Tokyo Museum, in the midst of the sumō stables and workshops of blue-collar Ryōgoku, both belies and reflects what's inside – this wonderful museum illustrates Tokyo's rise from the humble riverside origins of Edo (the Eastern capital) to today's fast-forward futuristic metropolis. The museum's layout is imaginatively designed, with a full-size replica of **Nihonbashi** dividing the vast display into recreations of Edo-period and Meiji-period Tokyo.

Large, life-size reconstructions of typical wooden homes and workshops depict scenes from everyday living; these are outdone only by the intricately constructed scale models of the riverside near Nihonbashi, the market and the residence compound of a *daimyō* (feudal lord). Displays also include examples of the wooden wells and water pipes that made up Edo's first waterworks system, and period prints and paintings of daily social life. Meiji-period displays trace the influence of international culture on Tokyo, with photographs, models and multimedia presentations, and there's a detailed exhibit on the Great Kantō Earthquake of 1923, which reduced much of Tokyo to rubble and killed more than 71,000 people.

Each exhibit has informative explanations in English; there's also an excellent free guide service (available in several languages). The docents who escort you around the six floors of the museum can explain the minutiae of Edo and post-Meiji life with an impressive precision and depth. Indeed, the whole museum is a treasure trove of artefacts and anecdotal evidence of life in the capital a century and a half ago.

JOHN ASHBURNE

MARTIN MOOS

The futuristic architectural façade of the Edo-Tokyo Museum

INFORMATION

- ☎ 3626 9974
- 🖥 www.edo-tokyo -museum.or.jp
- ✉ 1-4-1 Yokoami, Sumida-ku
- 💲 ¥600
- 🕙 10am-6pm Tue-Sun
- ⓘ free guided tours in English
- 🚃 Sōbu line to Ryōgoku
- 🅿 reserved car park for tour buses & parking for the disabled
- ♿ excellent
- 🍴 3 restaurants & 2 cafés

DON'T MISS

- The miniature animated model of a kabuki theatre, showing how special effects were cleverly created
- Gorgeous kimonos worn by the style-setting courtesans of Edo
- Checking out the marvellous individual people (and cats and dogs) in the scale model of the Edo market

SENSŌ-JI (11, B1)

The grand old temple Sensō-ji may attract millions of tourists annually, but it is still very much a living, working temple for the people of vibrant, working-class Asakusa.

Indeed, Sensō-ji's very origins are intertwined with the history of the local people. Legend has it that a golden image of Kannon, the Goddess of Compassion, was miraculously fished out of the nearby Sumida-gawa by two fishermen in AD 628. In time, a temple was built to house the image, which has remained on the same spot ever since, giving it its alternative name, Asakusa Kannon-dō.

INFORMATION

- ☎ 3842 0181
- ✉ 2-3-1 Asakusa, Taito-ku
- $ free
- 🕒 6am-5pm; temple grounds 24hr
- 🚇 Ginza & Toei Asakusa lines to Asakusa (exit 1)
- ♿ good
- 🍴 Edokko (p66), Owariya (p67)

The vibrant garden at Sensō-ji

When approaching Sensō-ji from Asakusa subway station, enter through **Kaminari-mon** (Thunder Gate) between the scowling protective deities: **Fūjin**, the god of wind, on the right; and **Raijin**, the god of thunder, on the left. Near Kaminari-mon, you'll probably be wooed by *jinrikusha* (rickshaw) drivers in traditional dress with gorgeous lacquer rickshaws; these energetic, fit guides can cart you around the temple and neighbourhood, providing commentary on architecture and history in English or Japanese. A 30-minute tour costs ¥8000 for two people.

Straight on through the gate is **Nakamise-dōri**, a shopping street set within the actual temple precinct. Everything from tourist trinkets to genuine Edo-style crafts are sold here. There's even a shop selling wigs to be worn with kimonos. Be sure to try the *sembei* (savoury rice crackers) that a few shops specialise in – you'll have to queue though, as they are very popular with Japanese tourists as well.

Nakamise-dōri leads to the main temple compound. Whether the ancient image of Kannon really exists inside is a secret – it's not on public display. Not that this stops a steady stream of worshippers making their way up the stairs to the temple, where they cast coins, clap ceremoniously and bow in a gesture of respect.

In front of the temple is a large incense cauldron, whose smoke is said to bestow health. You will see visitors rubbing the smoke into their bodies through their clothes. If any part of your body (modesty permitting) is giving you trouble, you should give it particular attention when applying the smoke.

Living History

Every day, in some overlooked nook in this ultramodern cosmopolis, an event takes place that probably harks back to centuries before Christ. The *matsuri* (festival), is an integral part of Japanese culture and dates back to the early days of communal rice-cultivation, when townships would gather to pacify the gods and consume vast amounts of fermented rice wine.

Call the local tourist information centre (TIC; p120) for *matsuri* information when you're in town; they are a daily highlight. Once you arrive in the neighbourhood, listen for the sound of *taiko* (drums) and *yokobue* (flutes), and look for crowds in traditional *happi* (half-coats) carrying *mikoshi* (portable shrines). If you follow the *mikoshi*, they'll eventually end up at a temple where you'll also find the fun stuff: people of all ages dressed in *yukata* (cotton kimonos), stalls that contain plastic toys and masks, shallow trays of goldfish to catch with a net of quickly-melting wafer for prizes and *matsuri* treats such as *takoyaki* (fried-octopus balls on a stick) or *okonomiyaki* (Japanese pancakes). But the treat of treats is that you'll be hanging with Tokyoites at their festive best.

Spectacular Sensō-ji lights up at dusk

HARAJUKU & OMOTE-SANDŌ (6)

These neighbouring 'hoods are a deliciously cool duo – a taste of the teenybopper fashion bastion that is Harajuku and the sophisticated flavour of Omote-sandō's couture and cafés.

INFORMATION
- ✉ Meiji-jingū-bashi
- 🚇 Yamanote line to Harajuku (Omote-sandō exit)
- 🍴 Le Bretagne, Natural Harmony Angolo (p72)

Omote-sandō, the boulevard running from Harajuku to Aoyama, is lined with shops carrying everything from Prada to Pokémon to French pastry. But even better are the small, labyrinthine alleys branching off Omote-sandō, where you'll find unique boutiques and charming little cafés rivalling those of Paris. The attraction is, arguably, less about the goods you'll find here than the treasure-trove of people-watching.

The cherry on top is Sunday – and Saturday. Weekends here are all about **Cos-play-zoku** (Costume Play Gang), a subculture consisting mainly of made-up teenage girls from the small towns and bedroom communities around Tokyo. Each weekend, Cos-play-zoku assemble at Harajuku's **Jingū-bashi** (the bridge linking Meiji-jingū with Omote-sandō). The Cos-play-zoku pose, preen and picnic, resplendent in both Goth and punk garb – a grab bag of S&M, queen arch-vamp, Victorian frill, colourful *anime* (animation) superheroes and nurses wrapped in bloodied bandages. Though their get-ups run the gamut, they are united in a sense of pride in their alienation.

DON'T MISS
- Hair salons around Takeshita-dōri alleys promising patrons the perfect puffy Afro or natty dreads
- Picking up a Gloomy Bear souvenir (the Goth Hello Kitty) – try Kiddyland (p61) on Omote-sandō
- Taking a short cut through trendy teen fashion-land to have a moment of peace in front of Tōgō-jinja

What you'll encounter is Tokyo's most fun circus, as each weekend hordes of excited photographers, bewildered tourists and plain voyeurs gather to catch the show. The girls revel in the attention of the paparazzi till dusk, when they hop back on the trains for the slow return to 'normal' life in the faceless housing blocks of Chiba and Kawasaki.

Omote-sandō intersection: where teenage attitude meets café sophistication

MORI ART MUSEUM (9, B3)

Making its debut in 2003, this contemporary art museum boasts an enviable location at the top of Mori Tower in the enormous **Roppongi Hills** development. Roppongi Hills was conceived by developer Mori Minoru, who envisioned that the centralisation of home, work and leisure into an urban microcosm could improve city dwellers' quality of life. The resulting shopping/eating/entertainment/housing complex is embellished with public art and a Japanese garden – it's so big as to warrant guided tours.

Exhibitions on show at the Mori Art Museum tend toward the (mind-bogglingly myriad) multimedia installation type and thus far have been of a respectably high calibre. Shows have included a dazzlingly curated examination of the meaning and history of colour in costume around the world, and the museum's opening exhibition entitled 'Happiness: A Survival Guide to Art and Life', is an intriguing look at the idea of happiness through such lenses as Nirvana and Desire with

INFORMATION

- ☎ 6406 6100
- 🖳 www.mori.art .museum
- ✉ 52 & 53F, Roppongi Hills Mori Tower, 6-10-1 Roppongi, Minato-ku
- 💲 around ¥1500; Tokyo City View ¥1500/500
- 🕓 10am-10pm Mon, Wed, Thu, 10am-5pm Tue, 10am-midnight Fri-Sun; Tokyo City View 9am-1am
- ℹ brochure with map in English; info booths with English-speaking staff
- 🚇 Hibiya & Toei Ōedo lines to Roppongi (Roppongi Hills exit)
- 🅿 car park with 2700 spaces
- ♿ excellent
- ✗ museum café; 200 restaurants at Roppongi Hills

contributing artists ranging from Claude Monet to Yoko Ono. As yet lacking a permanent collection, the museum is only open during its temporary exhibitions. Check the website for current exhibitions.

On the 52nd floor of Mori Tower, **Tokyo City View** offers 360-degrees' worth of just what you might expect. If the floor-to-ceiling windows don't give you enough of an eyeful, ¥500 more gains entrée to the open-air deck. Admission to Tokyo City View includes admission to Mori Art Museum.

DON'T MISS
- Meeting someone 'at the spider' – the sculpture whose given name is actually 'Maman'
- The mass of glass of the Museum Cone and a subway-bound escalator ride through the Metro Hat
- Getting away from the *über-*urbanity in the green Mori Garden

GINZA (12, C5)

Famed for being the Fifth Av of Tokyo, glitzy Ginza has some of the most expensive real estate on the planet. Lined up with their serious façades to the fashionable street are upmarket boutiques such as Hermés, Tif-

INFORMATION
- ℹ TIC brochure
- Ⓜ Ginza, Hibiya & Marunouchi lines to Ginza
- ♿ excellent
- ✗ Edogin Sushi (p69), Ten-Ichi (p70), Shin-Hi-No-Moto (p70)

fany, Chanel, Prada and the big-in-Japan Louis Vuitton. Ginza likes to show off its status, as do the ladies who can afford to shop there – look for crooked elbows proudly bearing designer-label shopping bags. Ginza is also renowned for its excellent, upmarket department stores – try Wakō, Mitsukoshi and Matsuya for starters (p53).

But that's just one facet of Ginza. Wander beyond the main boulevards to find local designers' shops, top-notch traditional *izakaya* (Japanese pubs), excellent Western restaurants, good cinemas and interesting architecture. In the 1870s Ginza was one of the first Tokyo suburbs to modernise, featuring novel Western innovations such as brick buildings, sidewalks and, that startling emblem of modernity, the gas lamp.

If innovation and creativity (coupled with an eye on the profit margins) are emblematic of Ginza, then nowhere is this more evident than in its art galleries. Ginza houses an array of them, each hoping to pro-

DON'T MISS
- Wakō department store's window displays
- The basement food halls of Mitsukoshi and Matsuya for sumptuous edible art
- Test-driving the latest high-tech toys in the ever-entertaining Sony Building

mote the Japanese art world's Next Big Thing. Most are free to enter and gallery-hopping makes a refreshing break between those arduous bouts of parting with heaps of cash everywhere else you go.

But for all the glitter of Ginza, notice the chanting Buddhist monk amid the commercial chaos. Such cameos put it all back into perspective.

Umbrellas indoors? Go check it out for yourself at Yakitori Alley, Ginza

KABUKI-ZA (12, C5)

Opened for the first time in 1889, Kabuki-za burned down in 1921 and was destroyed during its reconstruction in the 1923 Great Kantō Earthquake. The theatre was again destroyed during WWII bombing, although its exterior remained standing. Once again, it was rebuilt, and reopened in 1951. Today, its dramatic and imposing architecture pops out amid the modern buildings of Higashi-Ginza.

Kabuki (stylised Japanese theatre) began in the early 17th century and its first exponent was a maiden of Izumo Taisha shrine who led a troupe of women dancers to raise funds for the shrine. It caught on and was soon being performed with prostitutes in the lead roles. With performances plumbing even greater depths of lewdness, women were banned from kabuki. They were promptly replaced with attractive young men of no less availability. The exasperated authorities issued another decree, this time commanding that kabuki roles be performed by older men. Even today, there are male

INFORMATION
- ☎ 5565 6000
- 🖳 www.shochiku.co.jp/play/kabukiza/theater/index.html
- ✉ 4-12-5 Ginza, Chūō-ku
- 💲 ¥2520-16,800
- 🕑 times vary
- ℹ English earphone guide ¥650 (plus refundable deposit of ¥1000)
- 🚇 Hibiya & Toei Asakusa lines to Higashi-Ginza (exit 3)
- ♿ good
- 🍴 5 restaurants & food stalls

FRANK CARTER

Kabuki performer

actors specialising in female roles (called *onnagata*), as the tradition of an exclusively male cast is still in effect.

Of all Japan's performing arts, kabuki is the most accessible to a non-Japanese audience. Characterized by make-up, stylised movements and elaborate staging, the kabuki performance is accompanied by distinctive *shamisen* (three-stringed lute), flute and drum music called *nagauta*, and in combination they make for a colourful play. Without a doubt, the best place to catch a kabuki performance is at this venerable theatre in Ginza.

How to Kabuki

Kabuki performances can be quite a marathon, lasting from four to five hours. If you're not up to it, you can get tickets for the 4th floor from ¥600 to ¥1000 on the day of the performance and watch only part of the show (ask for *hitomakumi*, a one-act balcony seat); earphone guides are not available in these seats. There are generally two performances, starting at around 11am and 4pm. Call the TIC or the theatre itself for details on current performances and showtimes. Buy a *bentō* (boxed dinner) between acts so you don't run out of steam before the performance ends.

UENO-KŌEN (10)

This is where Tokyo comes to unwind, date, have illicit encounters, spruce up its *shamisen* technique and practise hip-hop dance routines. OK, so it houses dozens of museums, temples, shrines, a zoo, a pond and Tokyo's most architecturally adventurous police box, but its greatest attribute is that it's a park in Tokyo. You'll see folks here who you never dreamed existed.

INFORMATION
- ☎ 5685 1181
- ✉ Ueno-kōen, Taito-ku
- $ free
- ☼ 9am-6pm
- ⓘ info booth outside entrance
- 🚃 Yamanote line to Ueno (Park exit)
- ♿ good
- ✕ Ueno Yabu Soba (p79), Izu-ei (p79)

Say 'peace'

Though the park's official name is Ueno Onshi Kōen, the locals dub it Ueno no Oyama and Westerners call it Ueno Park.

Ueno Hill was the site of a last-ditch defence of the Tokugawa Shōgunate by about 2000 Tokugawa loyalists in 1868. They were duly dispatched by the imperial army and the new Meiji government decreed that Ueno Hill would become one of Tokyo's first parks. It's now home to major attractions such as the **Tokyo National Museum** (p8), the **National Science Museum** (p32), the **National Museum of Western Art** (p32) and the **Tokyo Metropolitan Museum of Art** (p33).

There are two entrances to the park. The main one takes you straight into the museum and gallery area, but it's better to start at the southern entrance near Ueno station and do a little temple viewing on the way to the museums. Slightly to your right at the top of the stairs is the popular meeting spot, the statue of the samurai **Saigō Takamori** walking his dog.

Bear to the far left and follow the wide tree-lined path until you reach the temple **Kiyōmizu Kannon-dō**, modelled on Kiyōmizu-dera in Kyoto. Women who wish to conceive a child leave a doll here for the *senjū* Kannon (the 1000-armed goddess of mercy) and the accumulated dolls are burnt ceremoniously on 25 September every year.

Tent City

Tokyo's homeless population is estimated at more than 30,000, although government figures peg it significantly lower. The most visible settlement of homeless people, though there are outposts under bridges and in parks across Tokyo, undoubtedly exists in Ueno-kōen. There's a vast tent-and-box community living in the park, where daytime is inundated with visitors soaking up museum culture and street performances, but night-time is ruled by this disenfranchised population.

Most of these people are middle-aged men who, despite their circumstances, are still fastidious enough to hang their laundry on plastic clotheslines and line up their shoes outside their makeshift shelters.

Continue along the road following the edge of the pond **Shinobazu-ike**. Through the red *torii* (shrine gate) is **Benten-dō**, a memorial to Benten, patron goddess of the arts, on an island in the pond. Behind the temple you can hire a peddle boat for 30 minutes or a row boat by the hour.

Make your way back to the road that follows the pond and turn left. Where the road begins to curve and leaves the pond behind there is a stair pathway to the right. Follow the path and take the second turn to the left. This path takes you into the grounds of **Tōshō-gū jinja**. Established in 1627 (the present building dates from 1651), this is a shrine which, like its counterpart in Nikkō, was founded in memory of Tokugawa Ieyasu. Miraculously, it has survived Tokyo's many disasters, making it one of the few early Edo structures extant. Don't miss the five-storey **Kanei-ji** (pagoda) to your right as you take the pathway into the shrine. The pathway is fronted by stone *torii* and lined with 200 stone lanterns given as a gift by *daimyō* during the Edo period.

Fun parlour machine slotted in amongst the jumble at Ameyoko Arcade (p54)

SUMŌ WRESTLING (3, F4)

If you're in town during January, May or September, you'd be crazy not to go see a sumō grand tournament. As a spectacle, it is stunning. As sport, it is very exciting. As a living history lesson, it's a chance to see how Shintō

impacted ordinary people's lives. Sumō's whole visual vocabulary is infused with Shintōist motifs and ideas. The wrestling matches that were precursors to sumō made up a part of Shintō ritual prayers for good harvests. This is an ancient, disciplined, tough sport. But best of all, it's seriously fun. The rules are simple: the victor causes any part of his opponent's body other than his feet to touch the ground inside the *dōyo* (ring), or pushes him outside the *dōyo*. Sumō wrestlers look like enormous flabby infants but that flab conceals some prodigious muscle.

INFORMATION

☎ 3623 5111

🖳 www.sumo.or.jp /eng/index.html

✉ 1-3-28 Yokoami, Sumida-ku

$ tickets ¥500-45,000

🕑 opening ceremonies 8.30am; ticket office 10am-6pm

ⓘ brochures in English, English earphone commentary free (plus refundable deposit of ¥2000)

🚇 Sōbu & Toei Ōedo lines to Ryōgoku

♿ fair

✕ arena food stalls

The action during the contests, or *basho,* takes place at the green-roofed **Ryōgoku Kokugikan**. The best ringside seats are bought up by those with the right connections. Box seats accommodate up to four people and are a good way to see sumō in style. Attendees in box seats can order food and tea from servers dressed smartly in *happi* and straw sandals. Non-reserved seats at the back sell for ¥1500, and if you don't mind standing, you can get in for around ¥500. Simply turn up on the day, but get there early as keen punters start queuing the night before. Only one ticket is sold per person to foil scalpers.

When a tournament isn't in session, you can enjoy the neighbouring **Sumō Museum** (☎ 3622 0366; admission free; 🕑 10am-4.30pm Mon-Fri) with its displays of humungous wrestler hand-prints, and the referees' ceremonial clothing. Unfortunately, there are no English explanations, and during tournaments the museum is open only to those attending the tournament.

Even more fascinating, if you can swing it, is a visit to a *heya* (wrestling stable) to witness *rikishi* – literally, 'the power men' – close-up. The most famous of all is **Kokonoe Beya** (4-22-4 Ishihara, Sumida-ku), run by the legendary wrestler-turned-big-boss, Chiyonofuji the Wolf, and you are invited to 'just turn up'. Other stables are not so open to outsiders, but during tournament season, you're likely to see *rikishi* walking around the neighbourhood in *yukata* and topknots. Keep your ears open for their *geta* (wooden sandals) clopping down the street.

Rituals of the Ring

At the beginning of each match, the victor of the last match offers a wooden ladleful of water to the next *rikishi* before entering the ring, for the incoming *rikishi* to perform a symbolic cleansing of the mouth and body. Before entering the ring, each *rikishi* takes a handful of coarse salt to scatter into the ring to purify it. Then, squatting at opposite ends of the ring to face each other, they outstretch their arms to the sides, palms raised, to show their intentions for a fair fight. As they both saunter to the centre of the ring, slapping thighs and bellies, with intimidating stares, they know this process will be repeated again and again for several minutes before they settle into a squat for the final staredown. When both *rikishi* are ready, they suddenly charge at each other and what happens next is an exciting, colourful ritual of unpredictability.

Rikishi perform a pre-bout warm-up, before the excitement begins

SUMIDA-GAWA CRUISE   (11, C2)

INFORMATION
- ☎ 3841 9178
- 🖥 www.suijobus.co.jp
  /english/index.html
- ✉ Azumabashi-mae,
  Asakusa, Taito-ku
- 💲 ¥660/330
- 🕙 9.55am-7.10pm
  (varies seasonally;
  call ahead)
- ⓘ English commen-
  tary and pamphlet
- 🚇 Ginza & Toei
  Asakusa lines to
  Asakusa (exits 4 & 5)
- ♿ good
- 🍴 Hanashibe (p73),
  Positive Deli (p73)

A direct route bringing you closer to Tokyo's river-borne heritage than any amount of terra firma temple-crawling ever could, the 40-minute boat ride from Asakusa down to Ōdaiba is the best way to travel. Locked in by concrete and plexiglass, it's easy to forget that Tokyo's vibrant river systems are the arteries through which its commerce has traditionally flowed from the Edo period to the present day.

Down at water level you see the timber- and landfill-hauling giant barges, the sports fishermen and the *yakata-bune* – floating restaurants where customers traditionally eat *ayu*, sweet fish washed down with sake, atop tatami mats. Alas, these are a dying breed. Along the waterfront, you'll spy hanging laundry and apartment blocks of regular Tokyo folk, and perhaps the prime riverfront encampments of Tokyo's more down-at-heel inhabitants.

As you head downstream from the Azuma-bashi pier in Asakusa, you'll pass under twelve bridges, each painted a different colour, en route for Hinode pier, then the 'entertainment island' Ōdaiba. Either hop off to take in the beautiful gardens at **Hama Rikyū Onshi-Teien** (p34) or stay on till Aomi and the delights of the **Museum of Maritime Science** (pp40-1) or **Venus Fort** (p37). The last boat that'll get you to Hama Rikyū leaves Asakusa at 3.25pm.

DON'T MISS
- The great view of Philippe Starck's Asakusa landmark (Beer foam? Burning flame? Poop? You decide)
- Fishermen in traditional garb
- Cityscape views from river level

Taking a picture of a picture from the Sumida-gawa cruise

YEBISU GARDEN PLACE   (7, C2)

Though not a garden, this place is balanced like a good garden should be – a blend of art, entertainment, dining and shopping, and a museum devoted to beer. Accessible by a moving walkway from the JR Ebisu station, this complex of shops, restaurants and cinema is topped with a 39-floor tower surrounded by an open mall – it's perfect for lazy summer evenings.

OLIVER STREWE

INFORMATION
- ☎ 5423 7111
- 🖥 www.gardenplace
  .co.jp/english
- ✉ 4-20-3 Ebisu,
  Shibuya-ku
- $ free
- ✿ beer museum
  10am-6pm Tue-Sun
- ⓘ pamphlets in
  English
- 🚇 Yamanote line to
  Ebisu (east exit to
  skywalk)
- P parking available
- ♿ excellent
- 🍴 many restaurants,
  cafés & bars on site

Yebisu Garden Place also features the headquarters of Sapporo Breweries and its **Beer Museum Yebisu**. There are lots of interesting exhibits here, the best of which is the 'Tasting Lounge', where you can sample Sapporo's various brews in a pleasant space decorated with European beer steins.

Outdoor cafés scattered around the complex serve light meals as well as cappuccinos and alcoholic drinks, and during the summer there are often live music performances in the courtyard. The restaurants on the 38th and 39th floors of Yebisu Garden Place Tower offer excellent views of Tokyo, and on the ground level the magnificent **Taillevent-Robuchon** (p68) out-Frenches the Gallic brethren themselves with top-notch cuisine.

Yebisu Garden Place is also home to the world-class **Tokyo Metropolitan Museum of Photography**. It is the city's largest, most progressive photographic exhibition space. The wing devoted to computer-generated graphics is highly regarded.

Photo Heaven

Japan's first large-scale museum devoted entirely to photography, **Tokyo Metropolitan Museum of Photography** (☎ 3280 0099; www.syabi.com/english /index_eng.html; 1-13-3 Mita, Meguro-ku; admission varies; ✿ 10am-6pm Tue, Wed, Sat & Sun, 10am-8pm Thu & Fri) is more than just its extensive collection of images. Though there's an emphasis on Japanese photography, the collection includes a respectable variety of international work. Visiting shows are a great mix of the classic and avant-garde. Rounding out the museum's resources are a searchable archive of images, workshops on different types of photographic media and the captivating Images and Technology Gallery, housing examples of photographic equipment old and new.

ŌEDO-ONSEN MONOGATARI (3, E9)

Using natural mineral water piped from 1400m beneath Tokyo Bay, the newly-opened Ōedo-onsen Monogatari is one of the less acquisition-oriented distractions out in Ōdaiba. This 'amusement park', as it bills itself, is modelled on old Edo times, and though the theme might sound a little hokey, the park is attractively designed, with lovely outdoor pools as well as traditional baths. The nude-bathing areas are same-sex only, but common areas where both sexes can mingle are clothing-required – it is a family-friendly destination, after all – and they include outdoor pools for soaking your travel-weary feet.

Admission fees cover the rental of *yukata* and towels, but you can also opt for massage and sand baths, or succumb to steam-induced unconsciousness in tatami resting rooms. Once you've scrubbed, soaked and slackened, wrap yourself in your *yukata* and check out the old-style restaurants and souvenir shops for a postbath bite and browse. Note that there are additional charges on weekends and holidays if you arrive after 6pm and stay for more than four hours.

INFORMATION

- ☎ 5500 1126
- 🖳 info@oom.jp
- ✉ 2-57 Aomi, Kōtō-ku
- $ ¥2700/1500; ¥1900/1500 from 6pm-2am
- 🕑 11am-9am, last entrance at 2am
- ⓘ pamphlet in English
- 🚃 Yurikamome line to Telecom Center
- Ⓟ parking available
- ♿ excellent
- ✕ many restaurants on site

JOHN ASHBURNE

Tattoo Blues

Long the mark of the *yakuza* (mafia), *irezumi* (tattoos) are still largely taboo in Japan. Though body art is becoming slightly more popular with younger people, tattoos are still not as commonplace as in the West. If your body bears a tattoo or few, be discreet when visiting an *onsen* (hot spring). They usually post signs prohibiting entry to tattooed individuals, ostensibly to keep out the *yakuza*. In reality, if the *yakuza* want in, they'll get in – and in all likelihood you won't be mistaken for one. Keep in mind, however, that in some places your ink may get you ejected.

JOHN ASHBURNE

AKIHABARA

Don't drink too much caffeine before braving an overload Akihabara. Incessant recorded sales ji

high-pitched, full-volume, pseudo-prepubescent-female-ebullience smack you in the face the minute you leave the relative sanctuary of Akihabara station. Welcome to **Denki-gai** (Electric Town) and Japanese techno-sales gone haywire. It's something akin to the

JOHN ASHBURNE

INFORMATION
- Yamanote line to Akihabara (Electric Town exit)
- Kanda Yabu Soba (p66)

maddest Asian market you've ever been in, but instead of selling mangosteens they're hawking motherboards – and the sellers are not only pushy, they're prerecorded.

Once Tokyo's dominant centre for discount cameras, then videos, then computers, Akihabara's role as discount-central is declining due to increased competition from huge stores in denser hubs like Shinjuku and Shibuya. Nowadays Akihabara has begun to turn to the boom market in animation and cartoon manga, particularly of the pornographic variety, to round out its fiscal activity. While electronics deals may be competitive with those you're used to at home, it's unusual to find prices that match those of dealers in Hong Kong or Singapore. Still, there is a massive range

DON'T MISS
- Plastic dolls embodying the latest virtual characters
- Bargain bins full of real electronics deals
- Japan's breed of *otaku* (tech geeks), browsing for the latest

of electrical appliances, and Akihabara is still the place to find a digital camera–equipped robot dog, wireless mouse or next year's computer, often at a steep discount. And if you have a short attention span, you'll be perfectly suited to spending half a day flitting from store to noisy store. Some larger stores – Laox (p57) and Softmap (p58) are reliable options – have tax-free sections with export models for sale; don't forget to ask for duty-free. Enjoy. And escape…clutching purchases.

FREDERIC SILVA

Electronic boom in Denki-gai (Electric Town): go haywire!

A blur of people rush around Shibuya

ShibuYA! Not a neighbourhood for contemplating old Edo, nor for museum-fuelled edification – Shibuya is where to head for a rush of Tokyo-today. Prime people-watching is everywhere, whether you're looking down from Starbucks onto the six-way intersection below, or wandering amongst the guys with voluminous Afros and girls in tiny skirts and sheepskin boots.

Leave the JR station via the Hachikō exit and the first thing you're likely to see before the **Hachikō statue** (often obscured by people waiting for their someones) are the giant TV screens of the buildings looming over Shibuya Crossing, notably the several-stories-high screen of the Q-Front Building. If you start down Bunka-mura-dōri (to the right of the 109 Building), you'll find excellent youth-oriented department stores for the knee-high striped socks and vinyl micromini you covet. Or if you seek a different kind of vinyl, you'll also hit a cluster of record shops in Udagawachō, specialising in genres from Motown to J-hip-hop. Stop by the top floor of **Loft** (p61) for souvenirs of toys and ¥200 capsule vending machines. Veering to the left of the 109 Building, you'll walk down Dōgen-zaka, a direct route to clubs and bars and love hotels on the hill to the right. Either way, make a loop around and get lost in the neighbourhood.

INFORMATION	
🚃	Yamanote line to Shi-buya (Hachikō exit)
✗	Reikyō (p76), Sakana-tei (p76)

A Dog's Life
In the 1920s, a professor who taught at what is now Tokyo University kept a small Akita dog named Hachikō. Hachikō accompanied the professor to Shibuya station every morning, then returned in the afternoons to await the professor's arrival. One spring day in 1925, the professor died of a stroke while at work and never came home. Hachikō continued to show up at the station daily to wait for his master until his own death 10 years later. The dog's faithfulness was not lost on the locals, who built a statue to honour his memory.

Sights & Activities

ARCHITECTURE

Roppongi Hills Development (9, B2)
This latest, greatest, gigantic development in Roppongi draws crowds for its mega-shopping complex, the plush cinema that has weekend all-night screenings, the Mori Art Museum and its massive coolness factor. The architecture here includes a cylindrical tunnel called the Metro Hat, a cone of glass leading into the museum tower, and surprisingly, kookily elegant public art everywhere.
☎ 6406 6000 ✉ Roppongi Hills, 6-10-1 Roppongi, Minato-ku $ free ☾ 24hr ◎ Hibiya & Toei Ōedo lines to Roppongi (Roppongi Hills exit) Ⓟ ♿ excellent

Sunshine City Alpa (2, C2)
Billed as 'a city in a building' this is another opportunity to partake in that quintessential Japanese pastime: shopping. Better than that, for a small fee you can get catapulted into the world's second-fastest elevator to the 60th-floor observatory, and peer out across Tokyo's hazy skyline. If you're lucky, you'll catch a glimpse of Mt Fuji out there.
☎ 3989 3331 ✉ 3-1 Higashi-Ikebukuro, Toshima-ku $ observation deck ¥620 ☾ 10am-8.30pm ◎ Yūrakuchō line to Higashi-Ikebukuro (exit 2)

Telecom Center Building (3, E9)
Ōdaiba is full of structures designed by architects gone wild, and the Telecom Center Building is one of those big, shiny baubles. A squat square shape with a hole in the middle of it, its observation deck affords a good view of the city – enlarged by a telescope – if you'd like to see what's going down in the streets of Ōdaiba.
✉ 2-38 Aomi, Kōtō-ku $ ¥600 ☾ 3-9.30pm Tue-Fri, 11am-9pm Sat & Sun ◎ Yurikamome line to Telecom Center ♿ good

Tokyo International Forum (12, B4)
It's a fantastic glass ship plying the urban waters of central Tokyo. No, it's a library, home to international ATMs, free Internet access and an art gallery. No, it's a nocturnal purple and orange-hued space colony, lifting off into the 22nd century. Whatever it is, you'd better check it out.
☎ 5221 9000 🖥 www.t-i-forum.co.jp/english ✉ 3-5-1 Marunouchi, Chiyoda-ku $ free ☾ 8am-11pm ◎ Yamanote & Yūraku-chō lines to Yūraku-chō (exit A4b) ♿ excellent

Tokyo Metropolitan Government Offices (4, A2)
Known as Tokyo Tochō, these colossal towers comprise Tokyo's bureaucratic heartland, and whizzing up to the twin observation decks, 202m or so above urban Shinjuku, is a treat. From the amphitheatre-like Citizen's Plaza below, check out the architecture and complex symmetry of the towers.
☎ 5321 1111 ✉ 2-8-1 Nishi-Shinjuku, Shinjuku-ku $ free ☾ Nth tower 9.30am-10pm Tue-Sun, Sth tower 9.30am-5.30pm Wed-Mon, 9.30am-7pm Sat & Sun ◎ Toei Ōedo line to Tochōmae (exits A3 & A4) ♿ excellent

Tokyo Stock Exchange (12, C2)
Watch the Japanese economy explode to the heavens or disappear up its own stock index – all from

Incredible design at the Tokyo International Forum

the comfort of the 2nd-floor observation deck. It's not quite as mad as during the bubble economy, but still quite a show of mania. Good tours in English require reservations in advance and there are stock trading simulation games for aspiring day-traders. ☎ 3666 0141 ✉ 2-1 Kabutochō Nihombashi, Chūō-ku $ free ⏰ 9-11am & 1-4pm

Mon-Fri ◉ Tōzai line to Kayabachō (exit 11) ♿ good

Tokyo Tower (3, D6)
Although it might play second fiddle to both the Eiffel Tower and Roppongi Hills' new Tokyo City View, Tokyo Tower still affords a great 360-degree view of the city. It retains a sort of oldster charm next to the architectural wonders that have succeeded it and a Wednesday night attraction is live music on the main observatory. ☎ 3433 5111 🖳 www .tokyotower.co.jp/2004 /web/eng ✉ 4-2-8 Shiba-kōen, Minato-ku $ adult/child/student ¥820/310/460 ⏰ 9am-10pm ◉ Toei Ōedo line to Akabanebashi (Akabanebashi exit) ♿ good

---

Station Identification

Ride the rails long enough and your ears will pick up on the cheery five-second-long electronic ditties played at each train station platform. Each station has its own distinct little tune, played when a train arrives at the platform. Some of those catnapping commuters who tune out the announcements broadcast inside the train will often jump up at the sound of their station song, just in time to pop out before the doors close.

GALLERIES

Art galleries in Tokyo usually don't charge an entry fee. They tend to be smaller and less exhausting than the big museums. The largest concentration of art galleries is in Ginza, but they can also be found in the chic neighbourhoods of Shibuya, Harajuku and Aoyama.

Contax Gallery (12, C4)
Contemporary Japanese photography courtesy of this camera maker provides proof that Japan's much vaunted obsession with nature is no myth – the nature and wildlife images are invariably the most impressive. Find classical-style shows at this gallery, next door to the San-ai building on Chūō-dōri. ☎ 3572 1921 ✉ 5F, Kyūkyodō Bldg, 5-7-4 Ginza, Chūō-ku $ free ⏰ 10.30am-6.30pm Tue-Sun ◉ Ginza, Hibiya & Marunouchi lines to Ginza (exits A1 & A2) ♿ good

Ginza Graphic Gallery (12, C5)
Excellent exhibitions featuring graphic design and related artwork are this gallery's forte. The gallery also hosts workshops and talks by visiting artists, covering everything from tiny typography to monumental architecture. ☎ 3571 5206 🖳 www .dnp.co.jp/gallery/ggg /index_e.html ✉ 1F, DNP Ginza Bldg, 7-7-2 Ginza, Chuo-ku $ free ⏰ 11am-7pm Mon-Fri, 11am-6pm Sat ◉ Ginza, Hibiya & Marunouchi lines to Ginza (exits A1 & A2) ♿ good

Laforet Museum (6, A1)
What's in a name? This museum, on the 6th floor of the teenybopper fashionista mecca that is Laforet department store, is gallery or performance space depending on the event. Small film festivals, art installations and launch parties are held here regularly – after browsing the art-as-streetwear on the floors below, check out art-as-art upstairs. ☎ 3475 3127 ✉ 6F, Laforet Bldg, 1-11-6 Jingūmae, Shibuya-ku $ ¥700/500 ⏰ 11am-8pm ☒ Yamanote line to Harajuku (Omote-sandō exit) ♿ excellent

Design Festa

If you're in Tokyo during May or November, be sure to get down to the Tokyo International Exhibition Centre, more fondly known as **Tokyo Big Sight** (3, F8; www.bigsight.jp/english/; Yurikamome line to Kokusai-Tenjijō Seimon), for the biannual Design Festa. Hundreds of young undiscovered designers rent spaces in the massive West Hall to reveal their creative genius.

Design Festa is the place to get your paws on a one-off T-shirt or piece of jewellery. Live bands and passels of DJs make for an excellent day out. Don't be fooled though – that big saw out front is a permanent fixture.

Nikon Salon (12, C5)
Taking a few more artistic risks than the Contax Gallery, the Nikon Salon holds occasional shows by leading overseas photographers as well as home-grown stars. The focus here is more on portraiture and the 'old masters' of photography.
☎ 3248 3783 ✉ 2F, Ginza Crest Bldg, 5-11-4 Ginza, Chūō-ku $ free ⏲ 10am-7pm Mon-Sat Ⓜ Toei Asakusa & Hibiya lines to Higashi-Ginza (exit A1) ♿ good

Parco Museum (5, B2)
The latest incarnation of Tokyo's most progressive independent photo gallery, this gallery exhibits works by leading international artists. High-profile locals such as Shinjuku native Kishin Shinoyama are also represented – Shinoyama opened the museum with luscious, documentary-style Tokyo photos from his book *Tokyo Addict*.
☎ 3477 5873 ✉ 7F, Shibuya Parco Part 3, 15-1 Udagawachō, Shibuya-ku $ ¥700/500 ⏲ 10am-8.30pm 🚆 Yamanote line to Shibuya (Hachikō exit) ♿ excellent

Spiral Building (6, B2)
It may not look very sinuous on the outside with its asymmetrical, geometric shapes, but the Spiral Building's name will make more sense upon entrance. The 1st-floor gallery features changing exhibits, shows, dining and live music. Check out the shop on the 2nd floor for more arty books, jewellery, stationery and stylishly designed loot.
☎ 3498 1171 ✉ 5-6-23 Minami-Aoyama, Minato-ku $ free ⏲ 11am-8pm Ⓜ Chiyoda, Ginza & Hanzōmon lines to Omote-sandō (exit B1) ♿ excellent

Toyota Amlux (2, C2)
Yeah, it's a *car* gallery – a collection of Toyota's classy, expensive works of art. If you want to take a drive in the virtual-reality car experience, you're actually required to have a valid driver's license. It's a six-storey multimedia extravaganza, with short movies, aerodynamic architecture and beauteous visions everywhere (for the mechanically minded). Look for the floor guide in English.
☎ 5391 5900 🖳 www.amlux.jp/english/access ✉ 3-3-5 Higashi-Ikebukuro, Toshima-ku $ free ⏲ 11am-7pm Tue-Sun Ⓜ Yūrakuchō line to Higashi-Ikebukuro (exit 2) P available for fee ♿ good

Winding Down

Has Tokyo chewed you up and spat you out? Or perhaps you have actually shopped 'til you've dropped? Treat yourself to a massage. Women might try **Mammy's Touch** (6, B2; ☎ 3470 9855; 6F, Kobayashi Bldg, 3-13-1 Aoyama, Minato-ku; ¥5000-10,000; ⏲ 11am-9pm Mon & Wed-Fri, 10am-8pm Sat & Sun; Chiyoda line to Omote-sandō, exit B2) for reflexology and calf-massage. Western-style and Shiatsu massage are available for both sexes at **Roppongi Oriental Studio** (9, C2; ☎ 3586 1329; Rm 301, Roppongi Five Bldg, 5-18-20 Roppongi, Minato-ku; ¥5000; ⏲ 10am-9pm; Hibiya line to Roppongi, exit 3).

MUSEUMS

Bashō Museum (3,F5')
Dedicated to the revered haiku poet Bashō, this little museum sits on the bank of the Sumida-gawa. Though there are no English translations, the peaceful place is filled with his poetry and personal possessions. There's also a small garden with a memorial shrine, and a statue of the poet – a contemplative spot.
☎ 3631 1448 ✉ 1-6-3 Tokiwa, Kōtō-ku $ ¥100 🕙 9.30am-5pm 🚇 Toei Ōedo & Toei Shinjuku lines to Morishita (exit A1)

Bunkamura Museum & Theatre Cocoon (5, A2)
The boat-like behemoth that is Bunkamura Arts Centre houses a cinema, theatre, concert hall and art gallery. Exhibitions here tend towards foreign modern art – an Andy Warhol retrospective, for example – and it's worth checking out the excellent shows, including its musical and theatrical performances.
☎ 3477 9111 🖳 www .bunkamura.co.jp /english ✉ 2-24-1 Dōgenzaka, Shibuya-ku

$ adult/18 & under/ student ¥1000/500/800 🕙 10am-7pm Sun-Thu, 10am-9pm Fri & Sat 🚇 Yamanote line to Shibuya (Hachikō exit) ♿ excellent

Fukagawa Edo Museum (3, F5)
It may not be quite as slick or well-outfitted as the Edo-Tokyo Museum (p11), but this is still a fun look at Edo. There's a life-size re-creation of a street with homes and shops, and the museum itself is located in an area that has retained some of those old Edo riverside roots.
☎ 3630 8625 ✉ 1-3-28 Shirakawa, Kōtō-ku $ ¥300 🕙 9.30am-5pm, closed 2nd & 4th Mon of the month 🚇 Toei Ōedo line to Kiyosumi-Shirakawa (exit 3) ♿ good

Hara Museum of Contemporary Art (3, C9)
This is an excellent, adventurous museum that showcases contemporary art by local and international avant-garde artists. As well

as exhibiting the works of controversial artists such as Gilbert & George (UK) and Cindy Sherman (US), the museum sponsors excellent workshops and presentations by those visiting artists.
☎ 3445 0651 🖳 www .haramuseum.or.jp /generalTop.html ✉ 4-7-25 Kita-Shinagawa, Shinagawa-ku $ ¥700 🕙 11am-5pm Tue-Thu, Sat & Sun, 11am-8pm Wed 🚇 Yamanote line to Shinagawa (west exit), then 5min by Tan 96 Otsu bus to Gotenyama (first stop)

Idemitsu Art Museum (12, B4)
Most famous for its collection of work by the Zen monk Sengai, this superb, eclectic collection of Chinese and Japanese art is brought to you courtesy of a petroleum zillionaire. There are also lovely views of the Imperial Palace from here. The museum is next to Teikoku Gekijō, the Imperial Theatre.
☎ 3213 9402 ✉ 9F, Teigeki Bldg, 3-1-1 Marunouchi, Chiyoda-ku

Got Grutto?

Museum-crawlers planning on visiting several museums during a Tokyo visit should grab a **Grutto Pass** (¥2000) at the **Tokyo Convention & Visitors Bureau (TCVB) TIC** (p120) near the Imperial Palace. The pass is a book of tickets entitling the bearer to free or discounted entry at more than forty Tokyo museums and zoos. It's valid for two months after the first visit, and it's a fabulous deal as it pays for itself in a few visits. The Grutto Pass is also available at most participating museums.

$ ¥800/500 ⏰ 10am-5pm Tue-Sun, 10am-7pm Fri ⊕ Yūrakuchō line to Yūrakuchō (exit A3) ♿ excellent

John Lennon Museum (1, B2)

Just 40 minutes from Tokyo is this wonderful memorial to John Lennon, housed in the Saitama Super Arena. A Beatles soundtrack accompanies your tour of Lennon's musical instruments, handwritten lyrics and photographs. For the day-tripper, the Beatle fan and the casual student of 20th-century pop history it is enthralling and unmissable.

☎ 048 601 0009 ⌨ www.taisei.co.jp/museum/index_e.html ✉ 4F & 5F, Saitama Super Arena, 2-27 Kami-Ochiai, Saitama-ken **$** ¥1500/1000 ⏰ 11am-6pm Wed-Mon 🚉 Keihin Tōhoku, Utsunomiya & Takasaki lines

to Shin-Toshin (main exit) **P** ♿ excellent

Kite Museum (12, C2)

This unusual museum feels like a kite-maker's store cupboard with everything crammed in tight. The kites are magnificent, especially the vintage ones depicting folk tales and kabuki. There could be a lot more explanatory material for visitors, but with some imagination you can picture the colours of the kites against the sky.

☎ 3275 2704 ⌨ www.tako.gr.jp/eng/museums_e/tokyo_e.html ✉ 5F, Taimeikan Bldg, 1-12-10 Nihombashi, Chūō-ku **$** ¥200/100 ⏰ 11am-5pm Mon-Sat ⊕ Tōzai line to Nihonbashi (exit C5) ♿ limited

Metropolitan Museum of Contemporary Art Tokyo (3, F5)

The 'MoT' is a must for architecture buffs as well as

art fans. Constructed from wood, stone, metal and glass, it creates an oasis of pure light. The museum houses a permanent collection of significant modern Japanese art, and each work has its own interpretive postcard with photo, title and artist biography written in both Japanese and English.

☎ 5245 4111 ⌨ www.mot-art-museum.jp/eng ✉ Metropolitan Kiba Park, 4-1-1 Miyoshi, Kōtō-ku **$** ¥500 ⏰ 10am-6pm Tue-Sun ⊕ Hanzōmon line to Kiyosumi-Shirakawa (exit B2)

National Museum of Modern Art (12, C4)

The National Museum of Modern Art has a magnificent collection of Japanese art from the Meiji period onwards. Your ticket (hold on to the stub) gives you free admission to the

Keeping the beat at Taikokan (p33)

nearby Crafts Gallery, which houses ceramics, lacquer-ware and dolls. ☎ 3214 2561 ☐ www.momat.go.jp/english ✉ 3-1 Kitanomaru-kōen, Chūō-ku $ adult/18 & under/student ¥420/70/130 ⏱ 10am-5pm Tue-Thu, Sat & Sun, 10am-8pm Fri ◎ Tōzai line to Takebashi ♿ excellent

National Museum of Western Art (10, B2)
It may seem odd coming all this way just to check out Rodin sculptures and Le Corbusier architecture, yet the Museum of Western Art is well worth a stop during its frequent visiting exhibits (for which there are extra admission fees). ☎ 3828 5131 ☐ www.nmwa.go.jp ✉ 7-7 Ueno-kōen, Taito-ku $ ¥420/130 ⏱ 9.30am-5pm Tue-Thu, Sat & Sun, 9.30am-8pm Fri 🚃 Yamanote line to Ueno (Park exit) ♿ excellent

National Science Museum (10, B2)
With most of its interpretive signage in Japanese only, this museum is really only visit-worthy for its excellent special exhibitions – usually around ¥500 extra. But it's a good place to bring the kids, especially combined with a trip to the Ueno Zoo. ☎ 3822 0111 ☐ www.kahaku.go.jp/english ✉ 7-20 Ueno-kōen, Taito-ku $ adults & students/18 & under ¥420/70 ⏱ 9am-4.30pm Tue-Sun 🚃 Yamanote line to Ueno (Park exit) ♿ good

Creating a big splash at the National Science Museum

Nezu Institute of Fine Arts (3, B6)
This is nirvana for all Asian art buffs, with exquisite ceramics, Buddhist sculpture and paintings from China, Vietnam and Japan. The slightly wild, statue-dotted gardens also make for a pleasant afternoon's escape from the congestion of Tokyo streets. It's well signposted and only a 10-minute walk east from the station. ☎ 3400 2536 ☐ www.nezu-muse.or.jp/index_e.html ✉ 6-5-1 Minami-Aoyama, Minato-ku $ ¥1000/700 ⏱ 9.30am-4.30pm Tue-Sun ◎ Chiyoda, Ginza & Hanzōmon lines to Omote-sandō (exits A4 & A5) ♿ good

Ōkura Shūkokan (8, C3)
Surrounded by a small but well-populated sculpture garden, this hotel-museum has an impressive collection of lacquer writing boxes and no less than three national treasures. The two-storey museum is definitely worth

a look if you're on this side of town. ☎ 3583 0781 ✉ 2-10-3 Toranomon, Minato-ku $ ¥700/500 ⏱ 10am-4.30pm Tue-Sun ◎ Hibiya line to Kamiyachō (exit 3)

Ota Memorial Art Museum (6, A1)
Leave your shoes in the foyer and pad in slippers through this museum to view its stellar collection of ukiyo-e (wood-block prints). The Ota Museum offers a good opportunity to see works by Japanese masters of the art, including Hiroshige. There's an extra charge for special exhibits. You'll find it up a hill on a narrow road behind Laforet. ☎ 3403 0880 ☐ www.ukiyoe-ota-muse.jp/english.html ✉ 1-10-10 Jingūmae, Shibuya-ku $ ¥700 ⏱ 10.30am-5.30pm Tue-Sun 🚃 Yamanote line to Harajuku (Omote-sandō exit) ◎ Chiyoda line to Meiji-jingūmae (exit 5)

Sake Plaza (12, B6)

Part museum, part shopping expedition – this is a brilliant showcase for sake, sponsored by the sake-makers' union. The 1st floor features an excellent sake shop, with tastings of the very finest (three/five samples ¥315/515). With books, sake accessories and of course the samples, this hard-to-find spot is the best place in town to buy up on your sake souvenirs.
☎ 3519 2091 ✉ 1-4F, Nihon Shuzo Kaikan, 1-21-1 Nishi-Shimbashi, Minato-ku ⏱ 10am-6pm Mon-Fri 🚇 Yamanote line to Shimbashi (Hibiya exit) ♿ fair

Shitamachi History Museum (10, B3)

Lots of interactive fun awaits here for the historically imaginative; poking around inside a Shitamachi tenement house (don't forget to take off your shoes), or pondering whether you would rather have been a copper-boiler, a sweetshop-owner or a merchant in a previous Japanese life. Try out the games and try on the clothes.
☎ 3823 7451 ✉ 2-1 Ueno-kōen, Taito-ku 💲 ¥300/100 ⏱ 9.30am-4.30pm Tue-Sun 🚇 Yamanote line to Ueno (Hirokōji exit) ♿ fair

Taikokan (Drum Museum) (11, A2)

It would be difficult to come here and deny the natural instinct to bash away on these gorgeous drums. Luckily, any item is fair game as long as it's not marked

with a red dot. It's on the 2nd floor of the Miyamoto festival goods store on Kokusai-dōri, opposite the *kōban* (police box).
☎ 3842 5622 ✉ 2-1-1 Nishi-Asakusa, Taitō-ku 💲 ¥300 ⏱ 10am-5pm Wed-Sun 🚇 Ginza line to Tawaramachi (exit 3)

Tepco Electric Energy Museum (5, B2)

Surprisingly, this is one of Tokyo's better science museums, offering seven floors of dynamic exhibitions on every conceivable aspect of electricity and its production. There are innumerable displays that are hands-on and an excellent, free English hand-out that explains everything.
☎ 3477 1191 ✉ 1-12-10 Jinnan, Shibuya-ku 💲 free ⏱ 10am-6pm Thu-Tue 🚇 Yamanote line to Shibuya (Hachikō exit) ♿ good

Tokyo Metropolitan Museum of Art (10, B1)

The Tokyo Met has several galleries that run temporary displays of contemporary Japanese art (admission fee varies). Galleries feature both Western-style art such as oil paintings and Japanese-style art such as *sumi-e* (ink brush painting) and ikebana (flower arrangement). Apart from the main gallery, the rental galleries aren't curated by the museum, so exhibitions can be of uneven quality.
☎ 3823 6921 🖳 www .tobikan.jp ✉ 8-36 Ueno-kōen, Taito-ku 💲 special exhibits ¥900-1000 ⏱ 9am-5pm

Tue-Sun, closed 3rd Mon of each month 🚇 Yamanote line to Ueno (Park exit) ♿ excellent

Watari Museum of Contemporary Art (6, C1)

Also known as the Watarium, this place showcases lots of brilliant conceptual and performance art, with visiting Scandinavians choreographing vacuum-cleaner ballets, and resident Japanese embalming themselves with glue. Ergo, lots of cutting-edge contemporary art can be found here, especially mixed-media art installations.
☎ 3402 3001 🖳 official@watarium .co.jp ✉ 3-7-6 Jingūmae, Shibuya-ku 💲 ¥1000/800 ⏱ 11am-7pm Tue-Sun 🚇 Ginza line to Gaien-mae (exit 3)

Yayoi Museum & Takehisa Yumeji Museum (3, D3)

These two charming brick museums focus mostly on illustrations from popular art, books and other precursors to Japan's manga tradition. The work represents graphic art from the Meiji, Taishō and Shōwa periods, including some Japanese-style art deco illustrations. The museums are on a side street facing the northeastern end of Tokyo University.
☎ 3812 0012 🖳 www .yayoi-yumeji-museum .jp/visit/guide.html ✉ 2-4-3 Yayoi, Bunkyō-ku 💲 adult/15 & under/student ¥800/400/700 ⏱ 10am-5pm Tue-Sun 🚇 Chiyoda line to Nezu (exit 1)

PARKS & GARDENS

Where to Run

Runners, rejoice – there are parks aplenty in Tokyo for jogs and power walks. Check out **Yoyogi-kōen** (opposite), **Meiji-jingū** (p9) and the **Imperial Palace East Garden** (below). Of course, for a real runner's high, those top-end hotel treadmills have pulse-racing views.

Hama Rikyū Onshi-Teien (12, C6-D6)

The shōgun used to have this magnificent place to themselves when it was Hama Rikyū, 'the beach palace'. Now mere mortals can enjoy this wonderful garden, one of Tokyo's best. Sometimes known as the **Detached Palace Garden**, it is impossibly elegant and a must for garden aficionados. Consider approaching it from Asakusa via the Sumidagawa cruise (p22).
☎ 3541 0200 ⊠ 1-1 Hamarikyū Teien, Chūō-ku 💲 ¥300 🕑 9am-4.30pm 🚇 Toei Ōedo line to Tsukiji-shijō (exit A2) ♿ good

Imperial Palace East Garden (12, A3)

Providing the nearest emergency exit from Ginza street chaos, the East Garden (Higashi Gyōen) is the only quarter of the palace proper that is open to the public. Its main feature is the Edo-period watchtower, Fujimi-yagura, designed to provide the aristocracy with a handy view of Mt Fuji. The store inside the garden sells a good map for ¥150.
☎ 3213 2050 ⊠ 1-1 Chiyoda, Chiyoda-ku 💲 free 🕑 9am-4pm Tue-Thu, Sat & Sun, last entry 3pm 🚇 Tōzai & Chiyoda lines to Ōtemachi (exit C10) ♿ good

Koishikawa Kōraku-en (3, D3)

A beautiful amalgam of Japanese and Chinese landscape design, this mid-17th-century garden is left off most tourist itineraries. It's a shame, because it's one of Tokyo's best gardens; then again, it's a blessing, since you'll be far from the madding crowds. The solicitous staff will help with wheelchairs although there are no specific facilities for them.
☎ 3811 3015 ⊠ 1-6-6 Kōraku, Bunkyō-ku 💲 ¥300 🕑 9am-5pm 🚇 Toei Ōedo & Tōzai lines to Iidabashi (exit A1) ♿ good

Nature Study Garden (3, C8)

Prosaic name, pulchritudinous garden – this is one of Tokyo's least known and most appealing getaways. Unique in Tokyo, it preserves the city's original flora in undisciplined profusion. Take a walk on Tokyo's wild side through woods and swamps in this haven for bird-watchers, botanists and those overdosing on urban rhythms.
☎ 3441 7176 ⊠ 5-21-5 Shirokanedai, Minato-ku 💲 adult/student ¥210/60 🕑 9am-4.30pm Tue-Sun, 9am-5pm Tue-Sun Jun-Aug 🚇 Yamanote line to Meguro (east exit) 🚇 Toei Mita & Namboku lines to Shirokanedai (exit 1) ♿ good

Rikugi-en (3, C2)

The poets' favourite, this is a 10-hectare (25-acre) Edo-style *kaiyū*, or 'many pleasure' garden, built around a tranquil, carp-filled pond. It's another garden good for strolling, with landscaped views unfolding at every turn of the pathways that crisscross the grounds. The design is said to evoke famous scenes from Chinese literature and Japanese *waka* (31-syllable) poetry.
☎ 3941 2222 ⊠ 6-16-3 Hon-Komagome, Bunkyō-ku 💲 ¥300 🕑 9am-5pm Tue-Sun 🚇 Yamanote line to Komagome (south exit) ♿ good

Shinjuku-gyōen (3, B5)

Dating back to 1906, this downtown park provides the perfect escape from the winter cold as it boasts a hothouse full of exotic tropical plants, including – it's rumoured – peyote! There's also a French garden and a pond full of giant carp. Keep this park in mind when you're exhausted by all that busy Shinjuku has to offer.
☎ 3350 0151 🖥 www.shinjukugyoen.go.jp/english/english-index

.html ✉ Naito-chō, Shinjuku-ku $ ¥200 ☯ 9am-4.30pm Tue-Sun ⊕ Marunouchi line to Shinjuku-gyōen (exit 1)

Yoyogi-kōen (3, A6)
At the edge of Harajuku, wooded Yoyogi-kōen is a sleepy skateboarder hang-out and always has some surprise around the corner (fire-eaters, for one). Though banned, punk bands and traditional musicians come here to practise and busk. Paired with a visit to Jingū-bashi (p14) to gawk at the Goth kids, a Sunday afternoon here makes for a perfect picnic. ☎ 3469 6081 ✉ 2-1 Yoyogi Kamizonochō, Shibuya-ku $ free ☯ dawn to dusk ⊛ Chiyoda line to Meiji-jingūmae (exit 3) ♿ excellent

Awesome Blossoms
Around April the whole nation excitedly waits for the first buds to appear on cherry trees. *Hanami* (cherry-blossom viewing) parties are held to celebrate the flowers during the week-long flowering season and both daytime parties and moonlit soirees are popular. There's plenty of sake, singing and dancing (beware of portable karaoke machines). At popular *hanami* spots the best sites are often taken by people who have camped out overnight for them. If you're in Tokyo during the spring, take in the *sakura* (cherry blossoms) at the **Imperial Palace East Garden** or **Shinjuku-gyōen**.

DAVID RYAN

PUBLIC BATHS & HOT SPRINGS

More than just a place to wash; the *sentō* (public bath) or *onsen* (hot spring) is a place to relax and socialise. The *sentō* is a vanishing institution in Tokyo, and it's worth visiting one while it's still possible.

Asakusa Kannon Onsen (11, B1)
The water at this traditional bathhouse is a steamy 40°C. Asakusa's historic ambience makes this a great place for a soul-soothing soak. ☎ 3844 4141 ✉ 2-7-26 Asakusa, Taito-ku $ ¥700 ☯ 6.30am-6pm Fri-Wed ⊕ Ginza & Toei Asakusa lines to Asakusa (exits 1, 3, 6 & 8)

Azabu-Jūban Onsen (9, B3)
Right in the middle of Tokyo, this is a good introduction to the pleasures of

a hot-spring bath. The dark, tea-coloured water here is from 500m underground and is scalding hot. A sauna, cold bath and tatami rooms complete the picture. ☎ 3404 2610 ✉ 1-5 Azabu-Jūban, Minato-ku $ ¥1260 ☯ 11am-9pm Wed-Mon ⊕ Namboku & Toei Ōedo lines to Azabu-jūban station

Finlando Sauna (4, B1)
This is a huge 24-hour complex of baths and steam rooms right in the middle of Shinjuku's Kabuki-chō. This

is a good place – for men only – to escape the madness of the streets outside. Massages (¥3060/45min) come highly recommended. ☎ 3209 9196 ✉ 1-20-1 Kabuki-chō, Shinjuku-ku $ noon-5pm ¥1900, 5pm-midnight ¥2100, midnight-noon ¥2600 ☯ 24hr ⊛ Yamanote line to Shinjuku (east exit)

Green Plaza Ladies Sauna (4, B1)
A central 24-hour bath and spa for women, this place is also in Shinjuku's Kabuki-chō

Making a Splash in the Sentō

As much for gossip as for hygiene, the *sentō* (public bath) is a great place for strengthening social bonds in Tokyo. Divided into men's and women's sections, you head for the appropriate changing room and pay the fee to an attendant. In the changing room, place your clothes in one of the wicker or plastic baskets and your toiletries in a *senmenki* (wash basin). With the basket in a locker, you're ready for your bath.

Before you step into the bath, you'll need to wash thoroughly at the banks of low showers and water spigots that line the walls. Grab a low stool and wash away, making sure you remove all soap so as not to cloud the water. Now choose your tub. At a good *sentō*, you can choose between a hot tub, scalding tub, cold tub, whirlpool bath, sauna and, best of all, electric bath (which is supposed to simulate the sensation experienced when swimming with electric eels). If you soak everything just right, you'll achieve the state of *yuddako* or 'boiled octopus'.

MASON FLORENCE

and a good place to take a little holiday from your holiday. A 40-minute massage costs ¥3260.
☎ 3207 5411 ✉ 1-29-2 Kabuki-chō, Shinjuku-ku
💲 6am-10pm ¥2700,

10pm-6am ¥3300
🕐 24hr 🚇 Yamanote line to Shinjuku (east exit)

Koshi-no-Yu Sentō (9, B3)
Downstairs from Azabu-Jūban Onsen is this *sentō*.

The water comes from the same source; the difference in price is only because the *sentō* offers a more stripped-down experience.
☎ 3404-2610 ✉ 1-5 Azabu-Jūban, Minato-ku
💲 ¥400 🕐 3pm-11.30pm Wed-Mon 🚇 Namboku & Toei Ōedo lines to Azabu-jūban station

Working Out

Most gym-goers in Tokyo belong to private gyms, but each ward subsidises community gyms. For a small fee, visitors can use the centrally located **Chiyoda Kuritsu Sogo Taiikukan** (3, E5; ☎ 3256 8444; 2-1-8 Uchi-Kanda, Chiyoda-ku; ¥600; 🕐 noon-8.30pm; Yamanote line to Kanda, exit 2), which has a reasonably sized pool and gymnasium.

Drop in to do the downward dog at the International **Yoga Center** (1, B2; ☎ 090 4596 7996; www.iyc.jp/iyc/en; 4F, Fukumura Ogikubo Bldg, 5-30-6 Ogikubo, Suginami-ku; Marunouchi line to Ogikubo, south exit). Ninety-minute classes (¥3300 with mat rental) in Ashtanga and Iyengar yoga are held in both Japanese and English.

Rokuryū (10, A1)
Boil away travel fatigue at this hot-spring bathhouse; the bubbling amber water is good for you. The setting isn't the most alluring, but it's clean and pleasant. Find it near the Suigetsu Hotel.
☎ 3821 3826 ✉ 3-4-20 Ikenohata, Taitō-ku
💲 ¥400/180 🕐 3.30-11pm Tue-Sun 🚇 Yamanote line to Ueno (Ikenohata exit)

QUIRKY TOKYO

23 Tiny Museums of Sumida-ku (3, F3)

Stumble on little gems in this corner of Tokyo, where life moves at a more traditional pace – the backstreets hide small workshop-museums exhibiting everything from indigo-dyed fabric to lighters to Noh masks. Staff at the city office don't speak much English, but they can give you a detailed map and point you in the right direction.

Sumida-ku Cultural Affairs Department ☎ 5608 6186 🖳 www.city.sumida .tokyo.jp/english/guide /museums ✉ 1-23-20 Azumabashi, Sumida-ku 🕓 8.30am-5pm Mon-Fri ⊖ Toei Asakusa & Ginza lines to Asakusa (exit 5)

Condomania (6, A1)

Inside this tiny shop you'll find more condoms than you can shake a stick at. For your love-hotel expeditions or footloose friends back home, pick up enigmatic prophylactics such as the 'Masturbater's Condom' or the more conservative glow-in-the-dark variety.
☎ 3797 6131 ✉ 6-30-1 Jingūmae, Shibuya-ku 💲 free 🕓 10.30am-11pm 🚉 Yamanote line to Harajuku (Omote-sandō exit)

Criminology Museum of Meiji University (3, D4)

Covering centuries of crime and punishment in Japan, this museum is the only one of its kind in Japan – the criminally minded (or the morbidly curious) will find it fascinating. There aren't

The smile says it all at Condomania

many English explanations, but much is self-explanatory. From the JR station exit, walk downhill on Meidai-dōri and look for the museum on a corner on your right.
☎ 3296 4431 ✉ 3F, Daigaku Kaikan, 1-1 Kanda Surugadai, Chiyoda-ku 💲 free 🕓 10am-4.30pm Mon-Fri, 10am-12.30pm Sat ⊖ Marunouchi line to Ochanomizu (exit B1) 🚉 Chūō & Sōbu lines to Ochanomizu (Ochanomizu exit) ♿ fair

Ghibli Museum (3, A4)

As utterly enchanting as the Ghibli Studio's *anime* (animation) – think *Spirited Away* – this museum will delight children big and small with gorgeous walls of art, displays to romp on and short films. And with limits on attendance: no crowds. You must reserve an appointment and purchase tickets in advance;

book on the web as far in advance as possible.
☎ 0570 05577 🖳 www .ghibli-museum.jp/ticket _info.html ✉ Inoka-shira-kōen 💲 ¥1000/400 🕓 10am-6pm Wed-Mon 🚉 Chūō line to Mitaka, bus to museum (¥200)

Meguro Parasitological Museum (7)

Those inclined to stifling shrieks upon encountering a spider won't find this museum to their liking, but for those with stronger stomachs, it's captivating. One of the more impressive exhibits is a nearly 9m-long tapeworm extracted from some unfortunate host. Kids will get a kick out of this place, and there's a terrific gift shop, too.
☎ 3716 1264 ✉ 4-1-1 Shima-Meguro, Meguro-ku 💲 free 🕓 10am-5pm Tue-Sun 🚉 Yamanote line to Meguro (main exit), then any bus to Ōtori-jinjamae

Venus Fort (3, E8)
Set in a building that mimics 17th-century Rome – then complete with ceilings simulating the sky turning from day to night – Venus Fort is a village's worth of 170 boutiques and restaurants all aimed at young women. It also boasts the distinction of having Japan's biggest lavatory (64 stalls). Perfect for Renaissance women bearing credit cards. ☎ 3599 0700 ✉ Aomi-itchōme, Kōtō-ku $ free ⏰ 11am-10pm, restaurants till 11pm 🚊 Yurikamome line to Aomi (main exit) P ♿ excellent

TEMPLES & SHRINES

Visiting a Shrine or Temple

Just past the *torii* (shrine gate) is a trough of water, or *chōzuya,* with long-handled ladles perched on *hishaku* (rack), above. This is for purifying yourself before entering the sacred precincts of the shrine. Some forego this ritual and head directly for the main hall. If you choose to purify yourself, take a ladle, fill it with fresh water from the spigot, pour some over one hand, transfer the spoon and pour water over the other hand. Then pour a little water into a cupped hand and rinse your mouth, spitting the water onto the ground beside (not into) the trough.

Once you've purified yourself, head to the *haiden* (hall of worship), which sits in front of the *honden* (main hall) enshrining the *kami* (shrine god). Toss a coin into the offerings box, ring the gong by pulling on the thick rope (to summon the deity), pray, then clap your hands twice, bow and then back away from the shrine. Amulets are sold (¥100 to ¥200) at the shrine office near the worship hall. Look for signs prohibiting photography; if it's allowed, be discreet so as not to disturb worshippers.

Unless the temple contains a shrine, you will not have to purify yourself before entry. The place of worship in a temple is in the *hondō,* which usually contains a Buddhist altar and one or more Buddha images. Entry is usually free; otherwise admission is around ¥500. The standard practice is to toss some change into the offerings box, which sits in front of the altar, step back, place one's hands together, pray, then bow to the altar before backing away.

Most temples sell *omikuji* (fortunes written on little slips of paper; ¥100). Pay an attendant or place the money in an honour-system box. Fortunes are dispensed randomly from a special box containing sticks with different numbers written on their ends. Shake the box until one stick drops out of a hole in its top. Take this to the attendant and you will be given a fortune matching the number on the stick. This will be written in Japanese under one of four general headings: *dai-kitchi* (big luck), *kitchi* (luck), *sho-kitchi* (small luck, moderately grim) and *kyō* (bad luck). You can also purchase amulets called *omamori* at temples. These usually cost a few hundred yen and come in a variety of shapes and sizes, the most common of which is a piece of fabric bearing the temple's name enclosed in a plastic case. Some temples have *omamori* for specific things such as traffic safety, good health and academic success. Hello Kitty *omamori* are still all the rage.

Black and white, but red all over: the colourful exterior of Hanazono-jinja

Hanazono-jinja (4, C1)

Nestled in ultra-urban, high-rise Shinjuku is this quiet, unassuming shrine. Hanazono-jinja is particularly pleasant when it's lit up in the evening, but it also makes for a quick escape from the seediness of Kabuki-chō. It only takes about 10 minutes to stroll around the grounds and it's a fine place to sit down and nibble on some *bentō* (boxed dinner).

☎ 3209 5265 ✉ 5-17-3 Shinjuku, Shinjuku-ku 💲 free 🕒 dawn to dusk 🚇 Marunouchi & Shinjuku lines to Shinjuku-sanchōme (exit B2)

Hie-jinja (8, B2)

One of the casualties of WWII bombing was Hie-jinja, which dates back to 1659 in its present location. Though the shrine itself isn't a major attraction, the highlight is the walk up, through a 'tunnel' of red *torii*. It's also the backdrop for one of Japan's most spectacular *matsuri* (festivals). Look for the concrete plaza-style entrance on Sotobori-dōri.

☎ 3581 2471 ✉ 2-10-5 Nagata-chō, Chiyoda-ku 💲 free 🕒 dawn to dusk 🚇 Ginza & Marunouchi lines to Tameike-sannō (exit 5)

Yasukuni-jinja (3, C4)

Yasukuni-jinja, the perennial fly-in-the-chardonnay in Japan-Asia relations, is the 'Peaceful Country Shrine' and a memorial to Japan's 2.5 million or so war-dead. No wonder it invites controversy. Politics aside, it has a beautiful, contemplative inner sanctum in the style of ancient Ise shrines – a stark contrast to the *uyoku* (right-wing activists) shouting their rhetoric outside.

☎ 3261 8326 💻 www .yasukuni.or.jp/english ✉ 3-1-1 Kudan-kita, Chiyoda-ku 💲 free 🕒 9.30am-4.30pm 🚇 Toei Shinjuku line to Kudanshita (exits 1 & 2) ♿ fair

Illusionary tunnel of red *torii* (shrine gates) at Hie-jinja

TOKYO FOR CHILDREN

Tokyo is a giant playground of a city for children. It's colourful, stimulating and a lot of activities are fun for both generations. Look for ☺ listed with individual reviews in other chapters for further kid-friendly options.

Noteworthy destinations for kids, not listed in this section, include the Ghibli Museum (p37) – for which reservations should probably be made before you arrive in Tokyo – the hands-on Shitamachi History Museum (p33) and Meguro Parasitological Museum (p37) for its phenomenal gross-out factor. Another fun activity is the Ōdaiba Day walking tour (p46), with lots of fresh air and a variety of stimulating stuff to check out.

Hakuhinkan Toy Park (12, C5)
Claiming to be one of the largest toy shops in the world, the Hakuhinkan Toy Park (p61) also features restaurants and theatres. Unless you're careful this is a dangerous spot to spend your entire holiday budget.
☎ 3571 8008 🖳 www .hakuhinkan.co.jp ✉ 8-8-11 Ginza, Chūō-ku ⏰ 11am-8pm 🚇 Toei Asakusa & Ginza lines to Shimbashi (exits 1 & 3) 🚃 Yamanote line to Shimbashi (Ginza exit) ♿ good

Kōraku-en Amusement Park (3, D4)
Adrenaline junkies of all ages will enjoy the Spinning Coaster Maihime and the Thrill Ride. Geopolis is a new hi-tech addition to the amusement park, with attractions such as the Geopanic indoor roller coaster. Once your equilibrium has been well and truly scrambled, head next door to the contemplative spaces of the Koishikawa Kōraku-en (p34) for a dose of serenity.
☎ 5800 9999 ✉ 1-3-61 Kōrakuen, Bunkyō-ku

💲 ¥1200/600, individual rides ¥600, unlimited rides ¥3300/2600 ⏰ 10am-10pm Jun-Aug, 10am-6pm Dec-Feb, 10am-8pm rest of year 🚇 Chūō line to Suidōbashi (east exit) 🚇 Marunouchi line to Kōraku-en (main exit)

Mega Web (3, E8)
Test-drive your favourite new Japanese-model Toyota on an actual lap course. A driver's license is required for this and for the zippy little electric vehicle that runs on a suspended track. And oh, right, for the kids: get the little ones hooked on motorcycles early and let them test-drive the child-friendly electric-powered vehicles.
☎ 3599 0808 🖳 www .megaweb.gr.jp/english ✉ Palette Town, Aomi-itchōme, Kōtō-ku 💲 individual rides ¥200-300 ⏰ 11am-6pm Mon-Fri, 11am-8pm Sat & Sun 🚃 Yurikamome to Aomi (main exit)

Museum of Maritime Science (3, E9)
Fune no Kagaku-kan is one of Tokyo's better museums:

Baby-sitters

Finding a baby-sitter can be tough in Tokyo, especially if you're only visiting for a short period. Popular among the foreign community is the professional childcare service **Kids World** (☎ 0120 001527), with native English speakers and fun activities. Drop-in services are available at many convenient locations in central Tokyo.

Agency baby-sitters usually charge a minimum of ¥1500 for two to three hours; some companies require that you pay a hefty annual membership fee. Reputable agencies include **Japan Babysitter Service** (☎ 3423 1251), **Kinder Network** (☎ 3486 8278) and **Poppins Service** (☎ 3447 2100).

A handy starting point for finding private sitters is www.tokyowithkids.com/babysitters/index.html.

four floors of excellent displays with loads of detailed models, lots of hands-on exhibits that kids will love, and a pool on the roof where, for ¥100, they can wreak havoc with radio-controlled boats and submarines.

☎ 5500 1111 ✉ 3-1 Higashi-Yashio, Shinagawa-ku $ ¥700/400 ⏱ 10am-5pm Mon-Fri, 10am-6pm Sat, Sun & holidays 🚇 Yurikamome line to Fune no Kagaku-kan (main exit) ♿ good

National Children's Castle (5, C2)

If you bring a brood, Kodomo no Shiro is by far the most comprehensive, child-friendly complex in the city. The castle (use your imagination!) has a pool, indoor and rooftop play areas, movies and activities, and diversions for accompanying adults. Stay next door at the Children's Castle Hotel (p99). Logically enough, the castle is located in upscale Aoyama.

☎ 3797 5666 🖳 www .kodomo-shiro.or.jp ✉ 5-53-1 Jingū-mae, Shibuya-ku $ ¥500/400 ⏱ 10am-5.30pm or 12.30-5.30pm (check website) 🚇 Chiyoda, Ginza & Hanzōmon lines to Omote-sandō (exit B2) 🅿 ♿ excellent

National Museum of Emerging Science and Innovation (3, E9)

Kids will love the engaging exhibits at this science museum, where most displays have excellent explanations in English and English-speaking guides fill in the

blanks. There's the spectacular planetarium (buy tickets for a show as soon as you arrive), demonstrations of robots and opportunities to interact with them, and tons of exhibits about space, medicine and the environment.

☎ 3570 9151 🖳 www .miraikan.jst.go.jp ✉ 2-41 Aomi, Kōtō-ku $ adult/child/6 & under ¥500/200/free, free on Sat ⏱ 10am-5pm Wed-Mon 🚇 Yurikamome line to Telecom Center 🅿 1st hr ¥300, per hr thereafter ¥100 ♿ excellent

Sunshine International Aquarium (2, C2)

Boasting the distinction of being the highest aquarium in the world, this high-rise water world has tanks full of electric eels, sharks and other intriguing sea life. It's also got some incongruous land-lubbin' critters as well, like lemurs. The building is full of stimulating stuff for kids, such as a planetarium, shopping mall and food-themed amusement park.

☎ 3989 3466 ✉ 10F, World Import Mart Bldg, 3-1-3 Higashi-Ikebukuro, Toshima-ku $ ¥1600/800 ⏱ 10am-6pm 🚇 Yūrakuchō line to Higashi-Ikebukuro (exit 2) ♿ good

Sunshine Planetarium (2, C2)

We may be in down-to-earth Ikebukuro but some of us are looking at the stars… Alas, the show is narrated in Japanese, but the visuals are spectacular enough to lift you out of

this earthly end of Tokyo.

☎ 3989 3475 ✉ 10F, World Import Mart Bldg, 3-1-3 Higashi-Ikebukuro, Toshima-ku $ ¥1600/800 ⏱ noon-5.30pm Mon-Fri, 11am-6.30pm Sat & Sun 🚇 Yūrakuchō line to Higashi-Ikebukuro (exit 2) ♿ good

Tokyo Disneyland (1, B2)

This legendary wonderland is a near-perfect replica of the California original, making it the second-happiest place on earth. Tokyo Disneyland has a **ticket office** (12, B4; ☎ 3595 1777; ⏱ 10am-7pm) in Hibiya. Its opening hours vary seasonally, so phone ahead or check the website to be sure; it's open year-round except for about two weeks, mostly in January.

☎ 045 683 3777 🖳 www.tokyodisney resort.co.jp ✉ 1-1 Maihama, Urayasu-shi, Chiba $ passport-ticket adult/child 12-17/child 4-11 ¥5500/4800/3700 ⏱ check website 🚇 Keiō line to Maihama (main exit) 🅿 per day ¥2000 ♿ excellent

Tokyo Joypolis (3, E8)

Located in the Decks Tokyo Beach complex, this is yet another hi-tech playland for overstimulating your kids. Run by Sega, it's the most sophisticated of the lot. Your visit here will be totally nonstop with crazy indoor roller coasters, video and computer games, virtual-reality experiences and, logically, lots of computer-generated fun.

☎ 5500 1801 ✉ 1-6-1 Daiba, Minato-ku 💲 ¥500/300, passport ¥3300/3100 🕑 10am-11pm 🚃 Yurikamome line to Odaiba Kaihin Kōen ♿ fair

Toy Museum (3, A4)

Exhibits here are eminently kid-friendly, meaning, of course, totally hands-on. Sure, there are museum-like glassed-in displays, but the beauty of this place is in the creative art projects and games to play. To really wind your kids up, combine this with a visit to Mandarake (p61). The museum is on Nakano-dōri, about three blocks north of the JR station.

☎ 3387 5461 ✉ 2-12-10 Arai, Nakano-ku 💲 ¥500

🕑 10.30am-4pm Wed & Thu, Sat-Mon ⊙ Chūō line to Nakano (north exit)

Transportation Museum (13, E2)

Not a trainspotting museum... although this place might turn you into a trainspotter – exhibits here are mostly dedicated to trains. In a place where you can pretend to 'drive' a virtual JR Yamanote train around Tokyo and not-so-secretly like it, no-one will think you're a nerd. It's great fun for both kids and grown-ups alike.

☎ 3251 8481 💻 www .kouhaku.or.jp/english /info.html ✉ 1-25 Kanda-Sudachō, Chiyoda-ku 💲 ¥310/150 🕑 9.30am-5pm Tue-Sun

⊙ Marunouchi line to Awajichō (exits A3 & A5)

Ueno Zoo (10, B2)

Established in 1882, Ueno Zoo was the first of its kind in Japan. It's a good outing if you have children; otherwise, it can be safely dropped from a busy itinerary. The zoo is very popular with Japanese visitors for its enchanting pandas (who are not on view on Fridays). Also impressive are the snow leopards, gorillas and okapi.

☎ 3828 5171 ✉ 9-83 Ueno-kōen, Taito-ku 💲 adult/concession /child ¥600/200/free 🕑 9.30am-5pm Tue-Sun ⊙ Chiyoda line to Nezu (south exit) 🚃 Yamanote line to Ueno (Park exit) ♿ excellent

ADINA TOVY AMSEL

School children on an excursion at Ueno Zoo; we're told they saw two pandas

Out & About

WALKING TOURS

Kabukichō Crawl

Surface around dusk at the My City exit, in front of the enormous **Studio Alta building** (**1**) video screen. Walk east down Shinjuku-dōri to **Kinokuniya** (**2**; p56) to browse its selection of English-language books. Three blocks further, also on the left, **Isetan** (**3**; p53) department store has fashionable boutiques and Isetan Museum, one of Tokyo's best galleries. Consider crossing Meiji-dōri for toothsome noodles at **Keika Kumamoto Rāmen** (**4**; pp77-8). From Meiji-dōri, turn left down Yasukuni-dōri and make a

distance 2km **duration** 3hr
▶ **start** 🚇 Yamanote line to Shinjuku (Kabukichō exit)
● **end** 🚇 Shinjuku (Kabukichō entrance)

Bright night lights, Shinjuku

first right into the alley leading to **Hanazono-jinja** (**5**; p39), which has a reputation for bringing good fortune to business. Exit onto **Golden Gai** (**6**; p83), a warren of alleyways devoted to small, stand-up watering holes, favourites of Tokyo bohemians – drop by before it's redeveloped. Continue in the same direction along the alleyways running parallel to Yasukuni-dōri and you reach **Kabukichō** (**7**), Tokyo's most notorious 'pleasure district'. Kabukichō plies the passing humanity with 'soaplands' (massage parlours), love hotels, peep shows and hostess bars. As you walk through neon streets crowded with drunken salarymen, young women call out invitations to their establishments. Eventually you'll arrive at **Koma Theatre square** (**8**), a popular night-time busking spot that's seen it all. From here, wander back to Yasukuni-dōri and take one of the lanes leading to Shinjuku-dōri and Shinjuku station.

Aoyama Art Walk

Cross Aoyama-dōri and stop by **Gallery 360** (**1**; ☎ 3406 5823; 2F, 5-1-27 Minami-Aoyama; ☽ noon-7pm Mon-Sat), a small white space exhibiting work related to the Fluxus movement. Just down Aoyama-dōri is the **Spiral Building** (**2**; p29), designed by Tokyo architect Fumihiko Maki. Stroll its 1st-floor gallery spiralling up to the airy museum shop.

Cross back over Aoyama-dōri at the next stoplight. Two streets past Kinokuniya International Supermarket, turn right. You'll soon hit an eclectic cluster of galleries. For a mix of the established and experimental, look for **Gallery Gan** (**3**; ☎ 3573 6555; 1F, 5-51-3 Jingūmae; ☽ 11am-7pm Mon-Sat), **Promo Arte** (**4**; ☎ 3400 1995; 2F, 5-51-3 Jingūmae; ☽ noon-7pm Tue-Sun) and **Gallery ES** (**5**; ☎ 3407 1234; 5-46-13 Jingūmae; ☽ 11am-7pm Tue-Sun).

Further on is arty **Las Chicas** (**6**; p71) – stop in for a bite. Backtrack and hang a left at **Cam Chien Grippe** (**7**; p71). When the street ends, turn left, walk another 50m and turn right. From here, head back to Omote-sandō-dōri. Take the pedestrian overpass, edge to the right of Itō Hospital, and turn left at the little café Apetito. About 100m on, look for the yellow entrance to **NADiff** (**8**; ☎ 3403 8814; B1F, 4-9-8 Jingūmae; ☽ 11am-8pm), one of Tokyo's best experimental galleries and supplier of art books. Make your way back to Omote-sandō-dōri and its eponymous station.

distance 2.5km **duration** 3-4hr
▶ **start** ⊖ Chiyoda, Ginza & Hanzōmon lines to Omote-sandō (exit B4)
● **end** ⊖ Omote-sandō subway station (entrance A2)

For all things art: NADiff, Jingūmae

Shitamachi Streets

Leave the Sensō-ji grounds through **Hōzō-mon** (**1**). Walk around the edge of the temple grounds and look out for **Chingo-dō-ji** (**2**), a shrine built for trickster *tanuki* (raccoon dogs). Pass the stalls selling kimonos, samurai wigs and other potential souvenirs. Turn right into **Hanayashiki Amusement Park** (**3**), which hasn't changed much since it was built in 1853 – nostalgia lovers should check out its Panorama Hall. Take a left, and then another, and you're in **Rokku** (**4**), Asakusa's old cinema district. It's a little down-at-heel nowadays, but try to imagine its glamorous heyday.

Have a wander along past the local *sembei* (rice cracker) shops to Kaminarimon-dōri and its excellent restaurants. You might want to sidetrack to **Owariya** (**6**; p67) for some *tempura udon*, then backtrack along Kaminarimon-dōri and cross Kokusai-dori to find the **Taikokan (Drum Museum)** (**5**; p33).

Turn right into **Kappabashi-dōri** (**7**) to unearth plastic food models, bamboo cooking utensils and *aka-chōchin* (red paper lanterns) that light the back alleys of Tokyo by night. At the end of the street, backtrack toward the building crowned with an enormous bust of a chef's head. Turn left at that building and the Tawaramachi subway station is straight ahead.

Tanuki; a protected species

distance 3km **duration** 2hr
▶ **start** Sensō-ji
● **end** ⊙ Tawaramachi (entrance 2)

Ōdaiba Day

After admiring bay scenery on your way over the Rainbow Bridge, hop off the monorail and follow the signs to **Fuji Television Japan Broadcast Center** (**1**). Check out the view from the spherical **observation deck** (¥500; 10am-9pm), then take a right from Fuji TV to **Decks Tokyo Beach** (**2**; 3, E8) for shopping and coffee. Backtrack towards Fuji TV, take the first right and head for the beach, reclaimed from the bay. Don't miss Tokyo's own **Statue of Liberty** (**3**) on your right. Keep to the shore-

line, and when you reach Shiokaze-kōen park turn left. The excellent **Museum of Maritime Science** (**4**; pp40-1) is just beyond the park. From here walk in a northeast-erly direction, follow-ing the monorail line. Look for the **Flame of Liberty** (**5**) – it's that big gold needle – on your way to **Palette**

A close encounter with Tokyo Big Sight (p29)

Town (**6**; ☎ 3529 1827; Aomi-itchōme; 10am-6.30pm), complete with humungous Ferris-wheel. Stop for lunch at the Renaissance-inspired shopping mall **Venus Fort** (**7**; p37). Next door is the state-of-the-art Toyota showroom–cum–amusement park **Mega Web** (**8**; p40). Cross Dream Bridge to get to the **International Exhibition Center, aka 'Tokyo Big Sight'** (**9**; p29). The centre re-sembles an inverted pyramidical spaceship, and the rooftop view of Tokyo is amazing. Find Kokusai-Tenjijō Seimon monorail station right outside Tokyo Big Sight.

distance 2.5km **duration** 4hr+
▶ **start** Yurikamome line to Daiba (main exit)
● **end** Kokusai-Tenjijō Seimon

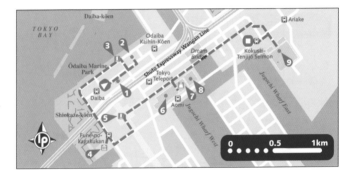

DAY TRIPS
Hakone (1, A3)

Among Hakone's varied pleasures are volcanic springs, an excellent open-air museum and serene **Ashino-ko** (Lake Ashi). This region is part of the huge Fuji-Hakone-Izu national park; Hakone, the town, covers around 25 sq km around Mt Komaga-take (1357m).

It's worth purchasing a Hakone Free Pass, which is valid on the Ōdakyū line from Shinjuku to Hakone-Yumoto and any transport within the Hakone region. Another bonus is the discounts it allows on entry to some sights.

Don't miss the excellent **Hakone Open-Air Art Museum** (☎ 0460 2 1161; ¥1600; 🕑 9am-5pm Mar-Oct, 9am-4pm Nov-Feb). It's only 100m south of Chokoku-no-mori station and set in a 30-sq-km park filled with August Rodin and Henry

INFORMATION
70km southwest of Tokyo
🚃 Ōdakyū line from Shinjuku station to Hakone-Yumoto; Hakone-Tōzan line to Chōkoku-no-mori
$ ¥5500/2750 Hakone Free Pass
ⓘ TIC pamphlets
✕ café at museum & ferry stop

Moore sculptures – perfect for picnics. Take the Sounzan Funicular from the next station, Gōra, up to **Ōwakudani** with its sulphurous hot springs.

From Ōwakudani, the cable car continues on to Tōgendai, the stop for Ashino-ko. From here you can experience one of the classic views of Mt Fuji (3776m), as well as enjoy a soak at one of the local *onsen* (hot springs). There are ferries across the lake to **Moto-Hakone** stop. Have a bite to eat here and contemplate the evocative red *torii* (shrine gates) of **Hakone-jinja**, rising from the water.

Serene Ashino-ko climbing up to the cloudy summit of Mt Fuji

Kamakura (1, B2)

Rife with notable temples and shrines, Kamakura has a wealth of relaxing walks that transport travellers a world away from manic Tokyo. As the capital of Kantō from 1192 to 1333, its myriad attractions – spread out in an inverted horseshoe shape around Kamakura station – make it one of Tokyo's most rewarding day trips. All can easily be seen by walking; the best route is to start at Kita-Kamakura station and visit temples between there and Kamakura. Temples are well signposted in English and Japanese.

Tōkei-ji (¥200; 9am-4.30pm) is famous for its shady grounds as much as for the temple itself. Women were once officially recognised as divorced if they spent three years as nuns here. Explore **Kenchō-ji** (¥300; 9am-4.30pm), Kamakura's most important Zen temple with its enormous temple bell. Surrounded by well-tended gardens, this temple is still a working centre for Buddhist meditation and study.

Dedicated to Hachiman, the god of war, the ornate **Tsurugaoka Hachiman-gū** (9am-4.30pm) is a dramatic contrast to the Zen temple. As most of Kamakura art is kept within its temples, the **National Treasure Museum** (0467 22 075; ¥150; 9am-4pm Tue-Sun) provides a unique opportunity to view Kamakura art.

The city's highlight, however, is the 11.4m-tall, 850-tonne **Daibutsu** (Great Buddha; ¥200; 7am-5.30pm), inspired by, but artistically superior to, the Great Buddha in Nara. Its home was washed away by a tsunami in 1495 and it now sits in silent, outdoor meditation.

Kamakura also harbours several **beaches**, that are better during the off-season when they aren't smothered with Tokyo escapees.

INFORMATION
50km south of Tokyo
- Yokosuka line from Tokyo station to Kita-Kamakura (55min)
- $ ¥1780 return
- TIC at east exit of Kamakura station (☎ 0467 22 3350; 9am-5pm)
- restaurants opposite Kamakura station

Meditative Daibutsu ponders offerings

CHRIS MELLOR

Mt Fuji (1, A2)

Although Fuji-san is one of the world's most famous mountains, the 3776m-high peak is notoriously reclusive, often hidden by cloud. Views are best in winter and early spring, when skies are clear and the snow cap adds solemn beauty. In summer the view is generally poor because it disappears behind heat-haze and pollution.

If you'd like a peek, the bus from Shinjuku stops at the Fifth Station on the northern side. The height at this point is 2393m. It isn't really a 'station', but a car park where climbers start from. You can then at least boast you've climbed on Mt Fuji.

> ## INFORMATION
> *80km west of Tokyo*
> 🚌 Chūō Highway bus from West Shinjuku bus terminal
> 💲 ¥5200 return
> ℹ️ 24hr taped English climbing information line ☎ 0555 23 3000; TIC pamphlets
> ✕ mountain lodges

From here there are excellent views to the west across **Lake Motso** (portrayed on the ¥5000 note) and the **Sea of Trees** (a favourite spot for suicides and disposal of murder victims). To the north it's possible to see **Lake Kawaguchi**, and to the east, **Lake Yamanako**.

Climbing Mt Fuji

Ascending to the peak of Fuji-san takes seven or eight hours and some planning. The climbing season is in July and August; mid-winter climbing is only for experienced mountaineers. Mt Fuji is high enough for altitude sickness, and oxygen is for sale at the higher stations. Because the weather is moody and the trek long, bring lightweight raingear, clothing that you can layer easily and plenty of water and snacks. A popular way to do the climb is to begin the night before – a dawn arrival at the summit ensures the sunrise experience of a lifetime.

Take time to reflect: snow-capped Mt Fuji from Lake Yamanako

Nikkō (1, B1)

There's an oft-trotted-out Japanese adage – 'Don't say *kekko* till you've seen Nikkō'. '*Kekko*' means fine or splendid – believe the hype. Nikkō, and its showpiece **Tōshō-gū** shrine, is unmissable. You'll need a full day and an early start from Tokyo, but it's worth the foray, no matter how short your stay. It's a 30-minute walk or short bus ride up the hill from the train station to the shrine area. On your way to the shrine, take a look at the arched bridge, **Shin-kyō-bashi**.

INFORMATION
110km north of Tokyo
- 🚆 Tōbu Nikkō line from Asakusa to Nikkō (2hr), then bus No 1, 2, 3 or 4 uphill to Shin-kyō-bashi bus stop; last train back at 7.42pm
- 💲 ¥3760 World Heritage Pass (return train ticket, admission to shrines, local Tōbu buses & trains)
- 🕐 shrines & temples 8am-4pm
- ℹ️ TIC Tōbu Nikkō station; purchase pass at Asakusa station
- 🍴 Hippari Dako (☎ 0288 53 2933; 🕐 till 7pm)

Detail of the eleborate Tōshō-gū shrine

At the very heart of Nikkō's shrine-filled mountain enclave is Tōshō-gū shrine. The mausoleum of Shōgun Tokugawa Ieyasu is 'pure 17th-century Disneyland', according to British art historian Gordon Miller. Ieyasu's shrine, crowded with detail, utilises every centimetre to remind you of its creator's munificence and power. Dragons, lions and peacocks jostle with gods and demigods among the glimmering gold-leaf and red lacquerwork. This is a loopy, visual roller-coaster ride – about as far as you can get from Zen minimalist architecture.

Don't dare miss **Rinnō-ji** and its **Sambutsu-dō** (Three Buddha Hall) with a trio of huge, remarkable gold-lacquered images; and **Hōbutsu-den** (Treasure Hall), featuring beautiful Buddhist artwork and the lovely Edo-period garden **Shōyō-en**. If you have time, bus it to lovely **Lake Chūzenji** and **Kegon Waterfall**, about half an hour from Nikkō town.

A popular spot to eat is **Hippari Dako**, which specialises in *yakitori* (grilled chicken), and is run by the very friendly Miki-san. It's on your left as you walk towards the shrine compound, just before Shin-kyō-bashi, identifiable by the large kite hanging above the entrance.

ORGANISED TOURS

Short on time and can't be bothered with planning? Consider taking an organised tour of Tokyo's major sights. The tour companies listed below have pick-up points city-wide. It's easiest to book tours over the phone or Internet, or to have the friendly folks at the JNTO's TIC (p120) arrange a tour for you.

Hato Bus (12, B3)

The yellow tour buses of Hato Bus ('Pigeon Bus', oddly) have been whisking foreigners around Tokyo for decades. The daytime **Panoramic Tour** (¥9800), which takes in most of Tokyo's major sights, includes lunch. They also offer night tours, some including dinner at a sukiyaki restaurant.

☎ 3435 6081 🖥 www .hatobus.co.jp/english ✉ World Trade Center Bldg, 2-4-1 Hamamatsu-chō, Minato-ku 🕐 9am-7pm 🚉 Yamanote line to Tokyo (Marunouchi exit) ♿ good

Mr Oka

The cheery Mr Oka guides you through Old Yamanote, Kanda and Asakusa. Half- and full-day options plus customised tours are available. Lunches, admission and subway fees are extra. Call between 10am and 10pm to arrange a meeting time.

☎ 0422 51 7673 🖥 www .mroka.homestead.com 💲 ¥2000/person 🕐 by appointment

Odakyū Q-Tours (4, B2)

Specialising in tours to Kamakura, Mt Fuji and Hakone, Odakyū's tours include an English guidebook. Tours meet at Odakyū Sightseeing Service Center, near the west exit of Odakyū-Shinjuku station. There's an **office** (☎ 3349 0111; 2-7-2 Nishi-Shinjuku, Shinjuku-ku; 🕐 10am-6pm Mon-Sat) in the Hotel Century Hyatt.

☎ 5321 7887 🖥 www .odakyu-group.co.jp /english ✉ 1F, Odakyū-Shinjuku, Shinjuku-ku 💲 ¥6800-9500 🕐 8am-6pm

Sunrise Tours

Sunrise offers general sightseeing tours around the city, but also longer excursions outside the city, including Mt Fuji and Hakone, Nikkō and Kamakura. Best though is their **Geisha Tour** (¥6800-18,800), which includes dinner, from Hamamatsuchō Bus Terminal to Ginza.

☎ 5796 5454 🖥 www .jtb.co.jp/sunrisetour/esun risetop.html 🕐 9am-6pm

Vingt-et-un

Vingt-et-un (Twenty-one) offers afternoon cruises and evening dinner excursions with excellent meals (usually featuring French *haute cuisine*), departing from Takeshiba Pier, near the Yurikamome line station. Reservations are essential.

☎ 3436 2121 🖥 www .vantean.co.jp ✉ 1-12-2 Kaigan, Minato-ku 💲 afternoon cruise from ¥2040, dinner cruise from ¥10,000 🚉 Yurikamome line to Takeshiba

---

Tramming It

Tokyo has one tram service still in operation. There used to be an extensive tram system across the city, but as car ownership became popular in the '60s and '70s, trams just got in the way. The Toden Arakawa tram line doesn't really go anywhere special, but it passes through a couple of areas that haven't (yet) been claimed by redevelopment. It runs from Waseda (west Tokyo) to Minowabashi (east Tokyo).

The best place to get on is at the **Zōshigaya cemetery** (2,C3; ¥160 one way; Yūrakuchō line to Higashi-Ikebukuro). It's the resting place of Lafcadio Hearn, remarkable cosmopolitan chronicler of everyday Meiji Japan, and of his contemporary, the popular writer Natsume Sōseki. From here the tram trundles east past Sunshine City and through Ōtsuka and Sugamo, passing a number of temples. After Ikebukuro, the tram is mostly off-road, winding through older residential areas.

Shopping

Shopping as leisure, as therapy, as appeasement, as socialising, as investment, as obligation, as identity both personal and collective – this is shopping in Tokyo. Shopping is a Tokyo lifestyle and gift-giving a tradition that has evolved into an art. It's no wonder, then, that this city is a candy store for the consumer with cash.

Even if you're on a budget, there are wonderful inexpensive things to take home: *washi* (handmade paper), lacquer bowls at the ¥100 shops, and dictionary-thick manga (comics). Clotheshorses can run amok in this city of cutting-edge style, finding fashions they can be sure no-one's wearing back home. And deals can still be found on electronics and camera equipment.

Stores are generally open every day, but sometimes closed on Mondays; large department stores *(depāto)* close one or two days each month. Shops tend to open around 10am or 11am, and stay open until 7pm or 8pm. Keep in mind that Japan may very well be the only Asian country where bargaining, unless you're at a flea market, is simply not done. Also, despite the changing of times, Japan remains a largely cash-based society. Plastic is being accepted in more shops nowadays, but always have a wad of yen as a backup. On luxury items such as electronics, the 5% VAT (value-added tax) can be waived for foreigners – bring your passport or lose out.

So out you go, shopaholics and shopaphobics alike: you will acquire something in Tokyo whether you want to or not. You cannot go into the streets without being swept up into the rush of commerce. But you can be sure you'll end up with something cute, quirky or chic, and you'll love it.

Shopping 'Hoods

For status, go straight to **Ginza** glam. Otherwise, take your acquisitional ways further afield. **Aoyama** is a good place to start – with the most elite of boutiques and cappuccino on the side.

Antique freaks should hit Aoyama's **Kotto-dōri** (Antiques St), where antique shops rub shoulders with trendy boutiques; head for **Jimbōchō** to look for used books in English.

Try **Akihabara** and **Shinjuku** for manga and electronics, and **Shibuya** and **Harajuku** for what Tokyo's trendy kids are wearing.

For old-style ambience roam around Asakusa's **Nakamise-dōri**, and for street-market style, stop by **Ameyoko Arcade** in Ueno.

DEPARTMENT STORES & MALLS

Get ready, set, go go go: shopping in a Tokyo *depāto* is a trip in itself. Know before you go that most *depāto* are closed on varying Mondays or Wednesdays each month.

Isetan (4, C2)
Long identified as *the* Tokyo department store, Isetan's window displays are always eye-catching if not downright bizarre. There's a customer service department on the 7th floor that provides English-speaking guides.
☎ 3352 1111 ✉ 3-14-1 Shinjuku, Shinjuku-ku ⏰ 10am-8pm 🚇 Yamanote line to Shinjuku (east exit) 🚇 Marunouchi line to Shinjuku-sanchōme (exits B3, B4 & B5)

Marui (4, C2)
Look for the Marui logo – OIOI – to find these department store branches. Here, you can pick up inexpensive but good quality youth-oriented clothing, as long as you're Japanese-sized. (Take heart, Japanese youth are getting a lot bigger.) Split into men's and women's buildings, you can't throw a coat hanger in Shinjuku without hitting a Marui.
☎ 3354 0101 ✉ 3-18-1 Shinjuku, Shinjuku-ku ⏰ 10am-8pm 🚇 Marunouchi & Toei Shinjuku lines to Shinjuku-sanchōme (exits A2, A3 & A4)

Matsuya (12, C4)
A boon for foreign visitors, Matsuya has the full works with packaging and international shipping service, tax-exemption assistance and useful, if haphazard, in-store English-speaking guides. Check out the latest exhibi-

tion at Matsuya's respectable art gallery on the 7th floor.
☎ 3567 1211 ✉ 3-6-1 Ginza, Chūō-ku ⏰ 10.30am-7.30pm 🚇 Ginza, Marunouchi & Hibiya lines to Ginza (exits A12 & A13)

Mitsukoshi (12, C4)
In the heart of Nihonbashi, Tokyo's oldest department store was originally modelled on that London bastion of commerce, Harrods. Mitsukoshi is a posh, polished leviathan filled to the gills with tempting wares. In the basement is a sumptuous food hall where the packaged gift foods seem like museum pieces rather than munchies.
☎ 3241 3311 ✉ 1-4-1 Nihombashi-muromachi, Chūō-ku ⏰ 10am-7pm 🚇 Hanzōmon & Ginza lines to Mitsukoshimae (exits A2, A3, A5, A7 & A8)

Sunshine City Alpa (2, C2)
Since Ikebukuro's shopping mecca is not as trendy as those in Shibuya and Shinjuku, it isn't as crowded – yet you're still deluged with shopping possibilities. Attractions include a good aquarium, planetarium, hypnotic car showroom and museum on site.
☎ 3989 3331 ✉ 3-1-3 Higashi-Ikebukuro, Toshima-ku ⏰ 10am-8pm 🚇 Marunouchi & Yūrakuchō lines to Ikebukuro (exits C4, C7, C8, 1b & 2a)

Takashimaya (4, B3)
Takashimaya's flagship store in Nihonbashi is worth a browse for its palatial architecture and white-gloved elevator and escalator attendants who bow demurely as you arrive and depart. But get terrifically lost in the newer, massive branch in the Times Square complex in Shinjuku. Both specialise in delivering expensive gifts during the New Year and midsummer gift-giving seasons.
☎ 5361 1111 ✉ 5-24-2 Sendagaya Shibuya-ku ⏰ 10am-8pm, restaurants 11am-11pm 🚇 Yamanote line to Shinjuku (east exit) 🚇 Toei Shinjuku line to Shinjuku (Shin-South exit) 🅿

Tōkyū Hands (5, A2)
Ostensibly a do-it-yourself store, Tōkyū Hands actually carries a comprehensive collection of everything you didn't know you needed, from blown-glass pens to chainsaws, hand-crafted tōfu-tongs and retro-mod lucite chairs. The Godzilla section is a must. The coolest branch is in Shibuya, but there are others in Ikebukuro and Takashimaya Times Square.
☎ 5489 5111 ✉ 12-18 Udagawachō, Shibuya-ku ⏰ 10am-8pm 🚇 Yamanote line to Shibuya (Hachikō exit) 🚇 Ginza & Hanzōmon lines to Shibuya (exits 6 & 7)

MARKETS

Pull yourself away from the magnetic allure of the giant, glittery department stores and shopping complexes, and like anywhere else in the world you'll find better deals and people in everyday mode at Tokyo's street markets.

Ameyoko Arcade (10, B3)
This thriving daily market is the nearest thing Tokyo has to an Asian street market. The city's African, Asian and Indian communities have joined the throng, so you can pick up Thai curry spices in the Ameyoko Center Building after snapping up that knock-off Gucci bag from a street stall.
✉ 4 Ueno, Taitō-ku ⊙ 10am-8pm ⊙ Ginza & Hibiya lines to Ueno (exit 5b) 🚈 Yamanote line to Ueno (Hirokōji exit)

Hanazono-jinja Antique Market (4, C1)
This place bills itself as an antique market – read: much the same stuff as at the flea markets, but with higher prices. But it's a pleasant market to poke around, right on the edge of Kabukichō.
☎ 3200 3093 ✉ 5-17-3 Shinjuku, Shinjuku-ku ⊙ 8am-4pm Sun ⊙ Marunouchi line to Shinjuku-sanchōme (exit C6)

Heiwajima Antique Festival (3, D9)
This huge three-day antique market usually takes place five times each year. Stuff you'll find covers the antique spectrum, from top-class ceramics to samurai armour to postage stamps. Call the TVCB TIC (p120) for exact dates.

☎ 3980 8228 ✉ 2F, Heiwajima Tokyo Ryūtsū Bldg Centre, 6-1-1 Heiwajima, Ōta-ku ⊙ 10am-6pm Mar, May, Jun, Sep & Dec 🚈 Tokyo Monorail to Ryūtsū Centre (main exit)

International Arcade (12, B5)
Built in 1960, this arcade is split into two parts, both conglomerations of stores specialising in Japanese souvenirs – fans, *happi* (half-coats) and 'I Love Tokyo' T-shirts. English is spoken, tax refunds are available, all major credit cards are accepted, and it's recommended mostly for the convenience factor. But a cut above are SI Brothers and Hayashi Kimono.
✉ 2-1-1 Yūrakuchō & 1-7-23 Uchisaiwaichō, Chiyoda-ku ⊙ 9.30am-6.30pm ⊙ Marunouchi & Hibiya lines to Ginza (exits A1 & C1)

Nogi-jinja flea market (9, B1)
This cheery market takes place once a month and is not as crowded as others. It's just around the corner from the Asia Centre of Japan.
☎ 3478 3001 ✉ 8-11-27 Akasaka, Minato-ku ⊙ 5.30am-3pm 2nd Sun of each month except Nov ⊙ Chiyoda line to Nogizaka (exit 1)

Tōgō-jinja flea market (6, A1)
Right in the heart of Harajuku, this great little flea market consistently produces interesting finds. Even if nothing good turns up, the shrine's grounds are a lovely setting for a market morning.
☎ 3403 3591 ✉ 1-5-3 Jingū-mae, Shibuya-ku ⊙ 5am-3pm 1st, 4th & 5th Sun of each month except Dec 🚈 Yamanote line to Harajuku (Takeshita-dōri exit)

Last-Minute Shibuya

So you've snagged some **fake food** on Kappabashi-dōri in Asakusa (it's a craft – expect to pay ¥4000 for a bowl of plastic *rāmen*), swung by Harajuku's **Oriental Bazaar** (p56) for a *yukata* (cotton kimono), and snapped up *washi* (handmade paper) in Ginza. But you're leaving Tokyo tomorrow and haven't found that perfect trinket for your sister. What to do? Head straight for Shibuya, where you'll find stupendous steals at **Daiso 100 Yen Plaza** (5, B2; ☎ 5459 3601; 27-4 Udagawachō, Shibuya-ku; ⊙ 11am-11pm) and stylish treats at **Loft** (p61), a sure-fire last stop.

ART & ANTIQUES

Fuji-Torii (6, B1)
This reliable antique dealer has been in the business since 1948 and stocks everything from exquisite *kutani* ceramics to inexpensive modern wood-block prints. It has an especially good selection of beautiful *byōbu* (antique folding screens).
☎ 3400 2777 ✉ 6-1-10 Jingūmae, Shibuya-ku ⏱ 11am-6pm Wed-Mon, closed every 3rd Mon Ⓜ Chiyoda line to Meiji-jingūmae (exit 4)

Inachu Lacquerware (8, B3)
Inachu is a renowned shop from Ishikawa prefecture, specialising in that area's prized and pricey *Wajima-nuri* lacquerware. Made from *keyaki* wood and painstakingly coated and burnished with many layers of lacquer, prices for the real article start at ¥30,000.
☎ 3582 4451 ✉ 1-5-2 Akasaka, Minato-ku ⏱ 10am-6pm Mon-Sat Ⓜ Ginza, Marunouchi & Namboku lines to Tameike-sannō (exit 9)

Japan Sword (12, A6)
This highly respected dealer in swords has a beautiful showroom and lots of experience in helping foreign tourists choose the right sword for their taste and budget. It also refurbishes swords, in case you've got one languishing with disuse. Priciest and spookiest are the *tameshi-giri* blades that have been 'used on humans'.

Dive into detail shopping for *yukata* (cotton kimonos)

☎ 3434 4321 🖥 www .japansword.co.jp ✉ 3-8-1, Toranomon, Minato-ku ⏱ 9.30am-6pm Mon-Fri, 9.30am-5pm Sat Ⓜ Hibiya line to Kamiya-cho (exit 3)

Japan Traditional Crafts Center (2, A2)
If you're at all interested in taking home some traditionally made gifts, take a detour through this centre to admire the lovely examples of handmade crafts – weavings, mosaics, bows and arrows, ceramics and *washi*. Temporary exhibitions are displayed on the 3rd floor.
☎ 5954 6066 ✉ 1F & 2F, Metropolitan Plaza Bldg, 1-11-1 Nishi-Ikebukuro, Toshima-ku ⏱ 11am-7pm 🚆 Yamanote line to Ikebukuro (Metropolitan exit)

Ohya Shobō (3, D4)
You could lose yourself for hours in this splendid, musty old bookshop specialising in ukiyo-e prints and ancient maps. The friendly staff can help you find whatever particular piece of antiquated trivia your heart desires.
☎ 3291 0062 🖥 www .abaj.gr.jp/ohyashobo /index-j.htm ✉ 1-1 Kanda Jimbōchō, Chiyoda-ku ⏱ 10am-6pm Mon-Sat Ⓜ Toei Shinjuku, Toei Mita & Hanzōmon lines to Jimbōchō (exit A7)

On Sundays (6, C1)
Connected to Watari Museum of Contemporary Art (p33), On Sundays carries a predictably unpredictable collection of avant-garde art for sale. It has a humongous selection of funky to classic postcards, and a marvellous array of functional arthouse objects, such as purses in the shapes of origami balloons and Scandinavian-style office accoutrements – as well as books on art, architecture and design.
☎ 3470 1424 ✉ 3-7-6 Jingūmae, Shibuya-ku ⏱ 11am-7pm Tue-Sun Ⓜ Ginza line to Gaien-mae (exit 2)

Oriental Bazaar (6, B1)
Carrying a wide-ranging selection of antiques and tourist items at very reasonable prices, Oriental Bazaar is an excellent spot for one-stop souvenir shopping. Good gifts to be found here include fans, folding screens, pottery, porcelain and kimonos. The branch at Narita airport opens at 7.30am for last-chance suit-of-armour purchases.
☎ 3400 3933 ✉ 5-9-13 Jingūmae, Shibuya-ku ⏱ 10am-7pm Fri-Wed ⊕ Chiyoda line to Meiji-jingūmae (exit 4)

Satomi Building (2, A3)
The locals call it this, but its real name is **Tokyo Ko-mingu Kotto Kan** (Tokyo Antiques Hall). It's a collection of around two dozen small antique shops, many specialising in items such as ceramics, ukiyo-e, masks, paintings and small statues from Japan and nearby Asian countries. Prices and quality vary.
☎ 3980 8228 ✉ 3-9-5 Minami-Ikebukuro, Toshima-ku ⏱ 10am-6pm Mon-Sat 🚃 Yamanote line to Ikebukuro (east exit)

Tolman Collection (3, D7)
For collectors interested in contemporary art, this well-respected, long-standing gallery represents a variety of printmakers, both Japanese and foreign. Though the artists here have a fairly broad range of styles, ranging from abstract to representative, all of the work has a distinctly Japanese feel.
☎ 3434 1300 🖥 www .tolmantokyo.com ✉ 2-2-18 Shiba-Daimon, Minato-ku ⏱ 11am-7pm Wed-Mon ⊕ Toei Asakusa & Toei Ōedo lines to Daimon (exit A3)

MUSIC & BOOKS

HMV (5, B2)
With many floors of music and video, His Master's Voice is challenging the domination of Tower Records. At five floors, its smaller scale makes for a far more chilled-out musical browse than in the frenetic tower of Tower. In addition to the listening stations, it has fancy video previews too.
☎ 5458 3411 ✉ 24-1 Udagawachō, Shibuya-ku ⏱ 10am-midnight ⊕ Ginza & Hanzōmon lines to Shibuya (exits 3 & 6) 🚃 Yamanote line to Shibuya (Hachikō exit)

Kinokuniya (4, C3)
Kinokuniya's annexe store in the Takashimaya Times Square complex surpasses the main Shinjuku store with its variety and depth of titles in English. Find foreign-language books on the 6th floor, and a rainy day's worth of art books,

> ## Tokyo Tomes
> Other guides you might find useful in your Tokyo travels include the excellent *Tokyo for Free* (Susan Pompian, 1998) and *Little Adventures in Tokyo: 39 Thrills for the Urban Traveler* (Rick Kennedy, 1998). Fiction fiends should consider finding a copy of Alan Brown's *Audrey Hepburn's Neck: A Novel* (1996), a humorously insightful story centring on sex in the city – it's contemporary, candid and a fun read.

magazines and manga everywhere else.
☎ 5361 3301 ✉ Annex Bldg, Takashimaya Times Square, 5-24-5 Sendagaya, Shibuya-ku ⏱ 10am-8pm, closed one Wed each month 🚃 Chūō line to Shinjuku (south exit)

Maruzen (12, C3)
Another centrally located bookshop, Maruzen in Nihonbashi has a respectably wide selection of English-language books. The place isn't as hectic as

Kinokuniya, so the book-browsing is more on the mellow side.
☎ 3272 7211 ✉ 2-3-10 Nihonbashi, Chūō-ku ⏱ 10am-7pm Sun ⊕ Ginza, Tōzai & Toei Asakusa lines to Nihonbashi (exit B1)

Tower Records (5, B2)
Tower is Tokyo's largest music store (and that's saying something). Despite its size, this place gets packed. If you can't get it here, you can't get it anywhere. Tower also carries a large selection

of English-language books and a fabulous array of magazines and newspapers from around the world. Magazines here are considerably cheaper than elsewhere around town.
☎ 3496 3661 ✉ 7F, Tower Records Bldg, 1-22-14 Jinnan, Shibuya-ku

🕑 10am-11pm 🚇 Ginza & Hanzōmon lines to Shibuya (exit 7) 🚃 Yamanote line to Shibuya (Hachikō exit)

Virgin Megastore (2, A1)
Virgin has landed a decent, though not gigantic spot in low-key west Ikebukuro.

There's a pretty good selection of home-grown J-pop to sample, and the staff here are very helpful in finding the tunes you desire.
☎ 3989 0210 ✉ 3-30-13 Nishi-Ikebukuro
🕑 10am-7pm 🚃 Yamanote line to Ikebukuro (west exit)

CAMERAS & ELECTRONICS

Remember to bring your passport to make duty-free purchases. And because prices sometimes vary significantly, shopping around a bit does pay off.

Bic Camera (2, B1)
Bic Camera claims to be the cheapest camera store in Japan, a claim hotly disputed by Yodobashi (p58) and Sakuraya (p58) camera stores. Its big bargain bins of film that is approaching its expiry date are good value – the merchandise is fine. Bic also has branches in Shibuya and Shinjuku.

☎ 3988 0002 ✉ 1-11-7 Higashi-Ikebukuro, Toshima-ku 🕑 10am-8pm 🚇 Marunouchi line to Ikebukuro (exits 23, 29 & 30)

Laox (13, E2)
The multilingual staff at Laox will help you figure out whether the voltage on your new superjuicer is

compatible with your home voltage before you lug it on the plane. This huge chain, selling discounted electrical equipment, has very competitive prices. Also check out Laox Duty Free, nearby.
☎ 3255 9041 ✉ 1-2-9 Soto-Kanda, Chiyoda-ku 🕑 10am-7.30pm 🚃 Yamanote line to Akihabara (Electric Town exit)

Electronics Buzz
While Tokyo's range of electronic products is astounding, many products are only for the domestic market, and it may prove impossible to have repairs done once you return home. Make sure the voltages (p115) of electronic products will be compatible with that of your country.

While Akihabara (Electric Town; 3, E1) is famous for bargains, the big stores in Ikebukuro and Shinjuku are giving Akihabara a run for its money. Shinjuku tends to have the best prices for cameras and film. Some stores have tax-free floors for nonresidents. And in all cases, as your mama told you: you'd better shop around.

Mac Store (12, C4)
O, haven of Apple goodness in Ginza! Apple opened its first Tokyo store in November 2003, filled with assorted baubles and perks – including games for kids and workshops for Mac users. Multilingual staff work all five floors of this sleek Ginza cube to help you find what you need.
☎ 5159 8200 ✉ 3-5-12 Ginza, Chuo-ku ☺ 10am-9pm ⊕ Ginza, Hibiya & Marunouchi lines to Ginza (exits A9 & A13)

Sakuraya Camera (4, B2)
Yodobashi Camera's chief rival offers much the same as others and at similar prices. It has an incredible selection of lenses and hot little digital cameras. You'll find some great deals here but like anywhere, comparison shopping is essential.
☎ 5368 1717 ✉ 3-17-20 Shinjuku, Shinjuku-ku

☺ 10am-8.30pm
⊕ Marunouchi line to Shinjuku (exits B7, B8 & B9)

Sofmap (13, E1)
Crafty marketing, ruthless discounting and a staff of tech geeks have helped Sofmap sprout more than a dozen branches within Akihabara alone. This company rules the cut-price computer world with a fist of silicon. Each shop specialises in new and used Macs, PCs and other cyber-goodies – but, as everywhere, buyer beware of used parts.
☎ 3253 3030 ✉ 3-14-10 Soto-Kanda, Chiyoda-ku ☺ 10.30am-8pm Mon-Sat, 10am-7pm Sun ⊠ Yamanote line to Akihabara (Electric Town exit)

T Zone Computers (13, E1)
In Akihabara, T Zone still has the best selection of machines with English-

operating systems and software. You'll find helpful, English-speaking staff here as well. There's another branch in Shinjuku.
☎ 3257 2659 ✉ 4-4-1 Soto-Kanda, Chiyoda-ku ☺ 10.30am-7pm Sun-Thu, 10.30am-7.30pm Fri & Sat ⊠ Yamanote line to Akihabara (Electric Town exit)

Yodobashi Camera (4, B2)
One of Tokyo's most famous camera stores, this emporium stocks anything from digital cameras to second-hand enlargers. Prices at Yodobashi are very competitive, and if you can't find it here then it probably can't be found in Japan.
☎ 3346 1010 ✉ 1-11-1 Nishi-Shinjuku, Shinjuku-ku ☺ 9.30am-9.30pm ⊕ Toei Shinjuku line to Shinjuku (exit 5) ⊠ Chūō line to Shinjuku (Minami-guchi & south exits)

CLOTHING

Comme des Garçons (6, C2)
When Rei Kawakubo hit international recognition status in the early '80s, it was with her revolutionary, minimalist, matte-black designs. Her lines have evolved from the simple black chic, but even with asymmetrical cuts, illusions of torn fabric and sleeves gone missing, her style is consistently a departure from the norm. This Aoyama wonder is her flagship store.
☎ 3406 3951 ✉ 5-2-1 Minami-Aoyama, Minato-ku ☺ 11am-8pm

⊕ Chiyoda, Ginza & Hanzōmon lines to Omote-sandō (exit A5)

Hanae Mori (6, B2)
Much beloved by the French (as indeed is Rei Kawakubo), Hanae Mori's 'European classic' style is also much emulated, but her real success lies in her adulation amongst hordes of *ojō-sama,* the conservative well-brought-up daughters of the Tokyo *riche.*
☎ 3423 1448 ✉ Hanae Mori Bldg, 3-6-1 Kita-Aoyama, Minato-ku ☺ 11am-7pm

⊕ Chiyoda, Ginza & Hanzōmon lines to Omote-sandō (exit A1)

Hysteric Glamour (6, A2)
It's really attitudinal tongue-in-cheek rather than hysteric glamour, but whatever you want to call it, it's sexy and fun. These designer confections are a good place to start for hip fashion with a Tokyo twist. There's even a toddler line, the ultimate in designer punk for your little rocker.
☎ 3409 7227 ✉ 6-23-2 Jingūmae, Shibuya-ku ☺ 11am-8pm

Your credit card won't get enough at Comme des Garçons

⊕ Chiyoda line to Meiji-jingūmae (exits 1 & 4)
🚇 Yamanote line to Harajuku (Omote-sandō exit)

Issey Miyake (6, C2)

Anarchic but chic conceptual fashion continue to flow from Issey Miyake. At the cluster of Aoyama shops along the south end of Omote-sandō, eye his famous pleated designs, or the A-POC garments – each made from a single piece of fabric. The gallery-like window displays are worth a look, after checking out the mirrored Prada spaceship across the street.
☎ 3423 1407 ✉ 3-18-11 Minami-Aoyama, Minato-ku ⏱ 10am-8pm
⊕ Chiyoda, Ginza & Hanzōmon lines to Omote-sandō (exit A4)

Laforet (6, A1)

Expressing identity and individuality is a function of fashion and Tokyo youth are famous for taking this concept to another level. Check out Laforet even if you're not looking for an artfully shredded, raw silk and vinyl micromini; watching the teenyboppers and twenty-somethings browsing for wardrobe elements is equal to the window shopping.
☎ 5411 3330 ✉ 1-11-6 Jingūmae, Shibuya-ku ⏱ 11am-8pm 🚇 Yamanote line to Harajuku (Omote-sandō exit)

CLOTHING & SHOE SIZES

Women's Clothing

Aust/UK	8	10	12	14	16	18
Europe	36	38	40	42	44	46
Japan	5	7	9	11	13	15
USA	6	8	10	12	14	16

Women's Shoes

Aust/USA	5	6	7	8	9	10
Europe	35	36	37	38	39	40
France only	35	36	38	39	40	42
Japan	22	23	24	25	26	27
UK	3½	4½	5½	6½	7½	8½

Men's Clothing

Aust	92	96	100	104	108	112
Europe	46	48	50	52	54	56

Japan	S	M	M		L	
UK/USA	35	36	37	38	39	40

Men's Shirts (Collar Sizes)

Aust/Japan	38	39	40	41	42	43
Europe	38	39	40	41	42	43
UK/USA	15	15½	16	16½	17	17½

Men's Shoes

Aust/UK	7	8	9	10	11	12
Europe	41	42	43	44½	46	47
Japan	26	27	27½	28	29	30
USA	7½	8½	9½	10½	11½	12½

*Measurements approximate only;
try before you buy.*

Muji (6, C1)

Muji – literally, 'no name' – is the paradoxical no-label designer brand that took Japan, then Paris, London and Hong Kong by storm. Everything is reasonably priced with simple design, from tea sets to cool toddler cycles. Best of all, it has reasonably priced clothing with an easy, clean style. This branch is the flagship store, but look for branches in department stores.

☎ 3478 5800 ✉ 2-12-18 Kita-Aoyama, Minato-ku ⏱ 10am-8pm Ⓜ Ginza line to Gaienmae (exit 2)

Undercover (6, C2)

Former punk band frontman Jun Takahashi has been domesticated – only in the fashion sense of the word. His line uses wallpaper and tablecloth, and though still dark and abstract, elements of the ugly have gone. True to Japanese fashion, he's edgy, hip and creative, almost to inaccessibility. But for you, perhaps not?

☎ 3407 1232 ✉ 5-3-18 Minami-Aoyama, Minato-ku ⏱ 11am-8pm Ⓜ Chiyoda, Ginza & Hanzōmon lines to Omote-sandō (exit A5)

UNIQLO (6, A1)

Like Muji and the Gap, UNIQLO has made a name for itself by sticking to the basics. Offering inexpensive, quality clothing with simple style, this chain has taken Tokyo by typhoon, with over 80 stores. You'll find the original outpost in Harajuku, and without even trying, you'll stumble over dozens more all over town.

☎ 5468 7313 ✉ 6-10-8 Jingumae, Shibuya-ku ⏱ 11am-9pm Ⓜ Chiyoda line to Meiji-jingūmae (exits 1 & 4)

FOOD & DRINK

Fukumitsuya (12, C5)

This sleek little shop, whose brewery has been around since 1625, is wedged amongst the elite boutiques around Ginza. In addition to selling high-quality sake, the shop stocks accoutrements such as ceramic flasks and iron tea sets, holds tastings, and even has a restaurant upstairs serving sake-centric cuisine. Stop by for a sample, and consider taking home something to sip.

☎ 3569 2291 ▢ www .fukumitsuya.co.jp /english/ginza/index ✉ 5-5-8 Ginza ⏱ noon-10pm Mon-Sat, noon-6pm Sun Ⓜ Ginza, Hibiya & Marunouchi lines to Ginza (exit B3)

Meidi-ya (9, B2)

Meidi-ya specialises in high-end groceries for foreign palates, carrying cheeses, wines, cookies and other titbits you might crave in this foreign land. Note there are other locations throughout the city, including branches in Akasaka and Ginza.

☎ 3401 8511 ✉ 7-15-14 Roppongi ⏱ 10am-9pm Ⓜ Hibiya line to Roppongi (exit 2)

National Azabu (3, C7)

Posher than posh can be, National Azabu is where the ambassadorial lackeys are sent to stock up on pâté de foie gras and truffles or their Japanese equivalents, *uni* (sea urchins) and *matsutake* (mushrooms). It's also got an awesome selection of imported wines and natural foods and has a pharmacy staffed with English-speakers.

☎ 3442 3181 ✉ 4-5-2 Minami-Azabu, Minato-ku ⏱ 9.30am-7pm Ⓜ Hibiya line to Hiro-o (exits 1 & 2)

Sweet! Japanese confectionery

HOMEWARES

Axis Building (9, C2)
Salivate over some of Japan's most innovative interior design at this Roppongi design complex. Of the 20 or so galleries and retail shops selling fabrics, furniture and art books, highlights are **Kisso** (specialising in ceramics) and **Yoshikin** for beautifully crafted, inexpensive kitchenware.
☎ 3587 2781 ✉ 5-17-1 **Roppongi, Minato-ku** 🕙 11am-7pm Mon-Sat 🚇 Hibiya line to Roppongi (exit 3)

Illums (2, B2)
Illums carries more of those designer items that you can justify purchasing because…hey, they're functional. It's a sleek emporium of Scandinavian homewares on the 1st and 2nd floors of Seibu Ikebukuro's east building.
☎ 5992 8678 ✉ 1-28-1 **Minami-Ikebukuro, Toshima-ku** 🕙 10am-9pm Mon-Sat 🚇 Yamanote line to Ikebukuro (west exit)

In The Room (2, A1)
In the Room is the well-designed nesting section of Marui department store, but it's located in its own building behind the main store in west Ikebukuro. Shops carry everything to outfit your home, from coffee cups to svelte Bang & Olufsen stereos.
☎ 3989 0101 ✉ 3-29-1 **Nishi-Ikebukuro, Toshima-ku** 🕙 10am-8pm Mon-Sat 🚇 Yamanote line to Ikebukuro (west exit)

Loft (5, B2)
Insert expendable income here. Loft offers an enormous range of useful goodies, such as silk washcloths, sleek furniture and kitchen appliances, but the best merchandise is the goofy, senseless goods such as miniature plastic sushi, plush shoe-fresheners in smiley-faced hedgehog shapes and other seductive silliness. Don't forego the 6th floor, filled with toys, travel gear and ¥200 capsule dispensers.
☎ 3462 3807 ✉ 21-1 **Udagawa-chō, Shibuya-ku;** 🕙 10am-8pm Sun-Wed, 10am-9pm Thu-Sat 🚇 Ginza & Hanzōmon lines to Shibuya (exits 6 & 7) 🚇 Yamanote line to Shibuya (Hachikō exit)

KIDS' STUFF

Hakuhinkan Toy Park (12, C5)
One of Tokyo's most famous toy stores, this 'toy park' is crammed to the ceiling with dolls, action figures, squawking video games, seas of colourful plastic and the softest plush toys ever invented. Hakuhinkan also harbours child-friendly restaurants and even a theatre in this huge children's attention-deficit paradise.
☎ 3571 8008 🖥 www.hakuhinkan.co.jp ✉ 8-8-11 Ginza, Chūō-ku 🕙 11am-8pm 🚇 Toei Asakusa & Ginza lines to Shimbashi (exits 1 & 3) 🚇 Yamanote line to Shimbashi (Ginza exit)

Kiddyland (6, B1)
Eep: five floors of products for your children to fall in lust with and which you may still be paying for next year. In fact, you yourself may be regressively seduced by plastic-bobbled barrettes, Pokémon paraphernalia or nostalgia-inducers like her feline highness Hello Kitty or Ultraman.
☎ 3409 3431 ✉ 6-1-9 Jingūmae, Shibuya-ku 🕙 10am-8pm, closed 3rd Tue of each month 🚇 Chiyoda line to Meiji-jingūmae (exit 4)

Mandarake (3, A4)
A must-stop for manga maniacs, Mandarake has more than a dozen shops spread throughout the Nakano Broadway mall. In addition to manga and *anime* offerings, there are toys on consignment, animation cells for sale and video games. The mall is across from the JR Nakano station; there are other branches are in Shibuya and Akihabara.
☎ 3228 0007 🖥 www.mandarake.co.jp/english/shop/nkn.html ✉ 5-52-15 Nakano, Nakano-ku 🕙 noon-8pm 🚇 Chūō line to Nakano (north exit)

JEWELLERY & ACCESSORIES

Atelier Magic Theater (6, B1)

A rarity in Tokyo, this studio is run by three friends who craft the jewellery in their on-site workshop. Their lovely pieces reflect themes and patterns in nature, and the jewellery lines range from plain-silver designs to sculptural work incorporating stones, wood and gold. Some of their jewellery is available online, but custom orders can also be arranged. ☎ 3478 5534 ⌨ www.magic-theater.org ✉ 3-20-21 J Meiji-jingūmae, Shibuya-ku ☽ noon-8pm ⍟ Yamanote line to Harajuku (Takeshita-dōri exit) Ⓒ Chiyoda line to Meiji-jingūmae (exits 2 & 3)

Mikimoto Pearl (12, C4)

Running since 1899, Mikimoto Pearl was founded by the self-made Mikimoto Kokichi. At an early age, he became fascinated with pearl divers and later developed the cultured pearl, building Mikimoto into the most famous of Tokyo's pearl shops. The store is located in glamorous Ginza, right next door to Wakō department store and opposite Mitsukoshi. ☎ 3535 4611 ⌨ www.mikimoto.com/html/en ✉ 4-5-5 Ginza, Chūō-ku ☽ 9.30am-6.30pm Ⓒ Ginza, Hibiya & Marunouchi lines to Ginza (exit B5)

Tasaki Shinju (12, C5)

Tasaki Shinju's six-floor monolith in Ginza is Mikimoto's chief rival. Tasaki is perhaps more experimental in his use of the gems and if the words 'diamond-encrusted' trigger your curiosity, this is your jeweller. There is also a branch in Akasaka. ☎ 3289 1111 ⌨ www.tasaki.co.jp/en/index-e.htm ✉ 5-7-5 Ginza, Chūō-ku ☽ 10.30am-7.30pm Ⓒ Ginza, Hibiya & Marunouchi lines to Ginza (exits A1 & A2)

Vending Machines

Not to put too fine a point on it, but where else in the world do you think you could find vending machines dispensing sex toys and cold beer? Toy stores, too, are a treasure trove of capsule machines – for ¥200 you can get your hands on Grateful Dead dancing bear keychains or Gloomy Bear cellphone charms. In subway stations or on the streets, pick up fresh bouquets, fresh eggs or fresh porn mags. Word to the wise: avoid the hot coffee. Also, who *is* that ubiquitous 'Boss', dispensing refreshing drinks to the masses – Vladimir Lenin?

Thirsty? Go quench yourself at a vending machine... Now, what to choose?

PAPER & STATIONERY

Most department stores have sections devoted to *washi* and stationery, but these specialty shops are particularly noteworthy for the quality of their *washi*, origami, stationery and handmade gems crafted from paper.

Haibara (12, C2)

Even the business cards at Haibara are made from handmade paper that resemble slivers of wood. Find gorgeous paper and tiny treasures such as wallets, hand mirrors and cellphone accessories made from printed paper in this jewellery box of a paper shop. ☎ 32723801 ✉ 2-7-6 Nihombashi, Chūō-ku ⏱ 9.30am-6.30pm Mon-Fri, 9.30am-5pm Sat Ⓜ Ginza & Tozai lines to Nihombashi (exit C3)

Itoya (12, C4)

Nine floors of stationery-shop love welcome paper (and paperclip) fanatics into Itoya. In addition to a comprehensive collection of *washi*, there are Italian leather agendas, erasable pens in the season's hippest shades and even *tenugui* – beautifully hand-dyed, all-purpose traditional handkerchiefs. ☎ 3561 8311 ✉ 2-7-15 Ginza, Chūō-ku ⏱ 9.30am-7pm Mon-Sat, 9.30am-6pm Sun Ⓜ Ginza & Hibiya lines to Ginza (exits A12 & A13)

SPECIALIST STORES

Puppet House (3, C4)

Possibly slightly scary for small children or puppet-fearing adults, this is a wondrous workshop of functional, not just decorative, marionettes. Peopled by an international collection of puppets, this place is run by a superfriendly couple who are happy to talk shop. Look for the sign of Punch in an alley near Mizuho Bank. ☎ 5229 6477 🖳 www.puppet-house.co.jp ✉ 1-8 Shimomiyabi-chō, Shinjuku-ku ⏱ 11am-7pm Tue-Sat Ⓡ Chūō line to Iidabashi (east exit)

Sekaido Stationery (4, C2)

After stocking up on art supplies, of which Sekaido has a blindingly broad array, check out its vast selection of manga. From the intricately penned to the brown-paper wrapper variety, Sekaido has what you're looking for. ☎ 5379 1111 ✉ 3-1-1 Shinjuku, Shinjuku-ku ⏱ 9.30am-9pm Ⓜ Marunouchi & Toei Shinjuku lines to Shinjuku-sanchōme (exit C1)

Yoshitoku (3, F4)

Doll-maker to the emperor, Yoshitoku has been in business since 1711. The dolls here are exquisitely crafted in silk and porcelain, dressed in sumptuous replicas of elaborate kimonos and accessories. It's possible to buy a smaller piece for around ¥2000. For the larger ones, unlace those purse strings. ☎ 3863 4419 ✉ 1-9-14 Asakusabashi, Taitō-ku ⏱ 9.30am-5.30pm Ⓡ Sōbu line to Asakusabashi (exit A2)

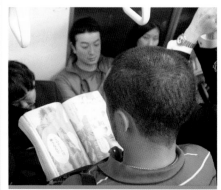
Subway storytelling with manga

Eating

Though Tokyoites are always on the move, eating's a serious business. From the simplicity of a convenience-store rice ball to *kaiseki-ryōri* restaurants orchestrating complex art on hand-thrown dishes, food in Tokyo is all in good taste – in flavour *and* presentation.

Rice is central to most meals, evinced in the term *gohan*, meaning both 'rice' and 'meal'. But there's a kaleidoscopic variety of food in Tokyo, from Ethiopian to Australian, French to Pakistani. Café culture thrives in the streets of Ebisu and Harajuku, with bistros and delis rounding out the mix for casual dining. Sophisticated wine lists offer savvy imported choices, and foreign and domestic beers appear on most menus. Stray from familiar Japanese favourites such as sushi and tempura, since Tokyo has it all. Try tempura on *udon* (dense, white, wheat noodles), *zaru soba* (thin buckwheat noodles, served cold), and rich, barbecued *unagi* (eel).

For novelty value, have drinks at a *kaiten-zushi,* where sushi travels by diners on a conveyor belt – but don't go there for quality. Or get a group together to have *sukiyaki* or *shabu-shabu,* where thinly sliced beef with tofu and vegetables is simmered in light broth at the table, and dipped into piquant sauces.

Cheap eats abound – *shokudō* (cheap mom-and-pop restaurants) and bistros offer great *teishoku* (lunch sets); standing-room-only *rāmen* (chinese-style noodles) shops dish out savoury broth and noodles; and *yakitori* (chicken skewers) stalls provide cheap fast food. Excellent lunch deals are everywhere for around ¥1000.

Grab a morning pastry and coffee in a *kissaten* (coffee shop); and late at night, seek out a train station *yatai* (street stall). In between: try something deliciously new.

> ## O-ikura Desu Ka?
> Prices indicate the cost of a dinner for one, excluding drinks. Tipping is not customary in Japan, but at top-end establishments, a 15% to 20% service charge will be added to your bill.
>
> | | |
> |---|---|
> | ¥ | under ¥2000 |
> | ¥¥ | ¥2000-5999 |
> | ¥¥¥ | ¥6000-11,999 |
> | ¥¥¥¥ | over ¥12,000 |

Tokyo Cuisine

Izakaya are rowdy, fun Japanese pubs, serving hearty drinking fare. *Robatayaki* (rustic bar-restaurant serving food grilled over charcoal) has a chef grilling dishes for you; at an *okonomiyaki,* it's DIY cooking of your pancake. Most common are *shokudō* for good deals on meal sets.

Okonomiyaki: DIY pancakes

But Japanese cuisine at its zenith is embodied in *kaiseki-ryōri* dining. All elements of a *kaiseki* meal, from ingredients to presentation, are carefully based upon the season and its available resources. Stemming from the tea ceremony tradition, meals are served in small courses, so the diner can admire the tastes, beauty and balance in each dish.

AKASAKA, NAGATA-CHŌ & TORANOMON

Asterix (8, A3)   ¥¥
French
A subterranean bistro that dreamed it was a wine cellar, Asterix is unpretentious enough to leave even its rough beams exposed. The prix fixe lunch menu is a steal, the 23-seat dining room a charmer. Look for the wine-crate lids that signal you've arrived at its dim, outer stairwell.
☎ 5561 0980 ✉ B1F, 6-3-16 Akasaka, Minato-ku ⏲ 11.30am-2pm & 6-10pm Mon-Sat Ⓜ Chiyoda line to Akasaka (exit 7) ♿

Mugyodon (8, B2)   ¥¥
Korean
This is a very popular and extremely friendly place. It's also a rare chance to sample the real Korean McCoy in Tokyo, not the usual toned-down version catering to Japanese tastes.
☎ 3586 6478 ✉ 2F, Sangyo Bldg, 2-17-74 Akasaka, Minato-ku ⏲ 5pm-midnight Mon-Sat Ⓜ Chiyoda line to Akasaka (exit 2)

Pho Garden (8, A2)   ¥
Vietnamese
Tune into the Viet-pop on the soundtrack and authentic dishes on the menu, and settle into a seat near one of the many windows to savour a taste of Vietnam. Enjoy *goi sen* (lotus root salad) or *pho* (beef noodle soup), accompanied by a Saigon beer.
☎ 5114 0747 ✉ 2-14-1 Akasaka, Minato-ku ⏲ 11.30am-11pm Mon-Fri, noon-11pm Sat, noon-

10pm Sun Ⓜ Chiyoda line to Akasaka (exit 2) ♿ Ⓥ

Rakutei (8, A3)   ¥¥¥¥
Tempura
If the Japanese have elevated the deep-fried to an art form, the chefs at Rakutei create masterpieces nightly. The freshest seafood and the lightest tempura batter are prepared to order, resulting in tender prawn and sweet potato that is transformed into something utterly heavenly.
☎ 3585 3743 ✉ 6-8-1 Akasaka, Minato-ku ⏲ 6-10pm Ⓜ Chiyoda line to Akasaka (exit 5) ♿

Sushi-sei (8, A2)   ¥¥
Sushi & sashimi
You'll find top-notch sushi at Sushi-sei, which traces its ancestry back to Tsukiji. Everyone sits at counters observing chefs in constant motion; and it's a serious business. Try to hit it during off-peak hours, or expect to queue with hungry government officials and financial movers and shakers.
☎ 3582 9503 ✉ 3-11-4 Akasaka, Minato-ku ⏲ 11.30am-2pm & 5-10.30pm Ⓜ Ginza & Marunouchi lines to Akasaka-mitsuke (Belle Vie exit)

Tofu-ya (8, B2)   ¥¥
Tofu
After finding its traditional wooden exterior on a small side street west of Sotobori-dōri, choose something equally traditional from the menu. On offer are myriad tofu dishes and a variety

of grilled fish. Lunch sets here are a great value, with thoughtfully balanced flavours.
☎ 3582 1028 ✉ 1F, Akasaka 3-5-2, Minato-ku ⏲ 11.30am-9pm Mon-Fri Ⓜ Chiyoda line to Akasaka (exit 2) Ⓥ

Toh-Ka-Lin (8, C3)   ¥¥¥¥
Chinese
Arch-rival to Aux Sept Bonheurs (p71), Toh-Ka-Lin claims to have the best Chinese food in Tokyo. It's a close call, but Toh-Ka-Lin holds one unbeatable trump card – it has access to Hotel Ōkura's indomitable wine cellar.
☎ 3505 6068 ✉ 6F, Hotel Ōkura, 2-10-4 Toranomon, Minato-ku ⏲ 11.30am-2.30pm & 5.30-9.30pm Ⓜ Ginza & Hibiya lines to Toranomon (exit 2) ♿ excellent ♿ Ⓥ

Trattoria Marumo (8, A1)   ¥¥
Italian
Serving respectable Italian fare, this pleasant pizzeria can quell your cravings for pasta without busting the bank. There are loads of food models in the window, but both the window and door may be difficult to spot behind the overgrown plants in front.
☎ 3585 5371 ✉ 1F, Tōyama Bldg, 3-8-14 Akasaka, Minato-ku ⏲ 11.30am-midnight Mon-Sat, noon-11pm Sun Ⓜ Ginza & Marunouchi lines to Akasaka-mitsuke (Belle Vie exit) ♿ fair ♿ Ⓥ

AKIHABARA & KANDA

Botan (13, E2)　　　¥¥¥
Japanese
Botan has been making flawless *torisuki*, an Edo-period pot-stew, in the same button-maker's house for more than 100 years. Savouring a meal here will be a culinary highlight of a visit to Tokyo. Reservations are recommended.
☎ 3251 0577 ✉ 1-15 Kanda-Sudachō, Chiyoda-ku ⏲ 11.30am-9pm Mon-Sat ⊖ Toei Shinjuku line to Ogawamachi (exit A3) ♿

Kanda Yabu Soba (13, E2)　　　¥¥
Soba
A Kanda stalwart, this *soba*'s authentic surroundings add to the atmosphere. Yet it's the noodles that make the day. Look for queues of customers in front of a traditional Japanese building in a garden setting, surrounded by a wooden fence.
☎ 3251 0287 ✉ 2-10 Kanda-Awajichō, Chiyoda-ku ⏲ 11.30am-8pm ⊖ Toei Shinjuku line to Ogawamachi (exit A3) ♿

Matsuya (13, E2)　　　¥¥
Soba
Rival to Kanda Yabu Soba and located almost next door, Matsuya is less crowded but still merry and bustling. Try plain *zaru soba*, then follow it up with the *kamo nanban*, *soba* with slices of roast duck. Soak it all up along with the crowd *de jour*.
☎ 3251 1556 ✉ 1-13 Kanda-Sudachō ⏲ 11.30am-8pm Mon-Sat ⊖ Toei Shinjuku line to Ogawamachi, (exit A3) ♿

Serious Business

Impressing a client with your pitch is enough to worry about. For business dining, consider the following establishments – all conducive to conversing, cocktails and closing deals. For quality Japanese cuisine, try **Rakutei** (p65), **Kyūbei** (p69) or **Echikatsu** (p79), or **New York Grill** (p78) for Western victuals.

As for the serious business of lunching with a Japanese friend or colleague, slurp noodles noisily at **Kanda Yabu Soba** (above), **Matsuya** (above) or **Muromachi Sunaba** (p70).

ASAKUSA

Edokko (11, B2)　　　¥¥
Tempura
Just outside the Senjō-ji complex is this famed restaurant named after the local folk. And in honour of Edo, this place serves the neighbourhood speciality, tempura (try the *tendon*, shrimp tempura on rice), in a very authentic atmosphere. Edokko has a traditional wooden façade and a white *noren* (curtain) outside.
☎ 3841 0150 ✉ 1-40-7 Asakusa, Taitō-ku ⏲ 11.30am-9pm Wed-Mon ⊖ Ginza & Toei Asakusa lines to Asakusa (exit 6) ♿ good ♿ Ⓥ

Khroop Khrua (11, B2)　　　¥
Thai & Vietnamese
In a neighbourhood known for its old Shitamachi spirit, you may hanker for something slightly less traditional. In that mood, head to Khroop Khrua for Southeast Asian classics such as spring rolls and spicy papaya salad, served in a cool, second-storey, wood-floored dining room.
☎ 3847-3461 ✉ 2F, 1-33-4 Asakusa, Taitō-ku ⏲ 11.30am-2pm & 6-10pm Tue-Sat, noon-9pm Sun ⊖ Ginza & Toei Asakusa lines to Asakusa (exits 1 & 6) ♿ Ⓥ

**Komagata Dojō
(11, B3)** ¥¥
Japanese
What Komagata does to
the humble *dojō* (loach, a
river fish similar to an eel)
is what makes this elegant
old Shitamachi restaurant a
local institution. Housed in
a very traditional-looking
building next to a small
park near the Sumida-
gawa, the restaurant has
tables at floor-level in
old-soul tatami rooms.
☎ 3842 4001 ✉ 1-7-12
Komagata, Taitō-ku
🕑 11am-9pm Ⓜ Ginza
& Toei Asakusa lines to
Asakusa (exit A1)

**La Ranarita Azumabashi
(11, C3)** ¥¥¥
Italian
After you've navigated to
La Ranarita tracking the
infamous golden *edamame*
(soya bean pod) atop the
Asahi Beer Tower, jet up to
the 22nd floor and enjoy
sigh-inducing views across
Asakusa and Sumida-gawa
and even better pizza *ca-
pricciosa*. Lunch and dinner
sets are substantial and rich
enough for a samurai.
☎ 5608 5277 ✉ 22F,
Asahi Beer Tower, 1-23-1

> **Eating Etiquette**
> As in most of Asia, refrain from sticking your
> chopsticks upright in your rice – this is how rice
> is offered to the dead. Passing food from your
> chopsticks to someone else's is also to be avoided.
> When taking food from shared plates, invert your
> chopsticks before reaching for that tasty titbit.
>
> Before digging in, it's polite to say 'Itadakimasu',
> literally 'I will receive'. At the end of the meal you
> should say 'Gochisō-sama deshita', a respectful way
> of saying that the meal was good.

Azumabashi, Sumida-
ku 🕑 11.30am-2pm
& 5-9pm Mon-Sat,
11.30am-3pm & 4-8pm
Sun Ⓜ Toei Asakusa line
to Honjo-Azumabashi
(main exit) ♿ excellent
♿ Ⓥ

Owariya (11, B2) ¥
Japanese
Along Kaminarimon-dōri,
Owariya has a welcoming
shopfront and serves that
Asakusa speciality, tempura.
It also does a variety of
good noodle dishes, but the
tempura donburi is especially
recommended. Be aware
that this popular place gets
crowded at lunch.
☎ 3841 8780 ✉ 1-7-1
Asakusa, Taitō-ku
🕑 11.30am-8.30pm

Ⓜ Ginza & Toei Asakusa
lines to Asakusa (exits 1)
♿ good ♿ Ⓥ

Vin Chou (11, A2) ¥¥
French yakitori
Tucked away in this corner
of Asakusa, Vin Chou is an
odd bird: a French-style
yakitori joint, offering foie
gras with your *tori negi*
(chicken and spring onion).
With cheeses and fowl
imported from Europe,
it's chic and unique. Find
it around the corner from
Taitō Ryokan (p102).
☎ 3845 4430 ✉ 2-2-13
Nishi-Asakusa, Taitō-ku
🕑 5am-11pm Mon-Sat,
4-10pm Sun Ⓜ Ginza
& Toei Asakusa lines to
Asakusa (exits 1, 2 & 3)
♿ Ⓥ

A feast for your eyes… Confused? Point to a picture!

EBISU & DAIKANYAMA

Café Artifagose (7, A1) ¥
Café

With appealing alfresco seating, Café Artifagose is easy to find by following your nose toward the heavenly, yeasty scent of fresh bread and flaky pastry. Reasons for queuing include superb breads, crispy pizza, European cheeses and a wide selection of tea, coffee, imported beer and wine.

☎ 5489 1133 ✉ 1F, 20-23 Daikanyama, Shibuya-ku 🕐 11am-8pm 🚉 Yamanote line to Ebisu (west exit) Ⓜ Hibiya line to Ebisu (exit 4) ♿ good 🚼 Ⓥ

Caffé Michelangelo (7, A1) ¥¥
Continental

Tokyo's best impersonation of Paris, Caffé Michelangelo is a prime place to watch the beautiful people. You'll pay for the pleasure, though – coffee starts at ¥600. Lunch sets (¥1360) are a much better deal, including soup, coffee and dessert.

☎ 3770 9517 ✉ 29-3 Sarugaku-chō, Shibuya-ku

🕐 11am-midnight 🚉 Yamanote line to Ebisu (west exit) Ⓜ Hibiya line to Ebisu (exit 4) ♿ good 🚼 Ⓥ

Ippūdō (7, C1) ¥
Rāmen

Nationally famous, this *rāmen* shop specialises in *tonkatsu* (pork cutlet) broth noodles. While the *akamaru shinmi rāmen* is tailored towards the Tokyo palate, the *shiromaru* is pure Kyūshū (grate fresh garlic over it for authenticity). You'll have to queue at peak periods, but it's well worth the wait.

☎ 5420 2225 ✉ 1F, Haines Bldg, 1-3-13 Hiroo, Shibuya-ku 🕐 11am-4pm 🚉 Yamanote line to Ebisu (east exit) Ⓜ Hibiya line to Ebisu (exits 1 & 2) ♿ fair 🚼 Ⓥ

Shunsenbō (7, C1) ¥¥
Shabu-shabu & tofu

Specialising in tofu dishes and *shabu-shabu*, courses here are a real bargain considering the quality of the food and the elegant sur-

roundings. Vegetarians can rejoice in the knowledge that the tofu is prepared in-house. Shunsenbō even offers an English menu.

☎ 5469 9761 ✉ 1F, Ebisu Prime Square Plaza, 1-1-40 Hiroo, Shibuya-ku 🕐 11am-3pm & 5.30-10pm 🚉 Yamanote line to Ebisu (east exit) Ⓜ Hibiya line to Ebisu (exits 1 & 2) ♿ excellent 🚼 Ⓥ

Taillevent-Robuchon (7, C2) ¥¥¥
French

Situated in a faithful reproduction of a Louis XV chateau, this very posh restaurant serves top-notch fare for lovers of all things French. On the ground floor is the more casual Café Français, open for lunch, early tea and dinner.

☎ 5424 1338 🖥 www.taillevent.com/japon ✉ Ebisu Garden Place, 1-13-1 Mita, Meguro-ku 🕐 noon-2pm & 6-9.30pm 🚉 Yamanote line to Ebisu (east exit) Ⓟ ♿ excellent 🚼 Ⓥ

A typical fast-food dish: *rāmen* (chinese-style noodles) with pork and *nori* (seaweed)

GINZA, NIHONBASHI, TSUKIJI & YŪRAKUCHŌ

Birdland (12, B4)   ¥¥
Gourmet yakitori
Who knew Gewurztraminer went so well with skewered chicken hearts? Before said hearts are set aflame, they belong to free-range chickens so pure that they can be ordered as *sashimi*. Upscale and in demand, Birdland limits your dinner to two hours but does take same-day reservations for its famous *yakitori*.
☎ 5250 1081 ✉ B1F, Tsukamoto Sozan Bldg, 4-2-15 Ginza, Chūō-ku 🕑 5-9pm Tue-Sat 🚇 Ginza, Hibiya & Marunouchi lines to Ginza (exits C6 & C8)

Chichibu Nishiki (12, C4)   ¥¥
Izakaya
You'll know this *izakaya* from its traditional wooden façade and tiled roof; inside, the tasty, inexpensive food is served with quality sake. It's tucked away a few blocks north of Kabuki-za and makes a perfect stop after taking in a kabuki performance.
☎ 3541 4777 ✉ 2-13-14 Ginza, Chūō-ku 🕑 5-10.30pm Mon-Fri 🚇 Toei Asakusa & Hibiya lines to Higashi-Ginza (exit A7) 🚻 fair Ⓥ

Edogin Sushi (12, D5)   ¥¥¥
Sushi & sashimi
Justly famous for its fresh, oversized, but reasonably priced Edo-style sushi, Edogin has a functional feel that only showcases its quality fish. At dinnertime it's worth shelling out for the *toku-jōnigiri* sushi set. There's no English sign outside, but it's easily identified by the plastic sushi in the window.
☎ 3543 4401 ✉ 4-5-1 Tsukiji, Chūō-ku 🕑 11am-9pm Mon-Sat 🚇 Toei Asakusa Hibiya & lines to Higashi-Ginza (exit 6) 🚻 fair 🚻

Kyūbei (12, C5)   ¥¥¥¥
Sushi & sashimi
It's not just sushi you're paying for at Kyūbei, but the wonderful surroundings in a sushi restaurant widely considered to be one of Tokyo's best. Discreet to the point of being almost unfindable, look for the very elegant Japanese façade set back from the street.
☎ 3571 6523 ✉ 8-7-6 Ginza, Chūō-ku 🕑 11.30am-2pm & 5-10pm Mon-Sat 🚇 Ginza line to Shimbashi (exit 2)

Lion Beer Hall (12, C5) ¥¥
Continental
Sapporo's Lion, Ginza's biggest beer hall, is a good place to slosh into Japanese beer-hall culture. The restaurant upstairs serves German comfort food such as sausage and fried onions. But you can also just park yourself in front of the 1930s mural downstairs and enjoy a beer with the convivial atmosphere.
☎ 3571 2590 ✉ 7-9-20 Ginza, Chūō-ku 🕑 11.30am-11pm 🚇 Ginza, Hibiya & Marunouchi lines to Ginza (exit A3) 🚻 excellent 🚻

Maxim's de Paris (12, B4)   ¥¥¥¥
French
Ever seen a Japanese waiter attempt a Gallic shrug? Superior French cuisine is graciously served in this basement restaurant. The interior and the menu are dead ringers for the original in Paris, assuring diners of a memorable, delectable dining experience.
☎ 3572 3621 ✉ B3F, Sony Bldg, 5-3-1 Ginza, Chūō-ku 🕑 11am-3pm & 5.30-11pm Mon-Sat 🚇 Ginza, Hibiya & Marunouchi lines to Ginza (exit B9) 🚻 excellent 🚻 Ⓥ

Mikuni's Café Marunouchi (12, B4)   ¥¥
Continental café
Multicourse Italian lunch sets (¥1260) fortify the diner for gallery-wandering and window-shopping. The circular pastry counter is worth a look for picking up something to nibble in the afternoon; the tiny scones verge on perfection.
☎ 5220 3921 ✉ 1F, Furukawa Sogo Bldg, 2-6-1 Marunouchi, Chiyoda-ku 🕑 11.30am-2pm & 5-9pm 🚇 Yamanote & Yūrakuchō lines to Yūrakuchō (exit A4b) 🚻 good 🚻 Ⓥ

Munakata (12, B5)   ¥¥¥
Kaiseki
If you're curious to try a *kaiseki* dinner but don't want to commit your firstborn, good value *kaiseki* sets can be found at this cheery little restaurant in the basement of the Ginza Mitsui Urban Hotel.

☎ 3574 9356 ✉ B1F, Mitsui Urban Hotel Ginza, 8-6-15 Ginza, Chūō-ku ◷ 11.30am-4pm & 5-10pm ⊖ Ginza line to Shimbashi (exit 3) ♿ good ♿

Muromachi Sunaba (12, B2) ¥¥
Soba
Relaxed and welcoming, with a small and pristine ornamental garden in front, Muromachi Sunaba has been drawing them in for ages. Try the excellent *tenzaru soba* – a divine contrast of crispy, hot tempura with silky cold soba. It has another branch in Akasaka.
☎ 3241 4038 ✉ 4-1-13 Nihonbashi-Muromachi, Chūō-ku ◷ 11am-8pm Mon-Sat ▣ Sōbu line to Shin-Nihonbashi (exit 4) Ⓥ

Nair's (12, C5) ¥¥
Indian
Oft-praised in the Japanese media, Nair's small scale allows proper attention to be paid to the food. Reservations are recommended and with luck you'll get a table next to one of the latest teenage pop idols.
☎ 3541 8246 ✉ 4-10-7 Ginza, Chūō-ku ◷ 11am-8.30pm ⊖ Toei Asakusa & Hibiya lines to Higashi-Ginza (exit 1) ♿ fair ♿ Ⓥ

New Torigin (12, C5) ¥¥
Yakitori
Just south of Harumi-dōri, the not-really New Torigin is hidden in a very narrow alley, but signposted in English (look for the chicken on a yellow sign). There's good

sake for sampling, an English menu and excellent *yakitori* and *kamameshi* (clay-pot steamed rice with chicken).
☎ 3571 3334 ✉ 5-5-7 Ginza, Chūō-ku ◷ 4-10pm Mon-Fri, 11.30am-9.30pm Sat & Sun ⊖ Ginza, Hibiya & Marunouchi lines to Ginza (exit C2) ♿

Robata (12, B4) ¥¥
Izakaya
Back near the railway tracks, this is one of Tokyo's most celebrated *izakaya*. A little Japanese language ability is helpful here, but the point-and-eat method works just fine. It's hard to spot the sign, even if you can read Japanese; better to look for the rustic, weathered façade.
☎ 3591 1905 ✉ 1-3-8 Yūraku-chō, Chiyoda-ku ◷ 5.30-11pm ⊖ Hibiya & Chiyoda lines to Hibiya (exit A4)

Sabatini di Firenze (12, B4) ¥¥¥¥
Italian
In a faithful reproduction of its twin in Florence, Sabatini serves over-the-top, authentic northern Italian fare for a special night out. Even better, prices are reasonable considering its Ginza digs.
☎ 3573 0013 ✉ 7F, Sony Bldg, 5-3-1 Ginza, Chūō-ku ◷ noon-3pm & 5.30-11pm ⊖ Ginza, Hibiya & Marunouchi lines to Ginza (exit B9) ♿ Ⓥ

Shin-Hi-No-Moto (12, B4) ¥¥
Izakaya
It's the travelling gourmet's dream come true – an *izakaya* in Tokyo run by a native English speaker. This

lively spot under the train tracks in Yūrakuchō offers a fun chance to enjoy the *izakaya* experience without language hassles. It's located opposite JAL Plaza.
☎ 3214 8021 ✉ 2-4-4 Yūraku-chō, Chiyoda-ku ◷ 5pm-midnight ⊖ Chiyoda, Hibiya & Yūrakuchō lines to Hibiya or Yūrakuchō (Yūrakuchō Denki Bldg exit) ♿ fair

Ten-Ichi (12, B5) ¥¥¥
Tempura
One of Tokyo's oldest and best tempura restaurants, the refined and gracious Ten-Ichi is where one should go to experience tempura the way it's meant to be: light, airy and crispy. You'll find several branches elsewhere in Tokyo, but the distinguished Ginza original is the smartest and the best.
☎ 3571 1949 ✉ 6-6-5 Ginza, Chūō-ku ◷ 11.30am-9.30pm ⊖ Ginza & Hibiya lines to Ginza (exit B7) ♿ fair ♿

Tsukiji Sushikō (12, D5) ¥
Sushi
Just a raw octopus' throw from Tsukiji Produce & Fish Market, you know that the sushi's always fresh here. This super clean and spacious sushi place is on the corner next to the Kyōbashi post office. The décor is as tasteful as the sushi is tasty.
☎ 3547 0505 ✉ 4-7-1 Tsukiji, Chūō-ku ◷ 11.30am-2pm & 5-11pm Mon-Fri, 11am-11pm Sat, 11am-10pm Sun ⊖ Hibiya line to Tsukiji (exits 1 & 2) ♿ fair ♿ Ⓥ

HARAJUKU & AOYAMA

Aux Sept Bonheurs
(6, B2) ¥¥¥
Chinese
Justly one of Tokyo's most highly regarded restaurants, Aux Sept Bonheurs serves Chinese cuisine in the style of a fine French restaurant. Like a *kaiseki* meal, the courses are a fabulous succession of small but wonderfully prepared delicacies.
☎ 3498 8144 ✉ 5F, Hanae Mori Bldg, Kita-Aoyama 3-6-1, Minato-ku ⏰ 11.30am-3pm & 5-11pm ⊙ Chiyoda, Ginza & Hanzōmon lines to Omote-sandō (exit A1)

Cam Chien Grippe
(6, B2) ¥¥
French
With a name translating to 'A Dog with the Flu', this bistro is located amongst its peers, some of the most irreverent visual art galleries in Harajuku. You'll associate neither dogs nor flu with the Japanese-tinged French items on the menu, which is deliciously designed and artfully executed.
☎ 3400 6885 ✉ 5-46-12 Jingūmae, Shibuya-ku ⏰ 11.30am-2pm &

6-11pm ⊙ Chiyoda & Ginza lines to Omote-sandō ♿ good ⬆ Ⓥ

Fonda de la Madrugada
(6, B1) ¥¥¥
Mexican
Fonda de la Madrugada serves the best Mexican food in Tokyo and is a favourite with expats. Complete with open courtyards and mariachi musicians, everything from the roof tiles to the chefs has been imported from Mexico. It's not cheap, but it's worth the expenditure.
☎ 5410 6288 ✉ B1F, Villa Blanca, 2-33-12 Jingūmae, Shibuya-ku ⏰ 5.30pm-2am Sun-Thu, 5.30pm-5am Fri & Sat ⓡ Yamanote line to Harajuku (Takeshita exit)

Fujimamas (6, A1) ¥¥
Fusion
Hugely popular for good reason, this commendable fusion restaurant pours quality California wines. Upstairs are some lovely rooms in what was once a tatami-maker's workshop. Like a good mama would, Fujimamas also offers a great children's menu. The

restaurant is in an alley just off Omote-sandō. Reservations are recommended.
☎ 5485 2262 🖳 www .fujimamas.com ✉ 6-3-2 Jingūmae, Shibuya-ku ⏰ 11am-10pm ⊙ Chiyoda line to Meiji-Jingūmae (exit 4) ♿ good ⬆ Ⓥ

Home (6, B2) ¥¥
Vegetarian
Appropriately named, sweet Home is a veritable vegetarian oasis in the carnivorous capital. The organic lunch is excellent and good value. Hiroba, its sister store right next door, offers similar takeaway fare. Both are in Crayon House building just off Omote-sandō, a block behind the Hanae Mori complex.
☎ 3406 6409 ✉ B1F, 3-8-15 Kita-Aoyama, Minato-ku ⏰ 11am-10pm ⊙ Chiyoda, Ginza & Hanzōmon lines to Omote-sandō (exits B2 & B4) ♿ good ⬆ Ⓥ

Las Chicas (6, B2) ¥¥
Brasserie
Chill with Tokyo expats in Las Chicas' pleasant, expansive surroundings. It's got everything from black coffee to fine dining, either out on the terrace or beside the fireplace – and the wine list is solid. There's a bar to repair to after dinner, and designer boutiques nearby to browse beforehand.
☎ 3407 6865 ✉ 5-47-6 Jingūmae, Shibuya-ku ⏰ 11am-11pm ⊙ Chiyoda, Ginza & Hanzōmon lines to Omote-sandō (exit B2) ♿ excellent ⬆ Ⓥ

Taking a well-earned break at Las Chicas

Le Bretagne (6, B1) ¥¥
Creperie
Though Le Bretagne's wonderful set menus creep into the higher price range, the sweet or savoury Breton-style crepes can be ordered à la carte for mere pocket change. And it's change well-spent – the buckwheat flour crepes are filled with only the freshest ingredients. ☎ 3478 7855 ✉ 4-9-8 Jingūmae, Shibuya-ku ⏰ 10am-11pm Mon-Fri, 10am-midnight Sat, 10am-10pm Sun ⊙ Chiyoda, Ginza & Hanzōmon lines to Omote-sandō (exit A2) ♿ good ♨ V

Mominoki House (6, B1) ¥¥
Organic vegetarian
Even if you're not of the vegetarian bent, you might be all *tonkatsu*-ed out. For herbivorous relief, stop into Mominoki House, where the largely macrobiotic menu covers the vegan to the vegetarian to…the chicken.

Hunting Grounds for Vegetarians

In the late 1800s, the centuries-old Buddhist prohibition against eating meat was repealed. It's been downhill for Japanese vegetarians ever since. Seek out one of the handful of organic restaurants, such as **Home** (p71) or **Mominoki House** (above). Tofu specialists are good bets, though they're usually not exclusively vegetarian; stick to the tofu, bean and vegetable dishes in an *izakaya*. Indian restaurants are always a good bet. Look for the Ⓥ with each review, and ask if a restaurant has any vegetarian meals: '*Bejitarian-ryōri wa arismasu ka?*' But be warned – Tokyo is a carnivorous city.

Though the rambling space is cosily welcoming, wafting cigarette smoke is a constant guest. ☎ 3405 9144 ✉ 1F, YOU Bldg, 2-18-5 Jingūmae, Shibuya-ku ⏰ 11am-10.30pm Mon-Sat ⊙ Chiyoda line to Meiji-jingūmae (exit 5) Ⓥ

Natural Harmony Angolo (6, C1) ¥¥
Vegetarian
Refreshingly smoke-free and dishing up live foods and excellent vegetarian fare, Natural Harmony is Tokyo's best-known natural food spot. Tall salads, creamy risottos and organic beer and sake entice those who trek to this veggie haven; there's also fish on the menu for those who partake. ☎ 3405 8393 ✉ 1F, Puzzle Aoyama Bldg, 3-28-12 Jingumae, Shibuya-ku ⏰ 11.30am-2.30pm & 5.30-9.30pm ⊙ Ginza line to Gaienmae (exit 2) ♨ Ⓥ

IKEBUKURO

Akiyoshi (2, A2) ¥¥
Yakitori
Akiyoshi is the establishment to try for a tasty *yakitori* in approachable, noisy, unpretentious surroundings. The picture menu is a boon to non-Japanese speakers, and these *yakitori* specialists know their stuff. There's no English signage outside, but you can easily spot the long counters and flaming grills from the street. ☎ 3982 0644 ✉ 3-30-4 Nishi-Ikebukuro, Toshima-ku ⏰ 5-11pm ⊙ Maru-nouchi & Yūrakuchō lines to Ikebukuro (exit 1a) 🚃 Yamanote line to Ikebukuro (west exit) ♿ fair ♨

Saigon (2, B1) ¥¥
Vietnamese
The pickings are slim in east Ikebukuro, not one of Tokyo's dining destinations. What a pleasure Saigon is then, with its red tablecloths and wooden floors, perched above the sex club touts and the convenience stores. Try the spicy *banh xeo* (Vietnamese crepes) for a departure from spring rolls. ☎ 3989 0255 ✉ 1-7-10 Higashi-Ikebukuro, Toshima-ku ⏰ noon-2.30pm & 6-10pm ⊙ Marunouchi & Yūrakuchō lines to Ikebukuro (exit 29) 🚃 Yamanote line to Ikebukuro (east exit) ♨ Ⓥ

Sasashu (2, A1) ¥¥¥
Izakaya
Serving rarities such as *kamonabe* (duck stew), Sas-

ashu is a high-quality sake specialist with a dignified old façade surrounded by strip joints. A little Japanese language ability would come in handy here, for pairing top-notch sake with complementary dishes. ☎ 3971 9363 ✉ 2-2-6 Ikebukuro, Toshima-ku ⏱ 5-10pm Mon-Sat

Ⓜ Marunouchi & Yūrakuchō lines to Ikebukuro (exit 3) ♿ fair

Tonerian (2, A1) ¥¥
Izakaya
One of Ikebukuro's many *izakaya*, this is a busy place with friendly staff. Turn up here to learn about good *jizake* (regional sake) – the

master, who speaks English, will be glad to make suggestions. Look for all the empty sake bottles piled up outside. ☎ 3985 0254 ✉ 1-38-9 Nishi-Ikebukuro, Toshima-ku ⏱ 5-11.15pm Ⓜ Marunouchi & Yūrakuchō lines to Ikebukuro (exit 12) ♿ fair

ŌDAIBA

Hanashibe (3, E8) ¥¥
Japanese
For Kyoto specialities and house-brewed sake, check out Hanashibe on the 3rd floor of the Mediage entertainment complex next to Aqua City. Try three types of sake in a tasting set (¥700) that you can match with small snacks or full meals. ☎ 3599 5575 ✉ Aqua City, 1-7-1 Daiba, Minato-ku ⏱ 11am-11pm Ⓜ Yurikamome line to Daiba Ⓟ ♿ excellent ⚑ Ⓥ

Khazana (3, E8) ¥
Indian
Come early to snag one of the coveted tables out on the deck for maximum sensory pleasure. This Indian restaurant serves a good all-you-can-eat buffet lunch and has a fair amount of vegetarian goodies on the menu. ☎ 5500 5082 ✉ 5F, Decks Tokyo Beach, 1-6-1 Daiba, Minato-ku ⏱ 11am-10pm Ⓜ Yurikamome line to Ōdaiba Kaihin-kōen (main exit) Ⓟ ♿ excellent ⚑ Ⓥ

Positive Deli (3, E8) ¥
Deli
The stylish and casual Positive Deli serves up *donburi* (rice bowls) to deli sandwiches, all of which you can wash down with a crisp glass of Australian wine. You'll find it on the 3rd floor of the Mediage complex, where you can enjoy the big bay view. ☎ 3599 4551 ✉ Aqua City, 1-7-1 Daiba, Minato-ku ⏱ 11am-11pm Ⓜ Yurikamome line to Daiba Ⓟ ♿ excellent ⚑ Ⓥ

Sampling

Go subterranean, to the basement food halls of swank department stores, to sample artful morsels. In central Tokyo, start with **Matsuya** (p53), **Mitsukoshi** (p53) and **Wakō** to admire candy maple leaves suspended in *yōkan* (azuki-bean gelatine), or persimmon-shaped *odango* (sweet, sticky rice dumplings). Though an exquisite feast for the eye, these treats are extremely perishable and don't make ideal souvenirs. Instead, content yourself with roaming around, picking up cocoa-dusted chocolate truffles, bits of *kanten* (seaweed-based gelatine), *sembei* (rice crackers), and perhaps snap some photos along the way as sweet souvenirs.

ROPPONGI & NISHI-AZABU

Bengawan Solo (9, B2) ¥¥
Indonesian

This eatery on Roppongi-dōri offers a taste of Indonesia. It's been around for ages, and though the indifferent interior disappoints, the food never does. The *gado gado* (salad with peanut sauce) lunch is a bargain and the beef in coconut cream is dreamy. Look for the food models displayed outside.
☎ 3408 5698 ✉ 1F, Kaneko Bldg, 7-18-13 Roppongi, Minato-ku ⌚ 11.30am-3pm & 5-10pm Mon-Sat ⊚ Hibiya line to Roppongi (exit 2) ♿ fair ⚇ Ⓥ

Bernd's Bar (9, C2) ¥¥
German

More a German *izakaya* than a bar, the very friendly Bernd's is slightly removed from the mad parade of Roppongi Crossing. Hearty, authentic German food goes with the German draught *bier*. The menus are in German, Japanese and English – languages that the owner speaks with aplomb. See also p82.
☎ 5563 9232 ⌨ www.berndsbar.com ✉ 2F, Pure Roppongi Bldg, 5-18-1 Roppongi, Minato-ku ⌚ 5pm-late Mon-Sat ⊚ Hibiya line to Roppongi (exit 3)

Fukuzushi (9, C2) ¥¥¥¥
Sushi

Care for a gin fizz with that raw tuna? Though the atmosphere here is upscale, Fukuzushi is decidedly more relaxed than some places in Ginza and Tsukiji. The sushi is some of the best in town, the portions are large, and there's even a cocktail bar.
☎ 3402 4116 ✉ 5-7-8 Roppongi, Minato-ku ⌚ 11.30am-1.30pm & 5.30-10pm Mon-Sat ⊚ Hibiya line to Roppongi (exit 3) Ⓥ

Havana Cafe (9, B2) ¥
Café

Fuel up or chill out at this casual spot that's open late for dance-floor burnouts. Respectably hefty burritos and sandwiches go for less than ¥1000 and Havana offers great happy-hour drink specials. The streetside seating and large-windowed dining room open onto a quiet backstreet, a quick escape from crowds.
☎ 3423 3500 ✉ 4-12-2 Roppongi, Minato-ku ⌚ 11.30am-5am ⊚ Hibiya line to Roppongi (exit 4a) Ⓥ

Humming Bird (9, C2) ¥¥¥
French/Vietnamese

Mixing French colonial and Vietnamese mood and food, the posh and relaxed Humming Bird wings its guests to gustatory bliss. Though we recommend indulging in a set dinner, there's an à la carte *pho* worth trying for ¥900.
☎ 3401 3337 ✉ Hanatsubaki Bldg, 3-15-23 Roppongi, Minato-ku ⌚ 6pm-3am Mon-Sat, 5pm-midnight Sun ⊚ Hibiya line to Roppongi (exit 3) ♿ good Ⓥ

The secret to making great noodles: a big knife

Japanese-style breakfast: where do you start?

Inakaya (9, B2) ¥¥¥¥
Kappo
Inakaya has gained fame as a top-end *robatayaki*. It does raucous, bustling, don't-stand-on-ceremony *robatayaki* with gusto. You'll spend wads of money here and have a rocking good time doing so.
☎ 5575 1012 ✉ 4-10-11 Roppongi, Minato-ku ⏰ 5pm-5am ⊖ Hibiya line to Roppongi (exit 3)

Kisso (9, C2) ¥¥¥
Kaiseki
Set in a contemporary, urban-style setting rather than a minimalist tatami room, Kisso is doubtless the most accessible place in Tokyo to sample Japan's gourmet cuisine, *kaiseki ryōri*. It's best to order a course and put your dining fate into the hands of the chef.
☎ 3582 4191 ✉ B1F, Axis Bldg, 5-17-1 Roppongi, Minato-ku ⏰ 11am-2pm & 5.30-10pm Mon-Sat ⊖ Hibiya line to Roppongi (exit 3) ♿ **good** ♨

Monsoon Café (3, C6) ¥¥
Southeast Asian
Monsoon serves Southeast Asian classics such as Vietnamese fresh spring rolls, Thai coconut and lemongrass soup, and chicken satay. With indoor-outdoor café-style seating, big rattan chairs and amiable staff, it's a relaxed hang-out for enjoying a tropical drink.
☎ 5467-5221 ✉ 2-10-1 Nishi-Azabu, Minato-ku ⏰ 5pm-5am Mon-Fri, 11.30am-5am Sat & Sun ⊖ Hibiya line to Roppongi (exit 1) ♿ **excellent** ♨ Ⓥ

Moti (9, B2) ¥¥
Indian
You'll get the red-carpet treatment at Moti not just because the carpets are, in fact, red, but because you'll dine on some of Tokyo's best Indian food served up by attentive and friendly staff, surrounded by lovely Indian décor. There are also branches in Akasaka.
☎ 3479 1939 ✉ 3F, Hama Bldg, 6-2-35 Roppongi, Minato-ku ⏰ 11.30am-10pm ⊖ Hibiya line to Roppongi (exit 1) ♨ Ⓥ

Olives (9, B2) ¥¥
Mediterranean
Hyped for its celebrity chef, Olives doesn't rest on its laurels – the prettily presented, creative Mediterranean cuisine balances innovation and tradition with delectable results. The décor isn't overly grandiose, and the view of Tokyo Tower lends external visual interest, but the focus is plainly on the food.
☎ 5413 9571 ✉ 5F, West Walk, Roppongi Hills, 6-10-1 Roppongi, Minato-ku ⏰ 11am-3.30pm & 5.30-11.30pm ⊖ Hibiya line to Roppongi (Roppongi Hills exit) ♿ **excellent** ♨ Ⓥ

Seryna (9, C2) ¥¥¥¥
Japanese
Though it feels vaguely aged, Seryna's three upstanding restaurants – all under one roof – are solid standbys for expats entertaining guests from abroad. Each restaurant has its speciality: *shabu-shabu* and *sukiyaki*, Kōbe beef and *teppanyaki* (table-top grilling), and crab, respectively, all surrounded by the pretty rock garden.
☎ 3402 1051 ✉ 3-12-2 Roppongi, Minato-ku ⏱ noon-11pm 🚇 Hibiya line to Roppongi (exit 5) ♿ good

Spago (9, C2) ¥¥
Californian
Like its older sister in Los Angeles, Tokyo's Spago celebrates California cuisine, using the freshest ingredients and lacing it with an Asian influence. To quell your cravings for architectural food or a glass of buttery California chardonnay, Spago is a reliable institution.
☎ 3423 4025 ✉ 2F, 5-7-8 Roppongi, Minato-ku ⏱ 11.30am-2pm & 6-10pm 🚇 Hibiya line to Roppongi (exit 3) ♿ fair 🚻 V

Tokyo Bellini Trattoria (9, C2) ¥¥
Italian
If you can snap a table in front, the excellent people-watching along Gaien-higashi-dōri is a complimentary side dish to the lunch specials. Pasta and pizza tend to be gloriously heavy on garlic, and the espresso drinks are served with a smile by friendly staff.
☎ 3470 5650 ✉ 3-14-12 Roppongi, Minato-ku ⏱ 11.30am-2am Sun-Thu, 11.30am-3am Fri-Sat 🚇 Hibiya line to Roppongi (exit 3) ♿ good 🚻 V

SHIBUYA

Arossa (5, A3) ¥¥
Italian
Reflecting its Australian background, Arossa is stylishly laid-back – the perfect mood for a wine bar in Shibuya. Oz-style Italian dishes are designed to go with Arossa's superb Australian wines, the selection of which rotates daily. By-the-glass prices are clearly marked, and discounted by 20% after 10pm.
☎ 3469 0125 ✉ 1-26-22 Shōtō, Shibuya-ku ⏱ 6pm-2am 🚉 Yamanote to Shibuya (Hachikō exit) 🚻 V

Kantipur (5, B3) ¥¥
Nepali
Happily for vegetarians, this Nepali restaurant has a broad range of acceptable menu items, and the portions are large. Kantipur is in the basement of its building, and the entrance is a little tough to spot. Look for

the small, brightly coloured signs on the street.
☎ 3770 5358 ✉ B1F, 16-6 Sakuragaoka-chō, Shibuya-ku ⏱ 11.30am-3pm & 5-11pm 🚉 Yamanote line to Shibuya (south exit) 🚻 V

Reikyō (5, A2) ¥¥
Taiwanese
A busy place that's been around for decades, Reikyō serves quality Taiwanese fare at reasonable prices. Look for the oddball, triangular red-brick building – then join the smoky, festive party.
☎ 3461 4220 ✉ 2-25-18 Dōgenzaka, Shibuya-ku ⏱ noon-2pm & 5pm-1am Fri-Wed 🚉 Yamanote line to Shibuya (Hachikō exit) ♿ fair

Sakana-tei (5, A2) ¥¥
Izakaya
This looks more like a concrete modernist bomb shelter than a good value, sort of

swish *izakaya* and sake specialist. But that's what it is, up in Dōgenzaka and handily placed for pre– or post–Love Hotel Hill trysts. Call ahead to reserve a spot.
☎ 3780 1313 ✉ 4F, Koike Bldg, 2-23-15 Dōgenzaka, Shibuya-ku ⏱ 5.30-11pm Mon-Fri, 3.30-10.30pm Sat 🚇 Hanzōmon & Ginza lines to Shibuya (exit 1) ♿ fair

Shizenkan II (5, C3) ¥
Vegetarian
Strict veggies looking to sample Japanese favourites may find it tough in Tokyo. Shizenkan II fills the gap with gluten-based versions of *katsudon* (breaded pork on rice), and tofu-centric dishes. Western selections, such as veggie burgers, are also available and seem fitting in this diner-like space fronted by a small grocery store.
☎ 3486 0281 ✉ 3-9-2 Shibuya, Shibuya-ku

11.30am-2pm & 6-9pm Tue-Sun 🚇 Yamanote line to Shibuya (east exit) Ⓥ

Sonoma (5, A2) ¥¥
Californian
Sonoma's well-balanced menu of California cuisine

is further enhanced by a warm, well-lit space. Mains on offer include pork chops with brown sugar, sage and apples, and seared tuna with a delicious red-onion jam. Dinner here gains you admission to the Ruby Room (p87) upstairs,

a fitting place for an all-night nightcap.
☎ 3462 7766 ✉ 2-25-17 Dōgenzaka, Shibuya-ku 🕐 5.30-11.30pm Sun-Thu, 5.30pm-4am Fri & Sat 🚇 Yamanote line to Shibuya (Hachikō exit) ♿ good Ⓥ

SHINJUKU

Court Lodge (4, B2) ¥¥
Sri Lankan
In this crammed, clean, cheerily busy restaurant, the superfriendly and efficient staff serve tasty Sri Lankan food. It's possible that the *dotamba* (flatbread) is actually manna. Chances are good, though, that it won't be falling from the sky; instead, try picking up takeaway from the streetside counter.
☎ 3378 1066 ✉ 2-10-9 Yoyogi, Shibuya-ku 🕐 11am-11pm 🚇 Yamanote line to Shinjuku (west exit) ♿ fair 🚹 Ⓥ

Daikokuya (4, C2) ¥
Shabu-shabu & sukiyaki
All-you-can-eat *yakiniku* (Korean barbecue), *shabu-*

shabu and *sukiyaki* courses bring in the students, making this a good place to get wrecked with the younger locals — especially since there's an all-you-can-drink option as well.
☎ 3202 7272 ✉ 4F, Naka-Dai Bldg, 1-27-5 Kabuki-chō, Shinjuku-ku 🕐 5-11.30pm Mon-Fri, 3pm-midnight Sat & Sun Ⓜ Marunouchi & Toei Ōedo lines to Shinjuku (Kabukichō exit) 🚇 Yamanote line to Shinjuku (east exit) ♿ fair

Ibuki (4, B2) ¥¥
Shabu-shabu & sukiyaki
Accustomed to foreign visitors, Ibuki is an excellent initiation into the pleasures of *sukiyaki* and *shabu-shabu*.

It accepts credit cards, has an English menu and hosts guests in a friendly and traditional atmosphere.
☎ 3352 4787 ✉ 3-23-6 Shinjuku, Shinjuku-ku 🕐 4pm-midnight Ⓜ Marunouchi & Toei Ōedo lines to Shinjuku (Kabuki-chō exit) 🚇 Yamanote line to Shinjuku (east exit) ♿ fair 🚹

Keika Kumamoto Rāmen (4, C2) ¥¥
Rāmen
This nationally famous *rāmen* shop, specialising in Kyūshū-style pork-broth-based noodles, is worth seeking out and queuing for. Try the *chāshū-men* (*rāmen* with sliced pork). There's no English sign

Verti-gohan

Skyscraper dining can make for one of Tokyo's more dizzyingly memorable experiences. The luxury hotels in west Shinjuku are ground-central for high-altitude *haute cuisine*. Try the **New York Grill** (p78) on the 52nd floor of the Park Hyatt, or head over to Asakusa and **La Ranarita Azumabashi** (p67) atop the Asahi Beer Tower. Or for a more humble repast in the clouds, take a rice ball to the observation deck of the **Tokyo Metropolitan Government Offices** (p27) or grab coffee at the café at the **Mori Art Museum** (p15).

To Go

Walk down the street eating a sandwich in Tokyo and you'll elicit more stares than a teenager sporting a furry bear costume in sweltering summer heat – which isn't to say Tokyoites don't eat on the run.

Provisioning a picnic with wine and cheese is simple, though not particularly cheap, at international groceries such as **Meidi-ya** (p60). For Japanese food, pick up beautifully packaged *bentō* (boxed dinner) or sushi in **department store food halls** (p53) or local groceries. If you're really short on cash, find ¥200 *onigiri* (rice balls) stuffed with *umeboshi* (pickled plum) or salty fish roe at convenience stores such as Sunkus and 7-11.

Go nuts for doughnuts; just don't eat 'em on the street!

outside, but it's the only *rāmen* restaurant located in the area; order and pay as you enter.
☎ 3354 4591 ✉ 3-7-2 Shinjuku, Shinjuku-ku
🕑 11am-10.45pm
🚇 Marunouchi & Toei Shinjuku lines to Shinjuku-sanchōme (exit C4)
♿ fair 🚹

Kurumaya (4, C2) ¥¥¥
Teppanyaki
One of the more elegant spots in east Shinjuku, Kurumaya's seafood and steak sets are excellent value. Highly recommended is the *ise ebi* (Japanese lobster). Kurumaya is on the corner directly across from Kirin City beer hall.
☎ 3352 5566 ✉ 3-21-1 Kabuki-chō, Shinjuku-ku
🕑 11.30am-2.30pm & 5-10.30pm 🚉 Yamanote line to Shinjuku (Kabukichō exit) ♿ good 🚹

New York Grill (4, A3) ¥¥¥
International
The drop-dead delicious view notwithstanding, this sky-high spot dazzles with its slabs of steak and well-prepared seafood. A treat worth waking and walking for is the Sunday brunch (¥5800; 🕑 11.30am-2.30pm Sun); the price includes a glass of champagne.
☎ 5323 3458 ✉ 52F, Park Hyatt Tokyo, 3-7-1-2 Nishi-Shinjuku, Shinjuku-ku
🕑 11.30am-midnight
🚇 Toei Ōedo line to Tochōmae (exit A4)
♿ excellent 🚹 Ⓥ

UENO

Echikatsu (10, A3)　¥¥¥
Sukiyaki
Within the exquisite environs of a grand old Japanese house, take in the beautiful ambience with your *sukiyaki* and *shabu-shabu*. Many of the tatami rooms overlook small gardens. The staff don't speak English, but will make a genuine effort to communicate; reservations are necessary.
☎ 3811 5293
✉ 2-31-23 Yushima, Bunkyō-ku ⊗ 5-9.30pm Mon-Sat ⊖ Chiyoda line to Yushima (exit 5) ♿ good ⛲

Hantei (10, A2)　¥¥
Japanese
To enter this *kushiage* (fried meat, fish and vegetables) specialist is to enter a world of wood and bamboo, and turn-of-the-20th-century aesthetics. Dishes come several at a time, after which you can order another wave. Because its cosy charm makes Hantei a favourite among nostalgia-crazed expats, reservations are recommended.

☎ 3828 1440 ✉ 2-12-15 Nezu, Taitō-ku ⊗ noon-2pm & 5-10pm Tue-Sun ⊖ Chiyoda line to Nezu

Izu-ei (10, B3)　¥¥
Unagi
Beautifully presented, authentic Japanese eel meals make this an excellent spot to take Japanese friends or colleagues to dinner. The Izu-ei *unagi bentō* (boxed dinner of eel) includes tempura and is best eaten near the window for a lovely view of the giant water lilies on Shinobazu-ike. There's a limited picture menu.
☎ 3831 0954 ✉ 2-12-22 Ueno, Taitō-ku ⊗ 11am-9.30pm ⊖ Chiyoda line to Yushima (exit 2) 🚃 Yamanote line to Ueno (Shinobazu exit) ♿ good

Sasa-no-Yuki (10, C1)　¥¥
Tofu
Sasa-no-Yuki, or 'snow on bamboo', opened over 300 years ago. Staying true to its roots, this establishment continues to serve

tofu in dozens of different dressings. Browse the English menu for a few courses; strict vegetarians should note than many dishes include chicken and fish stock.
☎ 3873 1145 ✉ 2-15-10 Negishi, Taitō-ku ⊗ 11am-9pm Tue-Sun 🚃 Yamanote line to Uguisudani (north exit) ♿ fair Ⓥ

Ueno Yabu Soba (10, B3)　¥
Soba
Near the arcade, this busy, famous place rustles up top-class *soba* (buckwheat noodles) and a richly filling *tenseiro* (noodles topped with shrimp and vegetable tempura) set. The picture menu makes ordering a snap. Look for the black-granite sign in front that says in English 'Since 1892'.
☎ 3831 4728 ✉ 6-9-16 Ueno, Taitō-ku ⊗ 11.30am-9pm Thu-Tue ⊖ Ginza & Hibiya lines to Ueno (exits 4, 5a & 5b) 🚃 Yamanote line to Ueno (Hirokōji exit)

Beautifully barbecued *unagi*: a rich, mouthwatering eel meal

Entertainment

What *can't* you do in Tokyo? Truly, the Big *Mikan* (mandarin) is a city that never sleeps. So the trains quit running at midnight – that doesn't mean you have to. Hit the town with Tokyoites, who love to drink and party. You'll be drowned in a sea of options; the only dilemma is finding a space that suits your taste. Underground lounges and sky-high cocktail bars can be found a hiccup and stumble away from one another. Dance clubs of the highest calibre and decibel pump out hip-hop, house, techno and trance. And if salsa, flamenco or tango are your passion, the Latin craze is still in fashion. Live contemporary music venues, called 'live house' in Tokyo, play host to punk, reggae, prog rock and noise pop. Beautiful people from Tokyo to Toronto preen and cruise the nightclub circuit. Better

Roppongi seizure-inducing neon after a few too many tequilas

yet, you can squeeze into an *izakaya* (Japanese bar) and depart having had a boisterous, quintessential Japanese pub night.

But Tokyo certainly has more to offer than backdrops for boozing. Traditional arts here are thriving, with kabuki and *Nō* (classical Japanese drama) performances showing regularly. Tokyo's contemporary theatre and dance scenes are also burgeoning, with increased accessibility for foreigners. Cinema offerings range from local art-house films to international blockbusters. In a city this big and eccentric, you can find almost any distraction your heart desires – and then some you didn't know existed.

Word Up

The local English-language papers are the best source for the latest music and theatre performances around Tokyo. *Metropolis* (weekly) and *Tokyo Journal* (monthly) can be found in bookshops (pp56-7) and are usually the best points to take Tokyo's pulse.

Strip-club advert, Kabukicho district, Shinjuku

FREE TOKYO

Tokyo is expensive, but the city offers a host of gratis attractions that cost no more than the train ticket to get you there.

Company Showrooms It's excellent PR for the companies and a form of free advertising, but some Tokyo showrooms are like small museums and they're all free. The **Sony Building** (☎ 3573 2371; www.sonybuilding.jp; 5-3-1 Ginza, Chūō-ku; 🕙 11am-7pm) in Ginza lets you test-drive all the hottest new-release video games.

Galleries Most private galleries don't charge admission, often because they're rented by individual artists who delight in foreign interest in their work. Ginza is the best place to hunt for them (see pp28-9). Department-store galleries (on upper floors) are another good bet; if not free, admission is often cheaper than museum entry fees.

Markets Watch the fish being flung around the world's biggest fish market, Tsukiji Produce & Fish Market (and its great external market, p10), for hours, for free. Flea markets (p54) are a staple in the city and worth a roam.

Nature Plum blossoms, dearly loved as early harbingers of spring, bloom from late February to early March. Cherry blossoms arrive some time in April. A stroll in a Tokyo park on a clear spring day through a riot of blossoms is unforgettable. During *koyō* (autumn foliage season) look out for maple trees which burn through a spectrum of yellows and oranges before exploding in a fiery red.

Parks Unlike Tokyo's gardens, Tokyo's parks are free – with the exception of Shinjuku-gyōen. They provide a welcome escape from the urban sprawl. Jog or picnic to your heart's content at Yoyogi-kōen (p35) and Ueno-kōen (p18).

Shrines & Temples Shrines are almost always free in Tokyo and most temples only charge to enter their *honden* (main hall). Sensō-ji (p12) in Asakusa and Meiji-jingū (p9) in Harajuku are two good places to start.

Skyscrapers Several skyscrapers have free observation floors, from where you can survey the city – stop by Tokyo Metropolitan Government Offices (p27) and Tokyo Big Sight (p29).

Banned: musicians busk at Yoyogi-kōen

BARS & PUBS

Whether you're up for the occasional G&T or classify as a functional alcoholic, Tokyo serves up infinite drinking possibilities. *Izakaya*, oft-listed in the Eating chapter (pp64-79), are half-restaurant, half-pub and a wholly unmissable Tokyo experience.

Abbey Road (9, B2)

Abbey Road is the first and last word in Tokyo Beatle-dom. Pull up a chair and prepare to be flabbergasted by the house Beatles cover band – all-Japanese, all seriousness, and appearances aside, pretty dang impressive. Cover charge includes one drink and one food item.
☎ 3402 0017 ✉ B1F, Roppongi Annex Bldg, 4-11-5 Roppongi, Minato-ku $ Mon-Thu/Fri & Sat ¥1900/2100 ⏰ 6pm-midnight Mon-Thu, 6pm-1am Fri & Sat ⦿ Toei Ōedo & Hibiya lines to Roppongi (exit 4)

Agave (9, B2)

You could probably convince yourself you're in Mexico after a few too many margaritas at Agave. Luckily, this amiable spot is more about savouring the subtleties of its 400-plus varieties of tequila rather than tossing back shots of Cuervo. Mariachi musicians will woo you as you sip *añejo* (aged tequila).
☎ 3497 0229 ✉ B1F, Clover Bldg, 7-15-10 Roppongi, Minato-ku ⏰ 6.30pm-2am Mon-Fri, 6.30pm-4am Sat ⦿ Hibiya & Toei Ōedo lines to Roppongi (exit 2)

Bernd's Bar (9, C2)

Drop by Bernd's (p74) for some German sausage, or for a quick escape from the crazier corners of Roppongi. Bernd's always has a jovial, lively atmosphere, which might distract you from appreciating the clean taste of your German beer or wine.
☎ 5563 9232 ⌨ www.berndsbar.com ✉ 2F, Pure Roppongi Bldg, 5-18-1 Roppongi, Minato-ku ⏰ 5pm-late Mon-Sat ⦿ Hibiya line to Roppongi (exit 3)

Bodeguita (9, C2)

Along with good Latin food, the draw here is the salsa (dancing, that is). Once dinner's over, the dance floor is cleared and you'll have to decide: dance, or be crushed. Every Wednesday, there's live *son* (crooning) and on the last Saturday of the month, awesome Cuban parties.
☎ 3796 0232 ✉ 3F, Arrow Bldg, 3-14-7 Roppongi, Minato-ku $ Wed, Fri & Sat ¥1000 ⏰ 6pm-1am Sun-Wed, 6pm-late Thu-Sat ⦿ Hibiya & Toei Ōedo lines to Roppongi (exit 3)

Drinking Etiquette

If you're out for a few drinks, remember that you're expected to keep the drinks of your companions topped up. But don't fill your own glass, as this implies your guests aren't taking care of you; wait for someone to pour yours. It's polite to hold the glass with both hands while it's being filled. And most importantly, remember to say, *'Kampai!'* – cheers!

For goodness: sake

Golden Gai

Despite the inexorable pull of progress, Golden Gai remains one of the city's most interesting little night zones. Even if you don't feel like a drink, take a nocturnal stroll through this warren of tightly packed, low-lying *nomiya* (drinking establishments) just to take in the atmosphere – you'll feel like you've entered a time warp, what with the Shinjuku skyscrapers and sleazy Kabukichō scene you left behind a few blocks ago. Though most of these tiny spots do not welcome foreigners, there are a handful that do: **Bon's** (below) or **La Jetée** (p84) are two favourites. Catch them while you can.

Bon's (4, C1)

One of the old-school bars in the Golden Gai (see above), this is a great place to enjoy a drink and soak up the cosy ambience while it can still hang on. Drinks start at ¥700. Look for it next to the police box near the Hanazono-jinja steps; it's hard to miss the signage painted on its wall.
☎ 3209 6334 ✉ 1-1-10 Kabuki-chō, Shinjuku-ku 💲 ¥500 🕙 7pm-5am 🚇 Marunouchi & Toei Shinjuku lines to Shinjuku-sanchōme (exit B5)

Enjoy House (7, B1)

Near What the Dickens (p85), this is one of Tokyo's better clubs/lounges, where you can kick back and listen to a variety of music, from rock to house, in an opium-den atmosphere. Best of all, there's no cover charge.
☎ 5489 1591 ✉ 2F, Kokuto Bldg, 2-9-9 Ebisu-Nishi, Shibuya-ku 🕙 1pm-2am Tue-Thu, 1pm-4am Fri-Sun, closed 1st Sun of each month 🚉 Yamanote line to Ebisu (west exit)

Gas Panic Bar (9, C2)

Gas Panic used to be one giant *gaijin*-bar, but it's been split into three venues, forming one of Roppongi's rowdier cul-de-sacs. All three are cheap places to drink, particularly during happy hour – but they do tend to get crammed with unpredictable yahoos. Look for the red stairwells and seizure-inducing neon.
☎ 3405 0633 💻 www .gaspanic.co.jp ✉ 2F & 3F, 3-15-24 Roppongi, Minato-ku 🕙 6pm-5am

Geronimo (9, B2)

Right at the corner of Rop-pongi Crossing, this kooky shot bar gets packed out with all sorts of off-work expats and their Japanese associates. Drinks are half-price at happy hour: 6pm to 9pm weeknights, and 7pm to 9pm weekends. Beer (including Red Hook!) is ¥800 no matter what time you go.
☎ 3478 7449 ✉ 2F, Yamamuro Bldg, 7-14-10 Roppongi, Minato-ku 🕙 6pm-6am Mon-Fri, 7pm-6am Sat & Sun 🚇 Toei Ōedo & Hibiya lines to Roppongi (exit 4a)

Highlander (8, C3)

Low on glitz, high on quality, the bar at Hotel Ōkura (p98) is the perfect place to wind down after a strenuous business day or wind up for an evening out in the bars and restaurants of upmarket Akasaka. This bar has a mind-boggling selection of 200 brands of whisky.
☎ 3505 6077 ✉ Hotel Ōkura, 2-10-4 Toranomon, Minato-ku 💲 afternoon tea ¥2300 🕙 11.30am-1am Mon-Sat, 11.30am-midnight Sun 🚇 Hibiya line to Kamiyachō (exit 2)

Hobgoblin Tokyo (8, A2)

Far better than your average British-pub replica, Akasaka's Hobgoblin is run by an Oxfordshire brewery. It serves good pub fare and excellent imported microbrews. You'll find this Hobgoblin, appropriately, lurking in the basement of the building next to the clearly marked Marugen 23 building.
☎ 6229 2636 💻 www .hobgoblin-tokyo.com ✉ 1F, Tamondo Bldg, 2-13-19 Akasaka, Minato-ku 🕙 11am-2pm & 5pm-1am Mon-Fri, 5pm-1am Sat 🚇 Chiyoda line to Akasaka (exit 2), Ginza & Namboku lines to Ta-meike-sannō (exit 9)

Insomnia Lounge (5, B2)

Red is the colour of Insomnia. Mirrored by reflective surfaces all around you, your red-eye will blend right into the ruby interior of this laid-back lounge. It doesn't promise any miracle cures for

insomniacs, but will keep the sleepless going 'til dawn with good beats and cocktails.
☎ 3476 2735 ✉ B1F, Ikuma Bldg, 26-5 Udagawachō, Shibuya-ku 🕙 6pm-5am 🚇 Yamanote line to Shibuya (Hachikō exit)

Kamiya (11, C2)
Once popular with the Tokyo literati, this splendid old place hasn't changed much since it was founded in 1880. The 1st floor is a beer hall where you pay for drinks as you enter. Its best-known offering is the brandy-based cocktail *denki-bran*. Upstairs, restaurants serve both Japanese and Western food.
☎ 3841 5400 ✉ 1-1-1 Asakusa, Taitō-ku 🕙 11.30am-10pm Wed-Mon 🚇 Ginza line to Asakusa (exit 3)

La Jetée (4, C1)
Kawai-san, the proprietor of this Golden Gai bar, knows more about film than most of us ever will. No English is spoken here, though you're more than welcome to practise your rusty Français. Unlike many Golden Gai establishments, this one's amenable to foreign visitors.
☎ 3208 9645 ✉ 1-1-8 Kabukichō, Shinjuku-ku 🕙 7pm-late Mon-Sat 🚇 Yamanote line to Shinjuku (east exit)

Las Chicas (6, B2)
Internet terminals and terminal trendiness mix at this Harajuku bar-restaurant that's perfect for a midafternoon glass of pinot grigio or a night of mingling with hip expats and locals. Drop by for a cocktail after browsing the local galleries and designer boutiques. See also p71.
☎ 3407 6865 ✉ 5-47-6 Jingūmae, Shibuya-ku 🕙 11am-11pm 🚇 Chiyoda, Ginza & Hanzōmon lines to Omote-sandō (exit B2)

Mix (6, B2)
Small and smoky, this reliable hole-in-the-wall near Omote-sandō crossing is as friendly as it is crowded. Reg-gae and hip-hop predominate, and even if the rest of Roppongi is dead, Mix won't be. It's a bit hard to find; look for the stairs heading down to the basement. Two drinks are included with the cover.
☎ 3797 1313 💻 www.at-mix.com ✉ B1F, 3-6-19 Kita-Aoyama, Minato-ku 💲 ¥2500 🕙 10pm-late 🚇 Chiyoda, Ginza & Hanzōmon lines to Omote-sandō (exit B4)

Motown House 1 & 2 (9, B2)
As the name might imply, these houses play a range of funk, hip-hop, pop and soul – plus the standard rock'n'roll. The crass might call it 'ho-town', but on the pick-up front, it's no worse (or better?) than its neighbours. Drinks start at ¥800.
☎ 5474 4605 💻 www.motownhouse.com ✉ 2F, Com Roppongi Bldg, 3-11-5 Roppongi, Minato-ku 🕙 6pm-5am 🚇 Toei Ōedo & Hibiya lines to Roppongi (exit 3)

Lost on Location
As you prowl the subdued halls of the **Park Hyatt Tokyo** (p97), travelling incognito in your starlet sunglasses, the sweeping views of Tokyo, elegantly understated rooms and dimly lit, swanky bars might look a bit familiar. That's because the luxurious hotel served as a locus for much of Sofia Coppola's similarly refined film, *Lost in Translation*. Unless you're a guest here, you won't gain entrée to the rooftop gym with the zillion-dollar view to work off your jet lag. You can, however, pose as a rock star in the hotel's New York Bar for a wake-up cocktail with a knockout view.

New York Bar (4, A3)
Located in the higher stratosphere, both physically and socially, the New York Bar towers over the city on the 52nd floor of the Park Hyatt Tokyo (p97) in west Shinjuku. With magnificent views, strong drinks and live jazz, this is the perfect location to impress your date.
☎ 5323 3458 ☐ www .parkhyatttokyo.com ✉ 3-7-1-2 Nishi-Shinjuku, Shinjuku-ku 💲 after 8pm ¥2000 🕑 5pm-midnight Sun-Wed, 5pm-1am Thu-Sat 🚇 Marunouchi & Toei Shinjuku lines to Shinjuku (exit 7) 🚋 Yamanote line to Shinjuku (west exit)

Old Imperial Bar (12, B5)
The terribly dignified Old Imperial possesses elements of its original Frank Lloyd Wright design, and a history it would probably like to tell you over a few bourbon-and-waters. The drinks aren't cheap, but you don't get a storied atmosphere like this in your usual modern hotel bar.
☎ 3504 1111 ✉ Imperial Hotel, Uchisaiwaichō 1-1-1, Chiyoda-ku 🕑 11.30am-midnight 🚇 Chiyoda, Hibiya & Marunouchi lines to Hibiya (exit A13)

Pink Cow (5, C2)
The Pink Cow has relocated not too far from its old digs, and with its animal-print décor and rotating display of local artwork, it's still a funky, friendly little place to hide away. There's also a terrific all-you-can-eat buffet (¥2625) every Friday and Saturday evening, with heaps of vegetarian choices.
☎ 3406 5597 ☐ www .thepinkcow.com ✉ B1F, Villa Moderna, 1-3-18 Shibuya, Shibuya-ku 🕑 5pm-late Tue-Sun 🚋 Yamanote line to Shibuya (Hachikō exit)

Scruffy Murphy's (6, A1)
Dust off your bodhrán, and head over to Omote-sandō for an evening of impromptu Gaelic music and good Irish stout. Murphy's has excellent live bands almost every night of the week.
☎ 3499 3145 ☐ www .geocities.com/scruffy murphystokyo ✉ 2F, Sampou Sogo Bldg, 6-5-6 Jingūmae, Shibuya-ku 🕑 5pm-5am Mon-Fri, noon-5am Sat & Sun 🚇 Chiyoda line to Meiji-jingūmae (exit 4) 🚋 Yamanote line to Harajuku (Omote-sandō exit)

Smash Hits (3, C7)
You may ask yourself, 'How did I get here?' Watch your friends wince as you deafen them with the Sid Vicious version of 'My Way'. Smash Hits provides excruciating fun of the highest order, karaoke style. There are 12,000 English-language songs to choose from for your 15 minutes of 'Fame'.
☎ 3444 0432 ✉ B1F, M2 Hiro-o Bldg, 5-2-26 Hiro-o, Shibuya-ku 🕑 8pm-3am Mon-Sat, 7pm-midnight Sun 🚇 Hibiya line to Hiro-o (exit 1)

Trading Places (9, C2)
What was that about separating business and pleasure? The Bloomberg news chatters away full-time here, as expat traders come to sink pints and discuss imminent mergers (not always of the financial variety). With DJ and movie screen, this place is a laid-back lair for this part of town.
☎ 3589 2442 ✉ B1F, Imperial Roppongi Bldg, 5-16-52 Roppongi, Minato-ku 🕑 6pm-3am Mon-Sat 🚇 Hibiya & Toei Ōedo lines to Roppongi (exit 3)

What the Dickens (7, B1)
One of Tokyo's better English-style pubs, this one has a pleasant, spacious feel, and there's usually a band in the corner playing good, mellow music. What the Dickens serves filling, hearty pub food and Guinness on tap. What more could you want?
☎ 3780 2099 ✉ 4F, Roob 6 Bldg, 1-13-3 Ebisu-Nishi, Shibuya-ku 🕑 5pm-1am Tue & Wed, 5pm-2am Thu-Sat, 3pm-midnight Sun 🚇 Hibiya line to Ebisu (exit 2) 🚋 Yamanote line to Ebisu (west exit)

XYZ Bar (9, C2)
It's the bar formerly known as G-Martini's, with a similar menu of more than 30 generously proportioned martinis. DJs keep the music flowing, and several rooms give you space to move, groove and schmooze.
☎ 3588 6147 ☐ www .xyzbar.com ✉ 4F, Five Plaza Bldg, 5-18-21 Roppongi, Minato-ku 🕑 7pm-6am 🚇 Hibiya & Toei Ōedo lines to Roppongi (exit 3)

Holy Cycling Xylophones!
Look, in that bicycle jersey: it's a road cyclist bearing a xylophone! No, wait, it's a globetrotting percussionist! Ah, in fact, it's Masahiro Tatematsu (and all of the above). If you don't recognise him by the self-designed folding wooden xylophone in front of him, then you will by the bike behind him, or by his toned bod and beaming smile in between as he makes unusual, brain-pleasing music in Ueno-kōen (pp18-19) or Tokyo International Forum plaza (p27). A rare breed in Tokyo, street performers must apply and audition to the metropolitan government to busk legally in Tokyo. And hooray, Masahiro Tatematsu made the cut.

DANCE CLUBS

Tokyo clubs heat up well after dusk and pump until dawn, with after-parties continuing into daylight. Since hot spots come and go, call ahead to check that a place still exists. Cover charges usually include a drink or two.

BuL-Let's (9, A2)
This mellow basement space plays worldwide trance and ambient sounds for barefoot patrons. Beds and sofas await for those who need a soft spot. But don't get the wrong idea – it's not all tranquillity and deadbeats. Get your groove on to live electronica and experimental rhythms.
☎ 3401 4844 ▯ www .bul-lets.com ✉ B1F, Kasumi Bldg, 1-7-11 Nishi-Azabu, Minato-ku ⑤ from ¥1500 ◉ Hibiya & Toei Ōedo lines to Roppongi (exit 2)

Club 328 (9, A3)
DJs at San-ni-pa (aka San-ni-hachi) spin a quality mix, from funk to reggae to R&B. With its refreshing un-Roppongi feel and a cool crowd of Japanese and *gaijin* (foreigners), 328 is a good place to boogie 'til the break of dawn. Two drinks are included with the cover.
☎ 3401 4968 ▯ www.02 .246.ne.jp/~azabu328 ✉ B1F, Kotsu Anzen Center Bldg, 3-24-20

Nishi-Azabu, Minato-ku ⑤ ¥2000-2500 🕒 8pm-5am ◉ Toei Ōedo & Hibiya lines to Roppongi (exit 1)

Club Asia (5, A3)
This massive techno/soul club is worth a visit if you're on the younger end of twenty-something. Events here are usually jam-packed every night. There's also a good restaurant serving a variety of Southeast Asian food if you need more fuel to burn on the dance floor.
☎ 5458 1996 ✉ 1-8 Maruyama-chō, Shibuya-ku ⑤ around ¥2500 🕒 11pm-5am 🚃 Yamanote line to Shibuya (Hachikō exit)

Gas Panic Club (9, C2)
Very slightly more upmarket than its rowdy progenitor, the Gas Panic Bar (p83), Gas Panic Club offers the same cheap-booze, cruisy sort of scene. The upside is, you're marginally less likely to get decked by testosterone-crazed military personnel here. If you're in the mood,

this international frat party is a gas.
☎ 3402 7054 ▯ www .gaspanic.co.jp ✉ 3-5F, 3-10-5 Roppongi, Minato-ku 🕒 6pm-5am ◉ Toei Ōedo & Hibiya lines to Roppongi (exit 3)

Harlem (5, A3)
Wanna see where all those Japanese Afros and fake corn-rows are heading? On the 2nd and 3rd floor of Dr Jeekahn's Building, this is *the* gathering place for Tokyo B-boys and B-girls. The music is soul and hip-hop spun by international DJs, and the cover includes one drink.
☎ 3461 8806 ✉ 2F & 3F, Dr Jeekahn's Bldg, 2-4 Maruyama-chō, Shibuya-ku ⑤ ¥2000-3000 🕒 10pm-5am Tue-Sat 🚃 Yamanote line to Shibuya (Hachikō exit)

Lexington Queen (9, C2)
The Lex was one of Roppongi's first discos and is still the place where every visiting celebrity ends up. The cover here starts around

¥2000 unless you've had your visage on the cover of *Vogue* or *Rolling Stone*. But, even noncelebrities get a free drink with admission.
☎ 3401 1661 🖳 www .lexingtonqueen.com ✉ B1F, Gotō Bldg, 3-13-14 Roppongi, Minato-ku 💲 from ¥2000 🕑 8pm-5am ◉ Hibiya & Toei Ōedo lines to Roppongi (exit 3)

Maniac Love (6, B2)

This techno mecca really comes into its own around 5am Sunday morning, when the after-hours crowd come to strut their freaky, funky stuff. It's a pig to find, behind an unmarked steel door in the basement of the Tera A Omote-sandō building. No one under 20 is admitted; bring your ID.
☎ 3406 1166 🖳 www .maniaclove.com ✉ B1F, 5-10-6 Minami-Aoyama, Minato-ku 💲 weekday/weekend ¥2000/2500 🕑 from 10pm ◉ Chiyoda, Ginza, & Hanzōmon lines to Omote-sandō (exit B1)

Flying Solo

Tokyo bursts with distractions, but solo travellers might feel odd pangs of loneliness amid the city's teeming crowds – Tokyoites in motion put on blank city faces, commune with cellphones and pop in headphones. But alienation is not an obligation; if you catch Tokyo dwellers at rest or at play, those aloof veneers fade away.

There are plenty places to meet other foreigners and friendly locals, especially in Roppongi, Shibuya and Harajuku. Try lively **Geronimo** (p83), low-key **Las Chicas** (p84) or the artsy **Pink Cow** (p85) for a cocktail, and hit the **Ruby Room** (below) or **Club 328** (opposite) for dancing.

Ruby Room (5, A2)

This cool, sparkly gem of a cocktail lounge is on a hill behind the 109 Building. With both DJed and live music, the Ruby Room is an appealing spot for older kids hanging in Shibuya. The cover includes one drink, but if you dine downstairs at Sonoma, admission is free.
☎ 3780 3022 ✉ 2F, Kasumi Bldg, 2-25-17 Dōgenzaka, Shibuya-ku 💲 around ¥1500 🕑 9pm-late 🚊 Yamanote line to Shibuya (Hachikō exit)

Salsa Sudada (9, B2)

Salsa is still big in Tokyo, and experienced salsa dancers can expect to shake some booty for hours; beginners can take lessons here on Sunday nights. Dancers from all over the world come regularly to this place, one of the most popular salsa joints in the city.
☎ 5474 8806 ✉ 3F, La Palette Bldg, 7-13-8 Roppongi, Minato-ku 💲 ¥1500 🕑 6pm-6am ◉ Hibiya & Toei Ōedo lines to Roppongi (exit 4a)

Gas Panic Bar (p83) after a few margaritas

Vanilla (9, B2)
Aimed more towards a Japanese clientele, Vanilla attracts fewer drunken *gai-jin* kooks than nearby clubs. Three floors of dance space are filled with different beats and crowds of peeps. It's at the end of a small alley off Roppongi-dōri, close to Roppongi crossing. ☎ 3401 6200 🖳 www .clubvanilla.com ✉ TSK Bldg, 7-14-30 Roppongi, Minato-ku 💲 from ¥1500 🕐 7pm-late 🚇 Hibiya & Toei Ōedo lines to Roppongi (exits 2 & 4)

Velfarre (9, B2)
On the club front, Velfarre is Roppongi's disco Hilton. Dance clubs don't get much bigger, flashier or better behaved than this place. The cover includes a drink or three. Velfarre is in the basement of what looks like a car park, down an alley behind the Hotel Ibis. ☎ 3402 8000 🖳 http ://velfarre.avex.co.jp ✉ 7-14-22 Roppongi, Minato-ku 💲 from ¥3000 🕐 7pm-midnight Thu-Sun 🚇 Hibiya & Toei Ōedo lines to Roppongi (exit 4a)

Womb (5, A3)
'Oomu' (as pronounced by the Japanese) is all about house, techno and drum 'n' bass. All four floors get jammed on weekends. Bring a flyer – check Shibuya record shops beforehand, or print one from Womb's website – and they'll knock ¥500 to ¥1000 off the cover. Photo ID required at the door.
☎ 5459 0039 🖳 www .womb.co.jp ✉ 2-16 Maruyama-chō, Shibuya-ku 💲 ¥1500-4000 🕐 8pm-late 🚃 Ya-manote line to Shibuya (Hachikō exit)

Yellow (9, A2)
Located by Nishi-Azabu crossing, this is one of the most progressive and hippest places in town. Everything from house to acid jazz, Brazil jazz to techno and foreign DJ nights are featured at Yellow. Look for the entrance to this inky basement space next to a 'coin parking' lot. ☎ 3479 0690 ✉ B1 & B2F, Cesaurus Bldg, 1-10-11 Nishi-Azabu, Minato-ku 💲 ¥2000-3500 🕐 8.30pm-late 🚇 Hibiya & Toei Ōedo lines to Roppongi (exit 2)

CINEMAS

Most of Tokyo's cinemas show Western films with Japanese subtitles, or domestic titles without English. Some smaller cinemas show funky, limited-release and art-house favourites, and classic Japanese movies with English subtitles. Check the *Japan Times*, *Metropolis* or the *Tokyo Journal* to see what's on.

Cine Amuse East & West (5, A2)
Equipped with two screens and an excellent sound system, Cine Amuse has regular screenings of Japanese movies subtitled in English as well as international releases. It's a small but comfy space, and well-located in Shibuya for post-cinema amusement. ☎ 3496 2888 ✉ 2-23-12 Dōgenzaka, Shibuya-ku 💲 ¥1800/1000, ¥1000 on 1st day of month (except Jan) 🕐 10am-11pm 🚃 Yamanote line to Shibuya (Hachikō exit)

Cinema Rise (5, B2)
Independent films, such as skater documentary *Dogtown and Z-Boys,* are what you'll find at Cinema Rise, another central cinema in the heart of Shibuya. It's also opened a smaller, even more indy-minded cinema around the corner, called Cinema Rise X. You're sure to catch a quality, nonmainstream movie here.
☎ 3464 0051 ✉ 13-17 Udagawachō 💲 ¥1800/1000, ¥1000 on 1st day of month (except Jan) 🕐 10am-11pm 🚃 Yamanote line to Shibuya (Hachikō exit)

National Film Centre (12, C4)
The third arm of the National Museum of Modern Art (pp31-2), this centre shows tremendous film series on everything from the history of Japanese animation to the masterpieces

of Cuba's film tradition. The centre also houses a library and a gallery that includes a permanent collection of antique cinematic articles.
☎ 3272 8600 ✉ 3-7-6 Kyōbashi, Chūō-ku 💲 varies 🕑 cinema 3-10pm Tue-Fri, 1-7pm Sat & Sun, gallery 11am-6pm Tue-Sat

Virgin Toho Cinemas Roppongi Hills (9, B3)
Virgin's nine-screen multiplex has the biggest screen in Japan, as well as luxurious reclining seats and Internet booking up to two days in advance for reserved seats. This state-of-the-art theatre also holds all-night screenings Thursday through Saturday, and on nights before holidays – bringing new meaning to 'movie night'.
☎ 5775 6090 ✉ 6-10-2 Roppongi, Minato-ku 💲 ¥1800-3000/1000, 1st day of month ¥1000, women on Wed ¥1000

> **Flick Tix**
> Tokyo movie-ticket prices are probably the highest in the world, ranging from ¥1800 to ¥2300. If you plan ahead, tickets can be bought at certain outlets at discounted prices. Typically, a ¥1800 ticket will cost ¥1300 or less this way.
>
> Discounted movie tickets are sold in the basement of the Tokyo Kōtsū Kaikan in Ginza, Shinjuku's Studio Alta (5th floor), Harajuku's Laforet (p59; 1st floor) and Shibuya's 109 Building (5, B2; 2nd floor).
>
> The hitch: discount tickets are sold for the film, not the venue, so you'll have to show up at least an hour early to shove your way to a seat when the doors open.

🕑 10am-midnight Sun-Wed, 10am-5am Thu-Sat 🚇 Hibiya & Toei Ōedo lines to Roppongi (Roppongi Hills exit)

Yebisu Garden Cinema (7, C2)
At Yebisu Garden Place (p23), where you can have a bite beforehand and a cocktail afterwards, this cinema is a good place to catch a

good variety of films. Patrons are called into the theatre in groups according to ticket numbers, so it's a stress-free stroll to your seat.
☎ 5420 6161 ✉ 4-20-2 Yebisu Garden Place, Ebisu, Shibuya-ku 💲 ¥1800/1000, on 1st day of month ¥1000 🕑 10am-11pm 🚇 Yamanote line to Ebisu (east exit), then Skywalk

LIVE MUSIC VENUES

Blue Note (3, B6)
Serious cognoscenti roll up at Tokyo's prime jazz spot, prepared to shell out much moolah on the likes of Maceo Parker, Sergio Mendes and Chick Corea. Walk down Kotto-dōri towards Nishi Azabu; it's opposite the Idee store.
☎ 3407 5781 ✉ Raika Bldg, 6-3-16 Minami-Aoyama, Minato-ku 💲 ¥6000-10,000 🕑 5.30pm-1.30am Mon-Sat 🚇 Chiyoda, Ginza, & Hanzōmon lines to Omote-sandō (exit B3)

Club Quattro (5, A2)
Club Quattro is another established showcase venue for local and international artists. Although it's located in the heart of Shibuya, it's actually one of the Parco department store buildings (and there's a lift) which makes for a slightly odd entry. Be sure to buy tickets in advance.
☎ 3477 8750 ✉ 5F, Club Quattro Bldg, 32-13 Udagawa-chō, Shibuya-ku 💲 varies 🕑 7pm-late 🚇 Yamanote line to Shibuya (Hachikō exit)

Crocodile (6, A2)
In Harajuku right on Meiji-dōri, Crocodile has live music seven nights a week. It's a spacious place with heaps of room for dancing if the music moves you. Tunes cover the gamut from night to night, be it jazz, reggae or rock'n'roll. The cover charge includes one drink.
☎ 3499 5205 ✉ B1F, New Sekiguchi Bldg, 6-18-8 Jingūmae, Shibuya-ku 💲 from ¥2000 🕑 6pm-2am 🚇 Chiyoda line to Meiji-jingūmae (exit 4)

Ichiko Hashimoto Trio playing at Shinjuku Pit Inn, older sister to Roppongi Pit Inn

La.mama (5, A3)

For a dose of current local-centric music, La.mama is a good bet for catching live, mainstream Japanese rockers. The room is fairly spacious, but even when the place gets crowded you'll be close enough to get sweat upon by the next rising star out of Tokyo.
☎ 3464 0801
🖳 info@lamama.net
✉ B1F, Primera Dogenzaka Bldg, 1-15-3 Dōgenzaka, Shibuya-ku 💲 around ¥2300
☽ 6pm-late 🚉 Yamanote line to Shibuya (Hachikō exit)

Liquid Room (7, B1)

Some of the world's greatest performers have graced the stage of the Liquid Room, from the Flaming Lips to Linton Kwesi Johnson. Settled into a new home in Ebisu, the venue is bigger and better than before. An excellent place to see an old favourite or find a new one.
☎ 5464 0800 🖳 www.liquidroom.net ✉ 3-16-6 Higashi, Shibuya-ku 💲 varies ☽ 7pm-late 🚉 Yamanote line to Ebisu (east exit)

Loft (4, C1)

Had they been Japanese, the Rolling Stones would have played at Loft long before they cut their first single. This Shinjuku institution is smoky, loud and lots of fun on a good night.
☎ 5272-0382 ✉ B2F, Tatehana Bldg, 1-12-9 Kabuki-chō, Shinjuku-ku 💲 varies ☽ 5pm-late 🚉 Yamanote line to Shinjuku (east exit)

Milk (7, B1)

One of Tokyo's best small live clubs, Milk features international and local punk, rock and underground. This is a cool space, with three underground levels and a crowd of weirdly wonderful local characters. Check out the food-less kitchen – a great place to chat and sip a vodka tonic between sets.
☎ 5458 2826 🖳 www.milk-tokyo.com ✉ B1F, Roob 6 Bldg, 1-13-3 Ebisu-Nishi, Shibuya-ku 💲 around ¥1000 ☽ 8pm-4am 🚉 Yamanote line to Ebisu (west exit)

Roppongi Pit Inn (9, C2)
It's not the pits; Roppongi Pit Inn is the younger branch of Shinjuku Pit Inn, a well-established jazz club in that central of neighbourhoods. This Pit focuses on fusion jazz and serves as an outlet for more experimental music-making.
☎ 3585 1063 ✉ 3-17-7 Roppongi, Minato-ku ⑧ varies ◷ 6.30pm-midnight ⊕ Hibiya & Toei Ōedo lines to Roppongi (exit 3)

Shibuya O-East (5, A3)
The rechristened O-East (formerly known as On-Air East) is another long-running club where you can catch good live acts with all sorts of wacky extras, such as bubbles, shadow puppets and video embellishments. You'll need to book ahead, as this is a popular place that tends to sell out.
☎ 5458 4681 ▯ www.shibuya-o.com ✉ 2-14-8 Dōgenzaka, Shibuya-ku ⑧ from ¥2500 ◷ 7pm-late ▣ Yamanote line to Shibuya (Hachikō exit)

Shibuya O-West (5, A3)
Another outpost in the O empire of Shibuya TV, O-West is just across the street from its eastern counterpart. While O-East hosts more electronica-style acts, O-West tends more towards punk rock and J-pop. As with its sister club, reserve your tickets in advance.
☎ 5784 7088 ▯ www.shibuya-o.com ✉ 2-3 Maruyama-chō, Shibuya-ku ⑧ from ¥2500 ◷ 7pm-late ▣ Yamanote line to Shibuya (Hachikō exit)

STB 139 (Sweet Basil; 9, B2)
A two-minute walk south of Roppongi station, this is a large, lovely space that draws similarly big-name acts. Performances are predominantly jazz, covering the spectrum from acid to big band. Even if the act is unknown to you, the ambience will be wonderful and the standards high.
☎ 5474 1395 ▯ http://stb139.co.jp ✉ 6-7-11 Roppongi, Minato-ku ⑧ ¥3000-7000 ◷ 6-11pm Mon-Sat ⊕ Hibiya & Toei Ōedo lines to Roppongi (exit 3)

CONTEMPORARY DANCE & THEATRE

Tokyo has a lively contemporary theatre scene tucked away and often off the beaten track. Language, of course, poses another barrier to the foreign theatre-goer. However, with the advent of Intrigue Theatre (see below) and the existence of various excellent dance studios, there are opportunities to access live performances.

Bunkamura Theatre Cocoon (5, A2)
This dance space in one of Tokyo's liveliest arts complexes (p30) and shows occasional works by international dance troupes. It has also been known to programme musical dramas, though these take place less frequently than dance programmes.
☎ 3477 9999 ▯ www.bunkamura.co.jp/english ✉ 2-24-1 Dōgenzaka, Shibuya-ku ⑧ varies ◷ varies ▣ Yamanote line to Shibuya (Hachikō exit) ♿ good

Intrigue Theatre
Tokyo's first professional theatre dedicated to English-language productions has finally arrived. Early offerings have included dramas by both Molière and García Lorca. Ticket sales have been brisk, which bodes well for the future of the troupe. Venues always vary, so check out the website for current locations, directions and ticket information.
☎ 090 9955 0200 ▯ www.intriguetheatre.com ⑧ ¥4000

Session House (3, C4)
Dance aficionados consider Session House one of the best traditional, folk and modern dance spaces in the city. The theatre seats only 100 people, which ensures an intimate feel for all performances. For news about what's on in the rest of the city, check the lobby's crowded notice board.
☎ 3266 0461 ✉ 158 Yaraichō, Shinjuku-ku ⑧ varies ◷ performances 7pm ⊕ Tōzai line to Kagurazaka (exit 1)

Special Events

January *New Year's Day* – the first shrine visit of the year; eating of buckwheat noodles
Dezome-shiki – 6 January; excellent photo opportunities at this firefighter's festival in front of Tokyo Big Sight, Ōdaiba
Hatsu-basho – sumō tournament at Ryogōku Kokugikan (see pp20-1 for more details)
Seijin-no-hi – 15 January; traditional display of archery at Meiji-jingū (p9)

February *Setsubun* – 13 February; demon-expelling, bean-throwing ceremonies, best experienced at Sensō-ji, Asakusa

March *Girls' day festival* – 3 March; a doll fair is held in Asakusabashi

March/April *Hanami* – cherry-blossom viewing across the city during outdoor picnics and parties

April *Jibeta Matsuri* – 15 April; Kawasaki festival that celebrates the vanquishing of a sharp-toothed demon residing in a young maiden, by means of an iron phallus
Kamakura Matsuri – 2nd Sunday; week of festival celebrations centred around Tsurugaoka Hachiman-gū in Kamakura

May *Hatsu-basho Sumō Tournament* – wrestlers settle grudges smouldering since January, at Ryogōku Kokugikan
Asakusa Sanja Matsuri – raucous festival in and around Asakusa-jinja shrine

June *Japan Derby* – tens of thousands flock to the races at Tokyo Racecourse
Iris viewing – across the city, especially at Meiji-jingū

July *Sumida-gawa fireworks display* – last weekend in July; the most popular *hanabi* of the year

August *Fuji Rock Festival* – three-day event that draws top international and local acts
O-bon – 13-15 August; Buddhist Feast of the Dead when Tokyoites return to their parents' home to welcome the visiting spirits of their ancestors
Asakusa Samba Festival – the Brazilian community dances in the street

September *Sumō Tournament Aki-basho* – last battle of the year at Ryogōku Kokugikan

October/November *Meiji Reidaisai* – 30 October to 3 November; displays of traditional horseback archery by riders at Meiji-jingū
Tokyo International Film Festival – held in late October or early November, this respectable film festival usually runs about 10 days (www.tiff-jp.net)

November *Shichi-go-san festival* – 15 November; for children aged 3, 5 and 7

December *All-Japan Kendo Championships* – check www.kendo.or.jp for exact dates for the national championships of this bamboo-sword martial art
Emperor's Birthday – 23 December; the Imperial Palace grounds are opened to the public
New Year's Eve – 31 December; at midnight the freezing populace flock to Shinto shrines to toll the bell 108 times to atone for their past year's sins; Meiji-jingū is especially festive

TRADITIONAL ARTS

In addition to kabuki and *Nō*, *bunraku* (puppet theatre) is another type of theatre unique to Japan. For current information on performances, check with a tourist information centre (TIC; p120) or the appropriate theatre for show times and ticket bookings.

Kabuki-za (12, C5)

Performances and times vary from month to month at Kabuki-za (p17), so you'll need to check with the TIC (p120) or with the theatre directly for programme information.
☎ 5565 6000 🖳 www.shochiku.co.jp/play/kabukiza/theater/index.html ✉ 4-12-5 Ginza, Chūō-ku 💲 ¥2520-16,800 🕙 varies 🚇 Hibiya & Toei Asakusa lines to Higashi-Ginza (exit 3) ♿ limited

Kanze Nō-gakudō (5, A2)

This theatre is attached to one of the traditional schools of *Nō*. By far the most exciting are the occasional outdoor night performances of Takigi Nō, where the masked actors are illuminated by huge burning torches. It's a transporting experience (and only a 15-minute walk from Shibuya station).
☎ 3469 6241 ✉ 1-16-4 Shōtō, Shibuya-ku 💲 from ¥3000 🕙 varies 🚇 Yamanote line to Shibuya (Hachikō exit)

Kokuritsu Geikijō (National Theatre; 8, C1)

Astonishingly lifelike, *bunraku* puppets are half to two-thirds life-size and are each operated by three hooded, visible puppeteers. A single narrator, standing on a dais to one side,

Signing a fan for a fan

intones the story using a different voice for each character. Performances take place in Tokyo in February, May, September and December.
☎ 3265 7411 🖳 www.ntj.jac.go.jp/english/index.html ✉ 4-1 Hayabusa-chō, Chiyoda-ku 💲 ¥1500-9200 🕙 tickets 10am-6pm, performances 11.30am & 5pm 🚇 Hanzōmon line to Hanzōmon (exit 1) ♿ limited

Kokuritsu Nō-gakudō (3, B5)

Also known as the National Nō Theatre, this venue has performances on weekends only. Exit Sendagaya station in the direction of Shinjuku on the left and follow the road that hugs the railway tracks; the theatre will be on the left.
☎ 3423 1331 ✉ 4-18-1 Sendagaya, Shibuya-ku 💲 tickets ¥2800-5600 🕙 varies 🚇 Chūō line to Sendagaya (west exit)

Nō Go?

Nō began over 600 years ago as a court performance and relies on understatement through stark sets and subtle masks to focus attention on the performers. Combining classical Japanese dance, music and poetry, *nō* is highly formulaic while at the same time improvisational; pre-performance rehearsals are generally eschewed.

Only two performers – *waki* or 'one who watches' and *shite* or 'one who acts' – are essential in *nō*. The *waki* unmasks the *shite*, who is never what he or she seems to be.

Nō can seem impenetrable even to Japanese audiences, but you can judge for yourself at venues listed in this section.

GAY & LESBIAN TOKYO

Shinjuku-nichōme has Tokyo's highest concentration of gay and lesbian nightlife. *Tokyo Journal*'s Cityscope section sometimes has a special insert called 'Tokyo Out'. See p116 for more information.

Out to the Cinema

Now in its teens, the annual **Tokyo International Lesbian & Gay Film and Video Festival** (TIL&GFF; ☎ 6475 0388; www.tokyo-lgff.org/e) takes to screens across the city during the summer and is definitely worth a look. There's a good mix of features and shorts, with films both Japanese and foreign. Depending on its origin, each film is subtitled in either Japanese or English.

Advocates Bar (3, B5)

Advocates Bar is just that – a bar. This place is so small that as the crowd gets bigger during the course of an evening, it becomes more like a block party and takes to the streets. Family of all genders are welcome here.
☎ 3358 8638 ✉ B1F, 7th Tenka Bldg, 2-18-1 Shinjuku, Shinjuku-ku $ varies ⏲ 8pm-4am ⊖ Marunouchi & Toei Shinjuku lines to Shinjuku-sanchōme (exits C7 & C8)

Arty Farty (3, B5)

Arty Farty is an easy place for guys to meet guys, with good all-you-can-drink specials. It's a sure-fire spot to start your evening and find out about the area's other possibilities. Women are only admitted Sunday and generally only with gay boys.
☎ 5362 9720 🖥 www .arty-farty.net ✉ 2F, 2-11-7 Shinjuku, Shinjuku-ku ⏲ 5pm-5am Mon-Sat, 4pm-5am Sun ⊖ Marunouchi & Toei Shinjuku lines to Shinjuku-sanchōme (exits C7 & C8)

Club Ace (3, B5)

At this laid-back ace of a place for both men and women, you can relax, enjoy some chill-out tracks and lounge on velvet sofas. Club Ace is an American-run joint and a great bar to meet fellow out-of-towners; some nights are men- or women-only events, so call ahead.
☎ 3352 6297 ✉ B1F, 2-14-6 Shinjuku, Shinjuku-ku $ from ¥1000 ⏲ 8pm-4am ⊖ Marunouchi & Toei Shinjuku lines to Shinjuku-sanchōme (exits C7 & C8)

Club Dragon (3, B5)

If you simply turn up here, you could arrive on a theme night and find yourself surrounded by hardcore leather daddies; however, some nights are free and it's a mixed – though largely male – crowd. Call ahead to get the scoop, or live on the edge.
☎ 3341 0606 ✉ B1F, Accord Bldg, 2-14-4 Shinjuku, Shinjuku-ku $ from ¥1000 ⏲ 9pm-5am Fri & Sat, 8pm-5am Tue-Thu & Sun ⊖ Marunouchi & Toei Shinjuku lines to Shinjuku-sanchōme (exit C8)

Kinswomyn (3, B5)

Counterbalancing all the male-dominated gay bars in the neighbourhood, Kinswomyn is a popular, welcoming lesbian bar run by well-known activist Tara. It's perfect for visitors as English is spoken, and a comfortable place for Japanese and foreign women alike.
☎ 3354 8720 ✉ 3F, Daiichi Tenka Bldg, 2-15-10 Shinjuku, Shinjuku-ku $ cocktails ¥750 ⏲ 8pm-4am Wed-Mon ⊖ Marunouchi & Toei Shinjuku lines to Shinjuku-sanchōme (exit C8)

Friday night frenzy at Club Dragon

SPECTATOR SPORTS

Baseball

Japan is baseball crazy and a trip to a Japanese ballpark is truly a cultural experience. The home team's fans often turn up in matching *happi* (half-coats) and perform intricate cheering rituals in perfect unison led by special cheerleaders, one for each section, who seem to make a job out of whipping fans into a well-ordered frenzy.

Tokyo Dome (3, D4; ☎ 5800 9999; www.tokyo-dome.co.jp/e; 1-3-61 Kōraku, Bunkyō-ku; ¥1800-3500; Marunouchi & Namboku lines to Kōraku-en, main exit) is the best place to catch a ball game. It's the home turf of Japan's most popular team, the Yomiuri Giants.

Hot-hitting Yomiuri Giants delight baseball fanatics at Tokyo Dome

Soccer

J-League soccer is booming in Japan, though naysayers had predicted its rapid decline with the departure of the 2002 World Cup (awarded to Japan, jointly with Korea). The increased interest in the game has remained, and the Japanese have decked it out with the hullabaloo of its baseball. Tokyo's own J-League team, Tokyo Verdy 1969, plays at the **National Stadium** (3, B5; ☎ 3403 1151; Kasumigaoka-machi, Shinjuku-ku; ¥3500/1000; Chūō line to Sendagaya, east exit).

Sumō

If your visit coincides with a Grand Tournament in Tokyo, don't miss your chance to witness this very Japanese of sports – a spectacle of ritual, tradition and pure physical power. See pp20-1 for more details.

Sleeping

Tokyo offers an uncommon array of accommodation options. Of the more conventional places to sleep, you can find anything from a world-class luxury hotel boasting its own art museum to a budget ryokan (Japanese inn) with fragrant tatami (woven floor matting) and a communal Japanese bath. The more adventurous might seek out a night in a bare-bones capsule, or a by-the-hour love-hotel room that features a Hello Kitty or race-car theme. Party animals can also rest assured that there is a place to nap when they have run out of steam – in a manga (comic book) café.

Luxury and top-end hotels in Tokyo provide the same high standards of comfort, style, efficiency and service you would find in these leagues anywhere else in the world, and they usually have the most coveted views and excellent restaurants. Many mid-range hotels cater to the transient trade of the Japanese business traveller and offer amenities such as in-room Internet access or a business centre. Hotels in this class may or may not take credit cards, so check ahead if you want to pay in plastic.

Whatever grade of hotel you're staying at, it's worth springing for a Japanese-style room. They're usually more spacious and aesthetically pleasing than Western-style rooms and arguably more comfortable. Above all, they remind you that you're not in London or New York, or any other world metropolis. Sleeping on a futon may work minor wonders on your back, and the delicate smell of a tatami floor will stay with you long after you return home.

Room Rates

These categories indicate the cost per night of a standard double room, including tax and service charges but exclusive of Tokyo's metropolitan accommodation tax (¥100 per person per night). During weekends and holidays prices may be slightly higher.

Deluxe	¥40,000 and over
Top End	¥25,000-39,999
Mid-Range	¥12,000-24,999
Budget	¥11,999 and under

Love Hotels

A night in one of Tokyo's love hotels (nowadays known as 'couples', 'fashion' or 'boutique' hotels) makes a fun change of venue. Rooms are rented by the hour, but after 10pm the overnight rates are quite reasonable. Starting at ¥7500, higher rates get kitschier and better-outfitted rooms (cavern-like bathtubs, sex toy vending machines).

Since many adults live with parents or in-laws, love hotels are used for romantic trysts by couples of all ages. Find a cluster of them in Shibuya, east of the station and up the hill. Select your room from the illuminated pictures in the empty foyer and pay the clerk. Ask for *tomari* (overnight) rates.

DELUXE

Four Seasons Hotel Chinzan-sō (3, C3)
Unquestionably Tokyo's most civilised Japanese-style accommodation, complete with ornamental ponds, gorgeous tatami rooms and all the trappings. You'll have easy access to central Tokyo and a peaceful retreat to return to at the end of the day.
☎ 3943 2222 ⌨ www .fourseasons.com/tokyo ✉ 2-10-8 Sekiguchi, Bunkyō-ku 🚇 Yūraku-chō line to Edogawabashi (exit 1A) 🅿 ♿ excellent ✗ 4 restaurants, bar & café 👶

Hotel Seiyo Ginza (12, C4)
With extravagant touches such as personal, 24-hour butler service for each guest, this doesn't feel like a hotel; rather, a very wealthy friend's impossibly dignified chateau. Because of its size, 77 rooms, be sure to book in advance.
☎ 3535 1111 ⌨ www .seiyo-ginza.com ✉ 1-11-2 Ginza, Chūō-ku 🚇 Yūraku-chō line Ginza-itchōme (exit 7) ♿ good ✗ 4 restaurants, bar, patisserie & tearoom 👶

Imperial Hotel (12, B5)
One of Tokyo's grand old, opulent hotels, the Imperial has regulars who wouldn't dream of staying anywhere else. The Imperial is within walking distance of Ginza, Tsukiji Produce & Fish Market and the Imperial Palace.
☎ 3504 1111 ⌨ www .imperialhotel.co.jp ✉ 1-1-1 Uchisaiwai-chō, Chiyoda-ku 🚇 Hibiya line to Hibiya (exit 5) ✗ 13 restaurants & 4 bars 👶

Park Hyatt Tokyo (4, A3)
Soaring over Tokyo on the upper floors of the 53-floor Shinjuku Park Tower, the Park Hyatt is all unfussy luxury. With a rooftop pool, an immaculate, sunlight-flooded spa, sauna facilities and sophisticated restaurants, it's a low-key, high-rise haven from manic Tokyo.
☎ 5322-1234 ⌨ tokyo .park.hyatt.com ✉ 3-7-1-2 Nishi-Shinjuku, Shinjuku-ku 🚇 Yamanote line to Shinjuku station (west exit) ♿ excellent ✗ New York Grill (p78), Kozue, Girandole & 2 bars 👶

TOP END

Akasaka Prince Hotel (8, A1)
The Akasaka Prince is a landmark, physically and socially. Much cachet is gained from dropping this name. Rooms at this skyscraper hotel provide excellent views and spaciousness; both commodities in short supply in central Tokyo. All top-end accoutrements are here.
☎ 3234 1111 ⌨ www .princehotels.co.jp /akasaka ✉ 1-2 Kioi-chō, Chiyoda-ku 🚇 Ginza & Marunouchi lines to Akasaka-mitsuke (exit D) 🅿 ♿ excellent ✗ 8 restaurants 👶

ANA Hotel Tokyo (8, B3)
Midway between Akasaka and Roppongi (halfway between business and pleasure?), this sleek 37-storey hotel is an excellent choice. It has all the amenities – fitness clubs, an outdoor pool, saunas, salons, shopping and lots of good bars and restaurants.
☎ 3505 1111 ⌨ www .anahotels.com/tokyo /e/index.html ✉ 1-12-33 Akasaka, Minato-ku 🚇 Ginza & Namboku lines to Tameike-sannō (exit 13) 🅿 ♿ excellent ✗ 8 restaurants & 4 bars 👶

Grand Hyatt Tokyo (9, B2)
Something of a master-piece, the new Grand Hyatt Tokyo shows off artful architecture with original designs that incorporate natural materials such as granite and bamboo. Rooms are both beautiful and plush, and the hotel is centrally located in Roppongi Hills.
☎ 4333 1234 ⌨ http ://tokyo.grand.hyatt.com ✉ 6-10-3 Roppongi, Minato-ku 🚇 Hibiya & Toei Ōedo lines to Roppongi (Roppongi Hills exit) 🅿 ♿ excellent ✗ 7 restaurants, 2 bars & patisserie 👶

Hotel New Ōtani (8, A1)
The New Ōtani is mega-famous, renowned for the beautiful Japanese garden around which it is constructed. The place is immense, with details you'd expect from a hotel of this class, including top-end boutiques, an art museum and a whiff of attitude. ☎ 3265 1111 💻 www1.newotani.co.jp/en/tokyo /index.htm ✉ 4-1 Kioi-chō, Chiyoda-ku 🚇 Ginza & Marunouchi lines to Akasaka-mitsuke (exit D) P ♿ good ✕ 34 restaurants ♨

Hotel Ōkura (8, C3)
This top hotel near the US embassy is popular with disgraced foreign presidents, celebrities and business travellers. With a fine Japanese garden, an art museum, elegant common areas and some of Tokyo's best restaurants, it also maintains a charming, unpretentious aesthetic. ☎ 3582 0111 💻 www.hotelokura.co.jp ✉ 2-10-4 Toranomon, Minato-ku 🚇 Hibiya line to Kamiyachō (exit 3) P ♿ good ✕ 8 restaurants, 3 bars & café ♨

Tea ceremony at Hotel Ōkura

Keiō Plaza Hotel (4, A2)
The Keiō Plaza is a comfortable, well-appointed hotel that's strong on business support. Rooms provide excellent views, and outside are the infinite distractions of Shinjuku after dusk. ☎ 3344 0111 💻 www.keioplaza.com/index.html ✉ 2-2-1 Nishi-Shinjuku, Shinjuku-ku 🚇 Toei Ōedo line to Tochōmae (exit A1) P ♿ good ✕ 6 restaurants ♨

MID-RANGE

Ginza Nikkō Hotel (12, B5)
The Nikkō is a quality mid-range hotel in a prime location. Perfect for *izakaya* (Japanese bar) hopping, shopping and taking off at dawn to Tsukiji Produce & Fish Market. It's right on Sotobori-dōri between Ginza and Shimbashi, near Shimbashi station. The rooms aren't huge but are quite comfortable. ☎ 3571 4911 💻 www.nikkohotels.com ✉ 8-4-21 Ginza, Chūō-ku 🚇 Ginza line to Shimbashi (exit 5) ✕ Kyūbei (p69)

Hotel Century Southern Tower (4, B3)
Soaring at the top end of this price range, this high-rise hotel towers over west Shinjuku. The relatively modest rooms are blessed with spectacular city and park views. It's quite posh, and especially good value if two share. ☎ 5354 0111 💻 www.southerntower.co.jp ✉ 2-2-1 Yoyogi, Shibuya-ku 🚇 Yamanote line to Shinjuku (Shin-minami exit) P ♿ good ✕ 3 restaurants & 1 bar ♨

Hotel Ibis (9, B2)
Smack bang in the middle of Roppongi party-land, this reasonably priced place is plenty used to dealing with late-night foreign revellers. Hardly the most relaxing neighbourhood to stay in, but if stay you must, this is super convenient. ☎ 3403 4411 💻 www.ibis-hotel.com ✉ 7-14-4 Roppongi, Minato-ku 🚇 Hibiya line to Roppongi (exit 4A) P ♿ good ✕ 2 restaurants & 2 bars

Gaijin Houses

Some *gaijin* (foreigner) houses offer nightly or weekly rates, but most are geared to foreigners working in Tokyo and charge by the month. If you plan to stay in the city for a month or more, you can reserve a room before arriving in Tokyo. Expect to pay from ¥40,000 to ¥90,000 a month.

Sakura House (4, B1; ☎ 5330 5250; www.sakura-house.com; 2F, Nishi-Shinjuku K1 Bldg, 7-2-6 Nishi-Shinjuku, Shinjuku-ku; ☉ 8.50am-5.50pm Mon-Sat) is a reliable agency with rentals in various central Tokyo neighbourhoods, but checking listings in *Metropolis* or asking other foreigners in Tokyo can yield good leads.

Hotel Parkside (10, B3)

Overlooking Shinobazu Pond, this a good choice near Ueno-kōen museums. Rooms in front with views of pond and park are particularly appealing. Japanese-style rooms are also available at reasonable rates.
☎ 3836 5711 ☐ www .parkside.co.jp ✉ 2-11-18 Ueno, Taitōku ☒ Yamanote to Ueno (Hirokōji exit) ✗ Izu-ei (p79) ♿ good

Hotel Sun Lite Shinjuku (4, C1)

Located in east Shinjuku, this is a good choice. The staff are friendly and relaxed, and the place is clean and quiet, with small but well-maintained rooms.
☎ 3356 0391 ☐ www .sunlite.co.jp/index-e.htm ✉ 5-15-8 Shinjuku, Shinjuku-ku ☒ Marunouchi line to Shinjuku-sanchōme (exit C7) ✗ restaurant & café

Hotel Sunroute Akasaka (8, A1)

A bright, friendly spot with well-designed rooms all equipped with high-speed Internet access, the Sunroute Akasaka is conveniently located near the Akasaka-mitsuke subway station.

It's a 15-minute walk from Roppongi nightlife.
☎ 3589 3610 ☐ www .sunroute.jp ✉ 3-21-7 Akasaka, Minato-ku ☒ Marunouchi & Ginza lines to Akasaka-mitsuke (exit A) ♿ good ✗ Sushi-sei (p65) & Trattoria Marumo (p65)

Hotel Yaesu-Ryūmeikan (12, B2)

Not only is this hotel the cheapest deal in the area, but the Japanese-style rooms are a steal – at rates comparable to the Western-style accommodation. Rates even include a Japanese breakfast.
☎ 3271-0971 ☐ www .ryumeikan.co.jp/yaesu _e.htm ✉ 1-3-22 Yaesu, Chūō-ku ☒ Yamanote line to Tokyo (Yaesu north exit) ℗ limited ✗ 2 restaurants

Kodomo no Shiro (Children's Castle) Hotel (5, C2)

This is a terrific option if you're in town with the kids. Rooms are spacious, and you get discount rates at the facilities of the adjoining Kodomo no Shiro (National Children's Castle; p41).
☎ 3797 5677 ☐ www .kodomono-shiro.or.jp /hotel ✉ 5-53-1 Jingū-mae, Shibuya-ku ☒ Chiyoda, Ginza & Hanzōmon lines to Omote-sandō (exit B2) ℗ ♿ excellent ✗ 1 restaurant (till 7pm) ⚐

Missing the Train

If you've missed the last train home, look for a manga (comic book) café. Full-night rates at manga cafés are a bargain, comparable to capsule hotels. Pre-pay for your stay and while away the wee hours in a comfortable private space. Manga cafés serve food, house libraries of DVDs and manga, provide Internet access and have staff making regular rounds to ensure safe surfing and sleeping.

Try **Manga Hiroba** (9, C2; ☎ 3497 1751; 2F, Shuwa Roppongi Bldg, 3-14-12 Roppongi, Minato-ku), **Café J Net New New** (5, A2; ☎ 5458 5935; 7F, Saito Bldg, 34-5 Udagawa-chō, Shibuya-ku) or **Manga@Cafe-Gera Gera** (4, B1; ☎ 5285 0585; 1-23-1 Kabuki-chō, Shinjuku-ku).

Mitsui Urban Hotel Ginza (12, B5)

Rooms at this well-located hotel have a polished feel and the usual mid-range amenities. With three in-house restaurants and easy access to Shimbashi station, this is a solid choice for comfort in Ginza.

☎ 3572 4131 ✉ 8-6-15 Ginza, Chūō-ku 🚇 Shimbashi (exit 3) P ♿ good ✖ Munakata (pp69-70)

Roppongi Prince Hotel (9, C1)

Just about every rock star deserving of the name has barfed, bonked, overdosed, or just graffitied here. Its curvy, groovy courtyard boasts a central outdoor heated swimming. Rooms are nothing special, but are only a 10-minutes walk from the excesses of Roppongi.

☎ 3587 1111 🖥 www .princehotels.co.jp /roppongi ✉ 3-2-7 Roppongi, Minato-ku 🚇 Hibiya line to Roppongi (exit 3) P ♿ good ✖ 4 restaurants & 1 bar 🛁

Shibuya Excel Hotel Tōkyū (5, B3)

Attached to Shibuya Station, this hotel isn't worn around the edges, unlike other hotels so near the tracks. Rooms are spacious, quiet and comfortable, with many having good views at night. The décor is simple, crisp and elegant.

☎ 5457 0109 🖥 www .tokyuhotels.co.jp/en /index.htm ✉ Shibuya Mark City Bldg, 1-12-2 Dogenzaka, Shibuya-ku 🚇 Yamanote line to Shibuya ♿ limited ✖ 2 restaurants & café

Shibuya Tōbu Hotel (5, B2)

Probably the smartest place to stay in trendy Shibuya, the rooms here are stylish, clean and relatively spacious. Common areas are bright and sleek, there are good in-house restaurants and the friendly, attentive staff speak English.

☎ 3476 0111 🖥 www .tobuhotel.co.jp/shibuya ✉ 3-1 Udagawa-chō, Shibuya-ku 🚇 Yamanote line to Shibuya (Hachikō exit) P ♿ good ✖ 2 restaurants & 1 bar

Shinjuku New City Hotel (4, A2)

On the far side of Shinjuku's Chūō-kōen, this hotel has bigger rooms than average, but the location is what recommends it. Some rooms have pretty park views, and staff here are very friendly.

☎ 3375 6511 🖥 www .newcityhotel.co.jp/eng /index.html ✉ 4-31-1 Nishi-Shinjuku, Shinjuku-ku 🚇 Toei Ōedo line to Tochōmae (exit A4) P ♿ good ✖ 2 restaurants

Sleeping Capsules

As private (and small) as coffins, capsule-hotel units come with bed, reading light, TV and alarm clock. Capsule prices range from ¥3300 to ¥4800. Capsule hotels are unused to hosting foreigners or women; most of their business comes from drunken office workers who've missed the last train home. Many have a well-appointed bath area similar to a good local *sentō* (public bath).

Two standouts that accept female guests include the cosy, inexpensive **Capsule Hotel Riverside** (11, C2; ☎ 3844 1155; 2-20-4 Kaminarimon, Taito-ku), and the upmarket **Capsule Hotel Fontaine Akasaka** (8, A2; ☎ 3583 6554; 4-3-5 Akasaka, Minato-ku), featuring lovely bath and sauna facilities.

Encapsulating!

Shinjuku Park Hotel (4, C3)

Just south of the Takashi-maya Times Square complex, the Shinjuku Park Hotel has larger rooms than most business hotels, and its prices are competitive. Best bets are Japanese-style rooms – or any rooms with a view of green Shinjuku-gyōen.

☎ 3356 0241 ⬜ www .shinjukuparkhotel.com ✉ 5-27-9 Sendagaya, Shibuya-ku 🚉 Yaman-ote line to Shinjuku (Shin-minami exit) 🍴 3 restaurants

Suigetsu Hotel Ōgaisō (10, A2)

The Western-style rooms here are fine, but the tatami rooms are far superior. Though Western in setup, it has several Japanese-style baths and is built around the former home of writer Mori Ōgai. It has a lovely Japanese garden as its centrepiece.

☎ 3822 4611 ⬜ www .ohgai.co.jp/index-e.html ✉ 3-3-21 Ikenohata, Taito-ku 🅿 ♿ good 🍴 3 restaurants

Tokyo Station Hotel (12, B3)

If, upon arriving at Tokyo station, you just can't travel any further: remain station-ary. Built in 1914, this hotel has a definite, red-carpeted charm. The rooms are fairly basic, but you can't beat the station-side location.

☎ 3231 2511 ⬜ www .tshl.co.jp ✉ 1-9-1 Maru-nouchi, Chiyoda-ku 🚉 Ya-manote & Marunouchi lines to Tokyo (Marunouchi central exit) ♿ limited 🍴 2 restaurants 🍴

Trimm Harajuku (6, A1)

Trimm verges on drab perhaps, but the location of this gym-equipped, above-average business hotel can't be beaten. It's on Meiji-dōri, a five-minutes walk south of Meiji-jingūmae station. Rooms are on the large side for this price range. The only drag is the 1am curfew.

☎ 3498 2101 ✉ 6-28-6 Jingū-mae, Shibuya-ku 🚉 Chiyoda line to Meiji-jingūmae (exit 4) 🍴 Fuji-mamas & Las Chicas (p71)

Villa Fontaine (8, B3)

A little bit country chateau, a little bit leather fetish, the Villa Fontaine lies between Roppongi and Akasaka, and is an excellent choice in this price bracket. Rooms are smartly decorated and comfortable.

☎ 5339 1200 ✉ 1-6-2 Roppongi, Minato-ku 🚇 Hibiya & Toei Ōedo lines to Roppongi (exit 5) 🅿 ♿ good 🍴 Fuku-zushi (p74) & Tokyo Bellini Trattoria (p76)

Yaesu Terminal Hotel (12, C3)

Between Tokyo station and Takashimaya depart-ment store, this recently refurbished hotel sports sleek, clean lines. Rooms are quite small, but prices are good for this area and it feels more refined than typical business hotels. The hotel restaurant's wall of windows look out on the streetside tree-tops.

☎ 3281 3771 ⬜ www .yth.jp ✉ 1-5-14 Yaesu, Chūō-ku 🚉 Yamanote line to Tokyo station (Yaesu north exit) 🍴 1 restaurant

Yama no Ue (Hilltop) Hotel (3, E4)

Like something out of a 1930s Hollywood movie, this quaint hotel is perched on a hill next to prestigious Meiji University. Oxygen and negative ions are circulated into the rooms for your health and re-freshment; rooms in the main building are more attractive.

☎ 3293 2311 ⬜ www .yamanoue-hotel .co.jp ✉ 1-1 Kanda-Surugadai, Chiyoda-ku 🚉 Chūō line to Ochano-mizu (exit B1) 🅿 ♿ good 🍴 7 restaurants & 4 bars

The bulk of the major hotels can be found at Shinjuku

BUDGET

Andon Ryokan (3, F2)

Exhibiting fresh architectural design and at ease with foreigners, this nontraditional ryokan is a cool place to crash, with all the comforts of a modern hotel. It's just two stops north of Ueno, and you can book in advance through its website, which also has a detailed map.
☎ 3873 8611 ☐ www .andon.co.jp ✉ 2-34-10 Nihonzutsumi, Taito-ku 🚇 Hibiya line to Minowa (exit 3)

Kimi Ryokan (2, A1)

Tokyo's best budget choice, Kimi Ryokan has clean, inexpensive Japanese-style rooms and the most convivial lounge area of Tokyo's ryokan. It's outfitted with showers and a Japanese-style bath. The owner's constantly changing ikebana (flower arrangements) adds colour. Be sure to book ahead; there's nearly always a waiting list.
☎ 3971 3766 ☐ www .kimi-ryokan.jp ✉ 2-36-8 Ikebukuro, Toshima-ku 🚇 Yamanote line to Ikebukuro (west exit) 🚹

Ryokan Katsutarō Annex (3, D3)

Bright, Japanese-style rooms at the cheery, spotless Annex have Western-style baths attached. There's LAN access in each room and free coffee in the lobby. Call ahead for directions in English, or print a map from its website. Credit cards are accepted.

Rules of the Ryokan

In the entrance area of a ryokan (Japanese inn), remove your shoes and put on a pair of slippers. Before entering any tatami rooms, remove your slippers. Since most ryokan are small and family run, there's often a curfew – check with the ryokan before booking if you think this will cramp your style. Most ryokan also have traditional Japanese baths – an experience not to be missed.

Typical ryokan: Japanese-style room with tatami floor

☎ 3828 2500 ☐ www .katsutaro.com ✉ 3-8-4 Yanaka, Taito-ku 🚇 Chiyoda line to Sendagi (exit 2) 🚹 excellent ♿

Sawanoya Ryokan (10, A1)

This cosy ryokan is run by a wonderfully friendly and helpful family, and the inn has English signs posted everywhere to explain what's what. It's within walking distance of Nezu subway station; print a map from its website or call for directions from the station. Major credit cards are accepted.
☎ 3822 2251 ☐ www .tctv.ne.jp/members

/sawanoya/eigo.html ✉ 2-3-11 Yanaka, Taitō-ku 🚇 Chiyoda line to Nezu (exit 1) ♿

Taito Ryokan (11, A2)

The intimate, wood-floored Taito Ryokan is great value, especially because of its English-speaking managers with whom conversing is a delight. It can be noisy, and palatial it ain't, but it's cheap and charming. The website has a map containing detailed directions to the easy-to-miss ryokan.
☎ 3843 2822 ☐ www .libertyhouse.gr.jp ✉ 2-1-4 Nishi-Asakusa, Taito-ku 🚇 Ginza line to Tawaramachi (exit 3)

About Tokyo

HISTORY
The Early Years

Around the mid-15th century, a poet named Ōta Dōkan constructed Edo's first castle on the site of an old fortress. When Portuguese traders first set eyes on 16th-century Edo, it was little more than an outpost for aristocrats and monks who had fled a civil war in Kyoto. Within three centuries, Edo would oust Kyoto as Japan's traditional seat of imperial power, and Tokyo would be born.

Tokugawa Edo

The father to this upstart child was the wily, madly ambitious shōgun (chief military commander), Tokugawa Ieyasu. His appointment by the emperor in 1603 was to change the fate of Tokyo (and Japan) forever.

A political survivor, Ieyasu knew he must 'divide and conquer' his political foes. In a masterstroke, he forced all *daimyō* (feudal lords) throughout Japan to spend at least one year of every two in Edo. This policy of dislocation made it difficult for ambitious *daimyō* to usurp the Tokugawas.

Ieyasu systematically created a rigidly hierarchical society, comprising, in descending order: nobility; *daimyō* and their samurai; farmers; and finally artisans and merchants. Class dress, living quarters and even manner of speech were strictly codified. Class advancement was prohibited, though

Edo-period samurai clothing catalogue

one could always, terrifyingly, descend to the underclasses, to the 'non-human' *hinin* and to *eta,* the untouchable class.

Isolation

After Ieyasu's death in 1616, his grandson Tokugawa Iemitsu, fearing Christian power, closed the country's borders in 1638. Japan was effectively removed from the world stage for nearly 300 years.

By the early 17th century, Edo (population over one million) was the largest city on earth. Its caste-like society divided Edo into the *daimyōs'* high city (Yamanote) and a low working-class city (Shitamachi). Destructive fires often swept through its shantytowns. The locals christened these fires *Edo-no-hana,* or 'flowers of Edo'. The cocky bravura of the expression sums up the tough Shitamachi spirit, still to be found in the backstreets of Ueno and Asakusa.

Tokyo Rising

When US Commodore Matthew Perry's armada of 'black ships' entered Edo (Tokyo) Bay demanding 'free trade' in 1853, despite spirited resistance from 2000 Tokugawa loyalists at the brief Battle of Ueno, the Shōgunate fell apart and power reverted to Tokyo.

Imperial Palace grandeur

The Meiji Restoration refers to this consequent return of power to the emperor; however, Emperor Meiji's rule was more revolution than restoration. A crash course in industrialisation and militarisation began and by 1889 Japan had adopted a Western-style constitution – and Western-style empire-building. Nowhere was revolutionary change more evident than on the streets of the country's new capital city. Job seekers flocked from the country and Tokyo boomed.

Catastrophe & War

The Great Kantō Earthquake struck the boomtown at noon on 1 September 1923. The subsequent fires, lasting some 40 hours, laid waste to the city. Though 142,000 lost their lives, worse was to come.

From the accession of Emperor Hirohito in 1926, nationalist fervour gripped the government. In 1931 the Japanese army invaded Manchuria, then China. By 1940 a pact with Germany and Italy had been signed and 'Greater Asia Co-Prosperity Sphere' was touted as the New Order. On 7 December 1941 the Japanese attacked Pearl Harbor.

WWII was catastrophic for Tokyo. Incendiary bombing of the mostly wooden city commenced in March 1944. On the nights of the 9th and 10th of March 1945, 40% of the city was engulfed in a terrible firestorm and between 70,000 and 80,000 perished. By the time Emperor Hirohito made his famous address to the Japanese people on 15 August 1945, much of Tokyo was wasteland.

Chiune Sugihara

One of the most compelling WWII stories is that of Chiune Sugihara, a Japanese diplomat who had been charged with starting a new consulate in a Lithuanian city called Kaunas. Several months after his arrival in early 1940, hundreds of desperate Jews thronged his office. They needed transit visas that would allow them to escape Nazi-occupied Europe via Russia. In defiance of his own government, Sugihara issued visas day and night until he and his family were finally forced to evacuate Lithuania. At the time of his departure, he had issued more than 6000 visas, most of whose recipients escaped.

Bubble & Bust

Tokyo rose phoenix-like from the ashes of WWII, and the economy flourished as almost no other in history. Ironically, it was sparked by US involvement in the neighbouring Korean War. The 1960s, '70s and early '80s saw unprecedented growth. Japan was suddenly an economic superpower – incredibly wealthy, globally powerful and omnipotent.

And then, suddenly it wasn't. The burst of the '80s 'bubble economy' dealt Japan a financial blow from which it has yet to recover. But the cracks ran deeper than the fiscal fault lines. In March 1995, when members of the Aum Shinrikyō cult released sarin nerve gas on a crowded Tokyo commuter train, killing 12 and injuring 5000, Japan's self-belief took a severe blow. The new millennium finds Tokyo's evolving identity being shaped by an aging population, recovering economy and changing social mores.

GOVERNMENT & POLITICS

Though recent years have seen much ado about who will succeed Emperor Akihito's son Prince Naruhito, who has only a daughter, the deeply respected Japanese emperor is but a figurehead. The governing body, known as the Diet, is made up of two houses. The party controlling the majority of seats in the Diet is the ruling party and has the right to appoint the prime minister. Since its inception in 1955, the conservative Liberal Democratic Party (LDP) has controlled the Diet, barring a few years during the mid-90s.

In theory, Japan is a democratic country, with members of the Diet elected by popular vote. However, in practice, real power is held by powerful political cliques descended from generations of the nation's elite who are allied with Japan's dominant *keiretsu* (business cartels). Until recently, this seemed to suit Japanese voters just fine, but present economic difficulties plus decisions by current prime minister Junichiro Koizumi have stoked more political fire among the populace.

Uyoku

Sinister black buses and vans occasionally prowl Tokyo's streets blaring out patriotic Japanese songs that sound like cheesy *anime* (animation) theme tunes. These vehicles are the propaganda arm of the *uyoku,* a collection of far-right political organisations.

While initially alarming, *uyoku* pose no threat to tourists with their messages aimed at the Japanese public. Bus speakers issue out diatribes damning Japanese politicians or glorying in nationalist sentiment including the catchcry 'Revere the emperor! Expel the barbarian!'

Although most Japanese dismiss them as cranks, there is a dark side to the boys in red and black. *Uyoku* intimidate critics of the emperor with threats of violence, which are occasionally carried out.

ECONOMY

Tokyo businessmen still look back to the economic halcyon days of the 1970s and early '80s with a barely concealed wistfulness bordering on melancholia. The word on everyone's lips at present is *fukeiki* – the depressed economy. The culprit is widely recognised as the shock of the late 1980s bursting of the 'bubble economy', but the Asia-wide financial collapse, ineffectual government response and tough competition from the USA are all key factors.

> **Did You Know?**
> - A bluefin tuna went for a record ¥20,200,000 at Tsukiji Produce & Fish Market
> - The number of Tokyo *pachinko* (pinball game) parlours is 1581
> - One sq metre of prime Ginza real estate has cost as much as ¥12,720,000
> - The ratio of Tokyoites to vending machines is 20:1
> - Around 780,000 people pass through Shinjuku station daily

Unemployment has risen – though it's a respectable 4.7% – and the concept of a job for life is no longer taken for granted by the younger generation, many of whom never knew life in the bubble economy. Part-time and sometime employment are on the rise, with younger people working merely to make a living, and living more alternatively than their elders. Occasionally 'parasite singles' are blamed for the sluggish economy – according to economic experts, they should be consuming more instead of living with (and mooching off) their parents.

ENVIRONMENT

The government seems all too happy to pander to big business interests. Pollution-related cases from decades ago are still dragging through the courts. It seems the government prefers grey suits to green action. The disposal of plastic is a major contributor to air pollution in Tokyo. While recycling programs have been established by most local governments and enthusiastically adopted by local residents, there is still too much plastic packaging in use in the first place.

Plastic food + plastic packaging = waste

On a more fundamental geographical level, Japan is part of the Pacific 'Ring of Fire', the tectonic activity of which created the majestic conical shape of Mt Fuji and crumbled the city of Kōbe in 1995. Though minor earthquakes occur all the time, there's no telling when the next big one will strike. There's little point in paranoia, but it pays to note where exits are located, and to remember to shelter under doorways or heavy furniture when big tremors begin.

SOCIETY & CULTURE

The life of the average Japanese citizen is bound by a massive network of obligation and counter obligation to family, colleagues, the guy next door, ancestors who passed away generations ago – the list is endless. Those individuals who just can't stand it flee – to Tokyo. The anonymity of the megalopolis is a magnet for misfits, rebels, artists and all the famous 'nails that stand out' (and duly get bashed down) in mainstream Japanese society. Thus it is, in many senses, the freest of Japanese cities. People scarcely know their neighbours, or care to.

With the disintegration of the family and continuing economic lethargy, the times are a-changing. The generation gap between conventional, self-sacrificing parent and pierced, part-time-employee child has never been greater. Younger people, more open to creativity, experimentation and failure, are colouring outside the lines in fashioning lives for themselves. It's a time of societal flux in Japan, and Tokyo today is all the more fascinating for that.

Expression exaggeration: Little Bo Peep meets Madam Goth

Etiquette

Given Tokyo's distinctly different place in Japanese society, it's difficult to offend. Moreover, Japanese people are highly forgiving of foreign visitors' minor social gaffes. But there are a few rules of etiquette that must always be followed. When entering a house or any tatami room, always take off your shoes. If in doubt, do as everyone else does. It's considered

Yellow Brick Road

Notice those bright yellow, bumpy pathways edging sidewalks and snaking through subway stations? They aren't the design flourishes of some wacky urban planner, but navigation aids for the blind and visually impaired. Working on a similar principle as Braille, these paths provide a tactile route through the Tokyo wilderness.

rude and disgusting to blow your nose in public – maintain a stoic and noisy sniffle until in private. Except for ice cream, eating while walking down the street is also out.

For those in Tokyo on business, *meishi* (business cards) carry a lot of weight in society and are ritually exchanged on first meetings. Politely accept a card with both hands and examine it before putting it away, and don't write on a card that someone has given you.

ARTS
Film
Akira Kurosawa, the most famous director of Japanese cinema's golden era, brought Japanese film into the spotlight when his *Rashōmon* (1950) took top prize at the Venice Film Festival. Illustrious filmmakers who followed include Shohei Imamura, who examines human behaviour with a piercing eye in works such as *The Profound Desire of the Gods* (1968).

More contemporary films include Jūzō Itami's *Tampopo* (1985), a characteristically quirky comedy about sex and food, and the award-winning *Zatoichi* (2003) featuring actor-director Takeshi 'Beat' Kitano as a blind swordsman. And Japan's gorgeous *anime* gems, such as Hayao Miyazaki's *Princess Mononoke* (1997), continue to issue from Tokyo onto international screens.

Literature
Often with a surrealist edge or a dose of subtle magical realism, Japanese contemporary literature – most of which is written by authors who've

Tokyo Anthro 101
Mamba Members of this tribe are unmistakable around Shibuya: look for long, bleached hair, white make-up on dark, artificial tans and colourful threads. Young guys (known as Center Guys) are likewise glamming it up.

OLs Short for 'office ladies', these women may be secretaries, but may equally be women who do the same work as their male bosses for half the pay. OLs usually travel in small groups wearing matching office uniforms of skirts, white blouses and vests.

Parasite Single These are women, usually, who continue to live with their parents well into their 20s and 30s, putting off marriage and spending their rent-free disposable income on fashionable clothing and travel.

spent most of their lives in Tokyo – provides a perspective on the more elusive emotional side of life in the city. Nobel Laureate Kenzaburo Õe's clear-eyed *A Personal Matter* tells the story of a man faced with a conflict of freedom and responsibility that transcends Japanese social mores. A departure from his more surrealist work, Haruki Murakami's celebrated *Norwegian Wood* chronicles the coming of age of a university student in late 1960s Japan. And for lighter, but surprisingly solid fare, pick up *Kitchen* by Banana Yoshimoto.

Music

Live gigs rock the 'live houses' every night of the week in Tokyo's basement bars, mostly on the city's west side. You name it, someone makes it – from Japanese hip-hop and punk rock to acid jazz and noise-spaz.

Japan has an enormous domestic record market, and Tokyo is very much a part of the international live-music circuit. Most of the top performers, from every genre of contemporary and classical music, do shows here. Along with Tokyo's better-known exports, such as composer Sakamoto Ryūichi and food-fetish rockers Shonen Knife, are musical collage artists Buffalo Daughter, and postmodern mixmaster Cornelius, who somehow successfully weaves heavy metal with birdsong.

Tokyo mainstream consists significantly of *aidoru* (idol singers) and girl-bands – manufactured J-pop confections sweetened to perfection for mass marketing. Don't overindulge, or you'll get a toothache.

English thrash-metal Goth band, Die Pretty, Shinjuku

Performance Arts

Kabuki, *Nō* (classical Japanese drama), and *bunraku* (puppet theatre) are well represented throughout the city, with several theatres (p93) featuring regular performances. *Taiko* (traditional Japanese drumming) is where music meets martial art and mysticism.

Traditional Japanese theatre performance

Tokyo is also a centre for Japan's enigmatic, challenging modern dance form, *butō*. Its bizarre movements, weird lighting, and long periods of inaction are not everyone's cup of green tea, but most certainly memorable. Check with a tourist information centre (TIC; p120), or *Tokyo Journal* for current performances. Seek out Dairakudakan (www.geocities.co.jp/Hollywood -Stage/8138/rakudakan/top.html), Sankaijuku (www.sankaijuku.com /sankaijuku_e.htm), or most powerful of all, Taihen (www.asahi-net .or.jp/~tj2m-snjy/eng/eprofile.htm), whose members are all severely physically disabled.

Visual Art

Tokyo's contemporary art scene is thriving. Its galleries possess a lack of pretension that is startlingly refreshing – it's easy to walk into a show and start a conversation with the artists themselves. Progressive spaces all over town give space to exciting work, much of it by the talented young artists of the city's prestigious art colleges.

Bigger museums tend to go for heavy-hitting names: Rodin, Renoir, Da Vinci, Degas. The superstars of Western art are most oft-found at the **National Museum of Western Art** (p32). But don't be surprised if they pop up, along with their Japanese counterparts, in the department-store galleries dotted around town. The greatest concentration of small galleries – with roughly 400 exhibition spaces – clusters in Ginza (see pp28-9).

Street art, Jingūmae

Directory

ARRIVAL & DEPARTURE   **112**
Air   112
Bus   112
Train   112
Travel Documents   113
Customs & Duty Free   113
Left Luggage   113

GETTING AROUND   **113**
Travel Passes   114
Train   114
Subway   114
Bus   114
Taxi   114
Car & Motorcycle   114

PRACTICALITIES   **114**
Climate & When to Go   114
Disabled Travellers   115
Discounts   115
Electricity   115
Embassies & Consulates   115
Emergencies   116

Fitness   116
Gay & Lesbian Travellers   116
Health   116
Holidays   117
Internet   117
Lost Property   117
Metric System   117
Money   118
Newspapers & Magazines   118
Opening Hours   118
Photography & Video   118
Post   119
Radio   119
Telephone   119
Television   119
Time   119
Tipping   120
Toilets   120
Tourist Information   120
Women Travellers   120

LANGUAGE   **120**

Easy rider, pushin' it real good, Sensō-ji, Asakusa (pp12-13)

ARRIVAL & DEPARTURE
Air

Tokyo's main international airport is Narita, 66km from the city. At its two terminals there are post offices, currency exchange counters and health clinics, as well as restaurants and duty-free shops. Terminal 2 has showers, day rooms for napping and a children's playroom for use after arrival. When flying out of Narita, be sure to check which terminal your airline departs from, as the distance between the two is significant enough to warrant separate train stops.

A few international flights still operate through Haneda, much closer to the city centre, most notably China Airlines. International traffic is expected to increase in the future.

NARITA   (1, C2)
Information

Flight information	☎ 0476 34 5000
General inquiries	☎ 0476 32 2802
Hotel booking service:	
Terminal 1	☎ 0476 32 8693
Terminal 2	☎ 0476 34 8518

Airlines

Air Canada	☎ 5405 8800
Air France	☎ 0476 32 7710
American Airlines	☎ 3214 2111
ANA	☎ 0120 029 222
British Airways	☎ 3593 8811
Cathay Pacific Airways	☎ 0476 32 7650
Japan Airlines	☎ 0120 25 5971
KLM	☎ 0476 32 5720
Korean Air	☎ 0476 32 7561
Lufthansa	☎ 0476 34 8130
Qantas Airways	☎ 0476 34 8285
United Airlines	☎ 3817 4411

Airport Access
Bus Limousine buses connect Narita with central Tokyo (¥3000, 1½hr).

Car Terminal 1 (☎ 0476 32 2253; ¥500/hr, overnight ¥3840); Terminal 2 (☎ 0476 34 5350; ¥500/hr, overnight ¥4080)

Taxi A taxi to Narita airport from Tokyo will cost about ¥30,000.

Train Several rail services connect Narita and Tokyo. The private Keisei line runs two services to Ueno – the Keisei Skyliner (¥1920, 1hr) and the Tokkyū (Limited Express; ¥1000, 1hr 11min). JR Narita Express goes to Tokyo station (N-EX; ¥2940, 55min) and Shinjuku (¥3110, 1½hr). Airport Narita Kaisoku also goes to Tokyo station (rapid train service; ¥1280, 1½ hr). All fares are one way.

HANEDA   (1, B2)
Information

Car park information ☎ 5757 8191; ¥400/hr

General inquiries & flight information ☎ 5757 8111

Hotel booking service: arrival terminal, tour desks 3 & 5

Airport Access
Bus Buses run between Haneda and Ikebukuro (¥1200) and Shinjuku (¥1200).

Taxi A taxi between Haneda and Tokyo station costs around ¥7000.

Train Haneda is connected by monorail to Hamamatsuchō station on the JR Yamanote line (¥470, 20min).

Bus

Domestic long-distance buses mainly arrive at Tokyo station's **Yaesu Highway Bus Terminal** (12, B3; ☎ 3215 0498). Services to both Osaka and Kyoto are operated by JR. Buy your tickets from a Green Window office at larger JR train stations.

Train

Japan Railways' (JR) famed *shinkansen* (bullet trains) serve Northern Honshū, Central and Western Japan and Kyūshū. The slower, less expensive *tokkyū* (limited express), *kyūko* (express) and *futsū* (ordinary) are options on every route between cities; however, not many people use them for long-distance travel. Typical one-way *shinkansen* fares are Kyoto–Tokyo ¥13,220, Fukuoka–Tokyo ¥21,210 and Osaka–Tokyo ¥13,750. The main terminals are Tokyo (3, E5) and Ueno (3, E3) stations.

Private lines running from stations on the Yamanote line are the quickest, cheapest bet to Kamakura, Mt Fuji, Hakone and Yokohama. They connect to Shinjuku (3, B5) and Shibuya stations (3, B6). The Tōbu line for Nikkō, runs from Asakusa (3, F3).

Travel Documents
PASSPORT
If you need a visa for entry to Japan, your passport will have to be valid for three months after the date of entry.

VISA
Tourists and business visitors of many nationalities (including Australia, Canada, Ireland, New Zealand, the UK and USA) are not required to obtain visas, if staying in Japan for less than 90 days. Those who wish to stay for lengthy periods or for work or study should check with their local Japanese embassy or consulate.

RETURN/ONWARD TICKET
An onward ticket may be requested before an entry permit is granted, as well as proof of adequate funds. Usually a valid credit card is sufficient proof of funds.

Customs & Duty Free
There are no limits on the import or export of foreign or Japanese currency; however, if the amount in Japanese yen exceeds one million yen, a customs declaration must be completed.

Limits for duty free items are three 760ml bottles of alcohol, 57g of perfume, 400 cigarettes, and gifts and souvenirs up to a value of ¥200,000.

Visit Japan Customs (http://www.customs.go.jp/index_e.htm) for further information on Japan's customs regulations.

Left Luggage
Both Narita terminals offer left-luggage services for around ¥500 per item per day. Baggage courier counters in the arrivals terminals can arrange delivery to addresses in Tokyo for about ¥2000 per large bag. At Haneda airport, left-luggage service is located near the south exit of the monorail station (¥420 per item per day).

There are coin lockers in all train and bus stations in Tokyo, with small ones starting at ¥300 per day. You can leave luggage for up to three days. There's a luggage-storage service at Tokyo station that will hold bags for up to two weeks, with rates starting at ¥500 per bag per day. Ask at the main information counter on the Yaesu side to direct you to this service.

GETTING AROUND
Short-term visitors and long-term residents alike mainly use the city's excellent subway system and the JR train lines, especially the Yamanote line. It rings the inner city, making anywhere accessible in under an hour. All stations have signposts and maps in English. Subway colour coding and regular English signposting make the system easy to use. The train and subway services in Tokyo are famed for their

punctuality, and trains are frequent. Nearest stations are listed after the 🚃 (for the Yamanote and above-ground lines) and Ⓢ (for subway lines).

Travel Passes

Short-stay visitors should consider getting the Tokyo Combination Ticket day pass that can be used on all JR, subway and bus lines within the Tokyo metropolitan area. It costs ¥1580 (¥790 for children aged six to 11) and is available from Pass offices at major stations. Stations with Pass offices are marked with a triangle on local subway maps.

Train

Tokyo is serviced by a combination of JR, private inner-city subway lines and private suburban lines, all of which are *gaijin* (foreigner) friendly. Trains run from around 5am to midnight. Most useful is the Yamanote line; fares begin at ¥130.

Subway

There are 13 subway lines, nine of which are TRTA lines and four of which are TOEI lines. The subway system is essential for getting to areas inside the loop traced by the Yamanote line. Both services are essentially the same, though ticketing is separate. Ticket vending machines that operate in English are available at every station. If you can't work out how much your fare will be, buy the cheapest ticket and pay the difference at a fare adjustment machine at your destination. Services run from around 5.30am to 1am.

Bus

Although buses crisscross the city, they are difficult to use as many routes and destinations are only explained in Japanese characters.

There's a flat rate of ¥200. On some routes, passengers enter at the back of the bus and pay the driver on leaving. But on most, it's pay as you enter. Most bus routes operate from around 6am to 9pm.

Taxi

Rates start at ¥660 per 2km (after 11pm it's 1.5km), then the meter rises by ¥80 every 274m (after 11pm it's every 220m or so). You also click up about ¥80 every two minutes while you relax in a typical Tokyo traffic jam.

Taxi vacancy is indicated by a red light; a green light means there's a night-time surcharge and a yellow light means that the cab is on call. Watch out for the automatic doors on taxis. Don't slam the door shut when you get in or leave – it will magically close itself.

Car & Motorcycle

On a short trip to Tokyo you're unlikely to need your own wheels, what with Tokyo's outstanding rail system. Traffic congestion and impossibility and cost of parking make driving here a missable experience. However, if you do need to hire a vehicle, be sure to obtain an International Driving Permit before you arrive in Japan as well as bringing a driver's licence from your own country.

Reputable car hire firms:

Dollar Rent-a-Car	☎ 3567 2818
Nippon Rent-a-Car	☎ 3485 7196
Toyota Rent-a-Car	☎ 5954 8008

PRACTICALITIES
Climate & When to Go

Spring (March to May) and Autumn (September to November) are the most balmy seasons. Typhoons usually occur in September and October. Summers are hot and humid, with temperatures getting into the high 30s. The *tsuyu* (rainy season), in June, means several weeks of torrential rain that can wreak havoc with a tight travel itinerary. In winter the weather is good with mainly clear, sunny skies and the occasional snowfall. Avoid major holidays such as Golden Week (29 April to 5 May) and the mid-August O-bon festival. The city tends to close down over New Year.

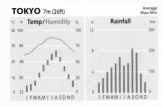

Disabled Travellers

Tokyo's size and complexity make it challenging for the mobility impaired, as well as the visually and hearing impaired. The upside is that attitudes to people with disabilities have vastly improved in the last two decades, and newer buildings tend to have excellent facilities. Advance planning is the key to a successful trip.

The ♿ icon throughout this guidebook denotes listings that are wheelchair-accessible, have toilets accommodating wheelchairs and are otherwise navigable for those with ambulatory challenges.

INFORMATION & ORGANISATIONS

Get the indispensable *Accessible Tokyo* guide from **Japanese Red Cross Language Service Volunteers** (☎ 3438 1311; http://accessible.jp/tokyo/en/; 1-1-3 Shiba Daimon, Minato-ku) or just check out the website for detailed, current information on getting around Tokyo.

Discounts

Many major sights offer discounts for children, and very young children may get in free. That said, many minor sights don't offer such discounts, as this practice isn't big in Japan.

STUDENT & YOUTH CARDS

An international student card will win you discounts on entry fees to some sights in Tokyo and discounted prices on long-distance train travel, but that's about it.

SENIORS' CARDS

Seniors can get discounts to some major sights, and Japanese domestic airlines (JAS, JAL and ANA) offer senior discounts of about 25% on some flights. But the picture's essentially the same as it is for youth discounts.

Electricity

Voltage	100V AC
Frequency	50Hz
Plugs	Two-pronged flat

Embassies & Consulates

Australia (3, C7; ☎ 5232 4111; www.australia.or.jp; 2-1-14 Mita, Minato-ku)

Canada (3, C5; ☎ 5412 6200; www.dfait-maeci.gc.ca/ni-ka/tokyo-en.asp; 7-3-38 Akasaka, Minato-ku)

Ireland (3, D4; ☎ 3263 0695; www.embassy-avenue.jp/ireland/index_eng.html; 2-10-7 Kōjimachi, Chiyoda-ku)

New Zealand (3, A6; ☎ 3467 2271; www.nzembassy.com/home.cfm?c=17; 20-40 Kamiyamachō, Shibuya-ku)

South Africa (8, B1; ☎ 3265 3366; www.rsatk.com; 414 Zenkyoren Bldg, 7-9-2 Hirakawachō, Chiyoda-ku)

UK (3, D5; ☎ 5211 1100; www.uknow.or.jp/be_e; 1 Ichibanchō, Chiyoda-ku)

USA (8, B3; ☎ 3224 5000; http://tokyo.usembassy.gov; 1-10-5 Akasaka, Minato-ku)

Emergencies

Crime and theft, though they exist, are rare in Tokyo; that said, you should exercise the same awareness of your surroundings as you would anywhere else. The emergency services listed here may not have English-speaking operators, but remain on the line so that your location can be traced by your call.

Ambulance	☎ 119
Fire	☎ 119
Police (emergency)	☎ 110
Police	☎ 3501 0110

Fitness

Chiyoda Kuritsu Sogo Taiikukan
(3, E5; ☎ 3256 8444; 2-1-8 Uchi-Kanda, Chiyoda-ku; pool/gym ¥600/350; ⏳ noon-8.30pm)

Chūō-ku Sogo Sports Centre
(3, F5; ☎ 3666 1501; 2-59-1 Nihonbashi Hamachō, Chūō-ku; pool/gym ¥500/400; ⏳ 9am-8.30pm)

International Yoga Center (1, B2; ☎ 090 4596 7996; www.iyc.jp/iyc/en; 4F, Fukumura Ogikubo Bldg, 5-30-6 Ogikubo, Suginami-ku; class ¥3300)

Gay & Lesbian Travellers

Tokyo is more hip and tolerant than many of its Asian counterparts, though public displays of affection are usually kept on the down-low. There's an active international scene that includes clubs, bars, newsletters and support groups.

INFORMATION

Two terrific, tried-and-true resources for what's on in gay Tokyo are:
www.fridae.com/cityguides/tokyo/tk-intro.php
www.utopia-asia.com/japntoky.htm

Health
IMMUNISATIONS

No immunisations are required for visitors to Japan.

PRECAUTIONS

Levels of hygiene in Tokyo are impeccable, and no serious health precautions are necessary.

Like anywhere else, practice the usual precautions when it comes to sex; condoms, the most popular form of contraception in Japan, are available in pharmacies and convenience stores, often in ambitious packs of 24.

MEDICAL SERVICES

All hospitals listed have English-speaking staff, and 24-hour accident and emergency departments. Travel insurance is advisable to cover any medical treatment you may need while in Tokyo. Medical treatment is among the best in the world, but also the most expensive.

Japanese Red Cross Medical Center (Nihon Sekijūjisha Iryō Sentā; 3, C7; ☎ 3400 1311; 4-1-22 Hiro-o, Shibuya-ku)

St Luke's International Hospital (Seiroka Byōin; 3, E6; ☎ 3541 5151; 9-1 Akashicho, Chūō-ku)

Tokyo Medical & Surgical Clinic (3, D6; ☎ 3436 3028; www.tmsc.jp; 2F, Mori Bldg 32, 3-4-30 Shiba-kōen, Minato-ku)

DENTAL SERVICES

Tokyo Clinic Dental Office (3, D6; ☎ 3431 4225; www2.gol.com/users/tward/clinic.html; 2F, Mori Bldg 32, 3-4-30 Shiba-kōen, Minato-ku) has English-speaking dentists licensed to practise in both Japan and the US. Phone for an appointment.

PHARMACIES

Pharmacies are easy to find and some have Japanese-English symptom charts. Staff speak English at the **American Pharmacy** (12, B3; ☎ 5220 7716; B1F, Marunouchi Bldg, 2-4-1 Marunouchi, Chiyoda-ku; ⏳ 9am-9pm Mon-Fri, 10am-9pm Sat, 10am-8pm Sun).

Holidays

Jan 1	New Year's Day
Jan 15	Adult's Day
Feb 11	National Foundation Day
Mar 21	Spring Equinox Day
Apr 29	Green Day
May 3	Constitution Memorial Day
May 5	Children's Day
Jul 20	Marine Day
Sep 15	Respect-for-the-Aged Day
Sep 23	Autumn Equinox Day
Oct 10	Sports Day
Nov 3	Culture Day
Nov 23	Labour Thanksgiving Day
Dec 23	Emperor's Birthday

Internet

Internet access is rapidly improving. Some bars and cafés offer net access for free, as do some governmental and prefectural offices and computer stores. Many mid-range hotels offer in-room LAN access.

INTERNET SERVICE PROVIDERS

Most major global ISPs have dial-up nodes in Japan; download a list of the dial-up numbers before you leave home. You can also get connected at a wireless hotspot; check www.freespot.net/users/map-e /map_tokyo.html for latest listings around Tokyo if you've a wireless-enabled laptop.

INTERNET CAFÉS

Though many mid-range hotels now provide in-room LAN access or business centres, you can alternatively head one of these cyber-cafés (all open 24 hours).

Café J Net New New (5, A2; ☎ 5458 5935; 7F, Saito Bldg, 34-5 Udagawa-chō, Shibuya-ku; per hr ¥500)

Manga Hiroba (9, C2; ☎ 3497 1751; 2F, Shuwa Roppongi Bldg, 3-14-12 Roppongi, Minato-ku; per hr ¥380)

Manga@Cafe-Gera Gera (4, B1; ☎ 5285 0585; 1-23-1 Kabuki-chō,

Shinjuku-ku; 1st hr ¥380, every 10min thereafter ¥30)

USEFUL WEBSITES

The LP website (www.lonelyplanet .com) offers a speedy link to many of Tokyo's websites. Others to try include the following:

Metropolis http://metropolis .japantoday.com

Tokyo English Life Line (TELLNET) www.telljp.com

Tokyo Journal www.tokyo.to

Tokyo Q http://club.nokia.co.jp/tokyoq

Lost Property

If you happen to leave something behind on the train, call JR trains on ☎ 3423 0111, TRTA subway on ☎ 3834 5577 and TOEI subway on ☎ 5600 2020. For property left in a taxi call ☎ 3648 0300. If you're still near enough, backtrack to the same spot, and then to the nearest police box or train station; chances are you'll find it waiting for you.

Metric System

Japan uses the international metric system; see the conversion table below.

TEMPERATURE
$°C = (°F - 32) ÷ 1.8$
$°F = (°C \times 1.8) + 32$

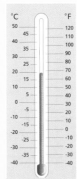

DISTANCE
1in = 2.54cm
1cm = 0.39in
1m = 3.3ft = 1.1yd
1ft = 0.3m
1km = 0.62 miles
1 mile = 1.6km

WEIGHT
1kg = 2.2lb
1lb = 0.45kg
1g = 0.04oz
1oz = 28g

VOLUME
1L = 0.26 US gallons
1 US gallon = 3.8L
1L = 0.22 imperial gallons
1 imperial gallon = 4.55L

Money
CURRENCY

The currency in Japan is the yen (¥). Banknotes and coins are easily identifiable; there are ¥1, ¥5, ¥10, ¥50, ¥100 and ¥500 coins; and ¥1000, ¥2000, ¥5000 and ¥10,000 notes. The ¥1 coin is made of lightweight aluminium; ¥5 and ¥50 coins have a hole in the middle (the former is coloured bronze and the latter silver). Newer-issue ¥500 coins won't be accepted by some vending machines.

TRAVELLERS CHEQUES

There's little difference in commission charged by banks and big hotels. All major brands are acceptable, but cheques in yen or US dollars are preferred over other currencies. Shinjuku's Isetan and Keiō department stores, and Ikebukuro's Seibu (7th floor), will change travellers cheques.

CREDIT CARDS

Visa, MasterCard, Amex and Diners Club are widely accepted, but Japan is predominantly a cash economy. Top hotels and restaurants usually accept credit cards, but check first with less exclusive places. For 24-hour card cancellations or assistance, call:

Amex	☎ 0120 020 120
Diners Club	☎ 0120 074 024
JCB	☎ 0120 500 544
MasterCard	☎ 00531 11 3886
Visa	☎ 0120 133 173

ATMS

Post offices all over Tokyo accept foreign-issued cash or credit cards, 9am to 5pm Monday to Friday. Some banks and department stores have 'Global ATM' which accepts Visa, MasterCard and Cirrus. Citibank is a sure bet, with many 24-hour global ATMs scattered around Tokyo. Find branches in Shinjuku (4, B2), Ginza (12, C5) and Roppongi (9, B2).

CHANGING MONEY

Banks offer the best exchange rates for cash and travellers cheques, and they also don't charge commission fees on travellers cheques. Most major currencies are exchanged at banks and post offices, and you can try top-end hotels to change cash. Major department stores usually have foreign exchange counters and trade at reasonable rates.

Newspapers & Magazines

The *Japan Times, Yomiuri Daily* and the *Asahi/International Herald Tribune* are English-language newspapers available at newsstands in or near train stations. *Tokyo Journal* is a good events magazine sold in bookstores, and the free *Metropolis* is a great weekly magazine available every Friday at cafés and bookstores around Tokyo.

Opening Hours

Banks	9am-3pm Mon-Fri, closed national holidays
Museums	9.30am-4.30pm
Offices	9am-5pm Mon-Fri (some open Sat am)
Post offices	9am-5pm Mon-Fri (major post offices 8am-8pm)
Public offices	9am-noon & 1-5pm Mon-Fri
Restaurants	11.30am-2.30pm & 6-10.30pm (family run restaurants open from 11.30am-11.30pm)
Shops	10am-8pm Mon-Sun

Photography & Video

Print, slide film, digital memory and camera gear are a snap to find in

Tokyo. A 36-exposure colour print film, without processing, costs about ¥420, slide film from ¥800 to ¥980. Disposable cameras are even sold from vending machines. Processing print film is fast and economical in Tokyo; usually a 36-exposure roll of film will cost from ¥1000 to ¥1800 to develop and print. Camera repairs, on the other hand, are extremely expensive.

Japan uses the NTSC format for video. Video cameras made in Australia and most of Europe use either PAL or SECAM tapes, which are unavailable in Japan.

Post

The government-run postal service is very reliable, and the best way to send packages and business papers overseas. You can buy stamps at most convenience stores. Tokyo's **Central Post Office** (12, B3; ☎ 3284 9540; 2-7-2 Marunouchi, Chiyoda-ku; ⏰ 9am-7pm Mon-Fri, 9am-5pm Sat) is conveniently located outside the west exit of Tokyo Station.

POSTAL RATES

The basic rates for all international letters is ¥110 (over 50g, ¥190). Airmail stamps for postcards to any overseas destination cost ¥70.

Radio

InterFM on 76.1FM broadcasts news and daily life information mainly in English, and in seven other languages, including Spanish and Chinese.

Telephone

Local telephone calls cost ¥10 for the first three minutes, and then ¥10 for each minute thereafter. Pink phones only accept ¥10 coins. Green and grey phones accept ¥10, ¥100 coins and phonecards.

PHONECARDS

Phonecards are available from both newsstands and convenience stores starting in denominations of ¥1000.

CELLPHONES

Currently Japan has the same system as North America, but not the GSM system used in the UK, Australia and the rest of Asia. Check with your service provider before you leave home that they have a roaming agreement with a local counterpart.

COUNTRY & CITY CODES

Japan	☎ 81
Tokyo	☎ 03
Toll free	☎ 0120

USEFUL NUMBERS

International directory inquiries	☎ 0057
International operator	☎ 0051
Local directory inquiries	☎ 104
Reverse-charge (collect)	☎ 0039
Time	☎ 117
Weather	☎ 177

INTERNATIONAL DIRECT DIAL CODES

Australia	☎ 0061
Canada	☎ 001
New Zealand	☎ 0064
South Africa	☎ 0027
UK	☎ 0044
USA	☎ 001

Television

NHK is the government-run TV station. Its 7pm news is bilingual. CNN and BBC World services are available in all major hotels.

Time

Japan is in one time zone, nine hours ahead of Greenwich Mean Time (GMT). Daylight-saving time is not used in Japan. In train stations, bus stations and airports, a 24-hour clock is used; eg 5pm is 17.00 and midnight is 24.00.

At noon in Tokyo it's:

10pm (previous day) in New York

7pm (previous day) in Los Angeles

3am in London

5am in Johannesburg

1pm in Sydney

3pm in Auckland

Tipping

Tipping is not standard practice in Japan. Expect to pay a service charge (10% to 20%) at more ex-pensive restaurants and hotels.

Toilets

Public toilets are everywhere, but the most comfortable are in the big department stores. They also tend to be high-tech, outfitted with bidet, dryer and rushing-water sound effects. Japanese-style toilets are the squat variety. Take care so that the contents of your pockets don't fall in!

Tourist Information

The Japan National Tourist Organ-ization's (JNTO) Tourist Informa-tion Centers (TIC) provide excellent information. They make reserva-tions for certain hotels and ryokan (Japanese inns). They also arrange free 'goodwill guides'.

JNTO Tokyo TIC (12, B4; ☎ 3216 1901; www.jnto.go.jp; 10F, Kōtsū Kaikan Bldg, 2-10-1 Yūraku-chō, Chiyoda-ku; ⏱ 9am-5pm Mon-Fri, 9am-noon Sat)

Narita Airport TIC (1, C2; ☎ 0476 34 6251; Terminals 1 & 2; ⏱ 9am-8pm)

Tokyo Convention & Visitors Bureau (TCVB) TIC (12, B4; ☎ 3287 7024; 1F, Tokyo Chamber of Commerce & Industry Bldg, 3-2-2 Marunouchi, Chiyoda-ku; ⏱ 10am-5pm Mon-Fri, 10am-4pm Sat, Sun & holidays)

Women Travellers

Tokyo is an extremely safe city for women travellers. Violent sexual crime is rare, but take the same precautions as you would in your own country. Beware of *chikan* (gropers), who take advantage of crowded rush-hour trains. Yelling *'chikan!'* may shame the offender into stopping, but look before you let loose – a crowded train is some-times just a crowded train.

Oral contraceptives can be found in Japan, but it is far more conven-ient to bring an adequate supply from home. Tampons are available but may differ slightly from those you're used to.

LANGUAGE

Japanese is the official language of Japan, but many Tokyoites under the age of forty have at least some basic skills in English. Although many Japanese spend years study-ing English, they often find com-municating in it difficult. This is partly due to the techniques of language teaching used in Japanese classrooms, but it also reflects the difficulty of translation. Japanese and English are so different that lit-eral translations are almost impos-sible. Fortunately, getting together a repertoire of travellers' phrases in Japanese should be no trouble – the only problem may be understand-ing what people say back to you.

If you'd like to delve deeper into the intricacies of Japanese, Lonely Planet's *Japanese Phrasebook* offers a convenient collection of survival words and phrases for your trip to Japan, plus a section on grammar and pronunciation.

Pronunciation

One of the pluses for Westerners is that, unlike other languages in the region (Chinese, Vietnamese and Thai among others), Japanese is not tonal and the pronunciation system is fairly easy to master. The following examples reflect British pronunciation.

a as in 'father'
e as in 'get'
i as in 'pin'
o as in 'pot'
u as in 'flu'

Vowels appearing in this book with a macron (or bar) over them (ā, ē, ō, ū) are pronounced in the same way as standard vowels except that the sound is held twice as long. Take care with this as vowel length can change the meaning of a word, eg *yuki* means 'snow', while *yūki* means 'bravery'. Consonants are generally pronounced as in English, with the following exceptions:

f purse the lips and blow lightly
g as the 'g' in 'goal' at the start of a word; and nasalised as the 'ng' in 'sing' in the middle of a word
r more like an 'l' than an 'r'

Meeting People

The title *san* is used after a name as an honorific and is the equivalent of Mr, Miss, Mrs and Ms.

Good morning.	*ohayō gozaimasu*
Good afternoon.	*konnichiwa*
Good evening.	*kombanwa*
Goodbye.	*sayōnara*
See you later.	*dewa mata*

Please/Go ahead. (when offering)	*dōzo*
Please. (when asking)	*onegai shimasu*
Thanks. (informal)	*dōmo*
Thank you.	*dōmo arigatō*
Thank you very much.	*dōmo arigatō gozaimasu*
Thanks for having me. (when leaving)	*o-sewa ni narimashita*

You're welcome.	*dō itashimashite*
No, thank you.	*iie, kekkō desu*
Excuse me/ Pardon.	*sumimasen*
Excuse me. (when entering room)	*o-jama shiamasu/ shitsurei shi-masu*
I'm sorry.	*gomen nasai*

What's your name?	*o-namae wa nan desu ka?*
My name is ...	*watashi wa ... desu*

Pleased to meet you.	*dōzo yoroshiku*
Pleased to meet you too.	*hajimemashite, kochira koso dōzo yoroshiku*
Where are you from?	*dochira no kata desu ka?*
How are you?	*o-genki desu ka?*
Fine.	*genki desu*
Is it OK to take a photo?	*shashin o totte mo ii desu ka?*

Basics

Yes.	*hai*
No.	*iie*
No. (for indicating disagreement)	*chigaimasu*
(less emphatic)	*chotto chigaimasu*
OK.	*daijōbu (desu)/ ōke*

What?	*nani?*
When?	*itsu?*
Where?	*doko?*
Which?	*dochira?*
Who?	*dare?*

Requests

Please give me this/that.	*kore/sore o kudasai*
Please give me a (cup of tea).	*(o-cha) o kudasai*
Please wait (a while).	*(shōshō) o-machi kudasai*
Please show me the (ticket).	*(kippu) o misete kudasai*

Language Difficulties

Do you understand English/Japanese?	*eigo/nihongo wa wakarimasu ka?*
I don't understand.	*wakarimasen*
Do you speak English?	*eigo ga hanase-masu ka?*
I can't speak Japanese.	*nihongo wa dekimasen*
How do you say … in Japanese?	*nihongo de … wa nan to iimasu ka?*
What does … mean?	*… wa donna imi desu ka?*
What is this called?	*kore wa nan to iimasu ka?*
Please speak more slowly.	*mō chotto yukkuri itte kudasai*

Getting Around

What time does the next … leave?	*tsugi no … wa nanji ni dema-su ka?*
What time does the next … arrive?	*tsugi no … wa nanji ni tsuki-masu ka?*
boat	*bōto/fune*
bus	*basu*
bus stop	*basutei*
tram	*shiden*
train	*densha*
subway	*chikatetsu*
station	*eki*
ticket	*kippu*

Accommodation

I'm looking for a …	*… o sagashite imasu*
hotel	*hoteru*
Japanese-style inn	*ryokan*
family style inn	*minshiku*
Do you have any vacancies?	*aki-beya wa arimasu ka?*
I don't have a reservation.	*yoyaku wa shiteimasen*
single room	*shinguru rūmu*
double room	*daburu rūmu*
twin room	*tsuin rūmu*
How much is it per night/per person?	*ippaku/hitori ikura desu ka?*
Does it include breakfast/ a meal?	*chōshoku/shokuji wa tsuite-imasu ka?*

Shopping

I'd like to buy …	*… o kaitai desu*
How much is it?	*ikura desu ka?*
I'm just looking.	*miteiru dake desu*
It's cheap.	*yasui desu*
It's too expensive.	*taka-sugimasu*
I'll take this one.	*kore o kudasai*
shop	*mise*
supermarket	*sūpā*
bookshop	*honya*

Food

I'm a vegetarian.	*watashi wa beji-tarian desu*
What do you recommend?	*o-susume wa nan desu ka?*
Do you have an English menu?	*eigo no menyū wa arimasu ka?*
I'd like the set menu please.	*setto menyū o onegai shimasu*
Please bring the bill.	*o-kanjō o onegai shimasu*
This is delicious.	*oishii desu*

Numbers

0	*zero/rei*
1	*ichi*
2	*ni*
3	*san*
4	*yon/shi*
5	*go*
6	*roku*
7	*nana/shichi*
8	*hachi*
9	*kyū/ku*
10	*jū*
100	*hyaku*
1000	*sen*

Index

See also separate indexes for Eating (p125), Entertainment (p126), Sleeping (p126), Shopping (p126) and Sights with map references (p127).

23 Tiny Museums of Sumida-ku 37

A

accommodation 96-102, *see also* Sleeping index (p126)
addresses 6
air travel 112
Akihabara 25, 52, 66
ambulance services 116
Ameyoko Arcade 52
amusement parks 24, 40-1
antiques 55-6
Aoyama 44, 52, 71-2
architecture 27-8
arts 8, 11, 15, 28-9, 30-3, 44, 55-6, 93, 108-10
Asakusa 6, 66
Asakusa Kannon Onsen 35
Ashi-ko 47
Ashino-ko 47
ATMs 118
Azabu-Jūban Onsen 35

B

baby-sitting 40
bars 82-5
baseball 95
Bashō Museum 30
bathrooms 120
beaches 48
Beer Museum Yebisu 23
Benten-dō 19
boat travel 22
books 56-7
Bunkamura Museum & Theatre Cocoon 30
bunraku 93, 109
business hours 52, 118
business travellers 66
busking 86
bus travel 112, 114
butō 110

C

cameras 57-8
capsule hotels 100
car travel 114
cellphones 119
chemists 116
cherry-blossom viewing 35, 81
children, travel with 40-2, 61
Chingo-dō-ji 45
Chiune Sugihara 104
Chiyoda Kuritsu Sogo Taiikukan 36
Chūzenji-ko 50
cinemas 88-9, 94
climate 114-15
climbing 49

clothing 58-60
clubbing 86-8
Condomania 37
consulates 115
Contax Gallery 28
Cos-play-zoku 14
costs 52, 64, 96
Costume Play Gang 14
credit cards 118
Criminology Museum of Meiji University 37
culture 5, 67, 78, 82, 107, 108
customs regulations 113

D

Daibutsu 48
Daikanyama 6, 68
Daiso 100 Yen Plaza 54
dance 91
dance clubs 86-8
Decks Tokyo Beach 46
Denki-gai 25
dental services 116
department stores 53
Design Festa 29
Detached Palace Garden 34
Diet 105
disabled travellers 115
Dōkan, Ōta 103
dolls 63
drinks 60
Drum Museum 33

E

earthquakes 106
Ebisu 6, 68
economy 106
Edo 11, 103
Edo-Tokyo Museum 11
electricity 33, 115
Electric Town 25, 57
electronics 25, 57-8
embassies 115
emergencies 116
entertainment 80-95
environmental issues 106

F

festivals 13, 92
film 84, 108
Finlando Sauna 35
fire services 116
Flame of Liberty 46
food 60, *see also* Eating index (p125)
football 95
Fūjin 12
Fuji Television Japan Broadcast Center 46
Fukagawa Edo Museum 30

G

galleries 8, 16, 28-9, 44, 81
Gallery 360 44
Gallery ES 44
Gallery Gan 44
Gallery of Eastern Antiquities 8
Gallery of Hōryū-ji Treasures 8
gardens 34-5
gay travellers 94, 116
Ghibli Museum 37
Ginza 6, 16, 52, 69-70
Ginza Graphic Gallery 28
Golden Gai 43, 83
government 105
Great Buddha 48
Great Kantō Earthquake 104
Green Plaza Ladies Sauna 35-6
Grutto Pass 30

H

Hachikō statue 26
Hakone 47
Hakone-jinja 47
Hakone Open-Air Art Museum 47
Hakuhinkan Toy Park 40
Hama Rikyū Onshi-Teien 34
Hanami 35
Hanazono-jinja 39
handicrafts 55-6
Haneda airport 112
Harajuku 6, 14, 52, 71-2
Hara Museum of Contemporary Art 30
Hato Bus 51
health 116
Heiseikan 8
Hie-jinja 39
Hirohito 104
history 103-5
Hōbutsu-den 8
holidays 117
homelessness 19
homewares 61
Honkan 8
Hōryū-ji Hōmotsukan 8
hot springs 35-36, 47
Hyōkeikan 8

I

Idemitsu Art Museum 30-1
Ikebukuro 6, 72-3
Imperial Palace 6
Imperial Palace East Garden 34
Internet access 117
itineraries 7

J

jewellery 62
Jimbōchō 52
John Lennon Museum 31

K

kabuki 17, 93, 109
Kabukichō 43
Kabuki-za 17
Kamakura 48
Kaminari-mon 12
Kanda 66
Kawaguchi-ko 49
Kanei-ji 19
Kappabashi-dōri 45
Kegon Waterfall 50
Kenchō-ji 48
Kinokuniya 43
Kite Museum 31
Kiyōmizu Kannon-dō 18
Koishikawa Kōraku-en 34
Kokonoe Beya 20
Koma Theatre square 43
Kōraku-en Amusement Park 40
Koshi-no-Yu Sentō 36
Kotto-dōri 52

L

Laforet Museum 28
Lake Ashi 47
Lake Ashino 47
Lake Chūzenji 50
Lake Kawaguchi 49
Lake Motso 49
Lake Yamanako 49
language 120-2
left luggage 113
Lennon, John 31
lesbian travellers 94, 116
literature 108-9
Lost in Translation 84
lost property 117
love hotels 96

M

magazines 118
malls 53
Maman 15
Mammy's Touch 29
manga 99
markets 10, 54, 81
massage 29, 35-6
matsuri 13, 92
measures 117
medical services 116
Mega Web 40
Meguro Parasitological
    Museum 37
Meiji-jingū 6, 9
Meiji-jingū-gyoen 9
Meiji Restoration 104
Metropolitan Museum of
    Contemporary Art Tokyo 31
mobile phones 119
money 115, 118
Mori Art Museum 15
Motso-ko 49
Moto-Hakone 47
motorcycle travel 114

Mt Fuji 47, 49
Mr Oka 51
museums 7, 8, 11, 15, 20, 23,
    30-3, 37-8, 40-1, 44, 47, 48
Museum of Maritime Science 40-1
music 56-7, 89-91, 109

N

NADiff 44
Nagata-chō 65
Nakamise-dōri 12, 52
Narita airport 112
National Children's Castle 41
National Museum of Emerging
    Science and Innovation 41
National Museum of Modern
    Art 31-2
National Museum of Western
    Art 32
National Science Museum 32
National Treasure Museum 48
Nature Study Garden 6, 34
newspapers 118
Nezu Institute of Fine Arts 32
Nihonbashi 11, 69-70
Nikkō 50
Nikon Salon 29
Nishi-azabu 74-6
Nō 93, 109

O

Ōdaiba 6, 46, 73
Odakyū Q-Tours 51
Ōedo-Onsen Monogatari 24
Ōkura Shūkokan 32
Omote-sandō 14
onsen 35, 47
opening hours 52, 118
orientation 6
origami 63
Ota Memorial Art Museum 32
Ōwakudani 47

P

Palette Town 46
Parco Museum 29
parking 114
parks 9, 18-19, 34-5, 81
passports 113
pearls 62
pharmacies 116
photography 23, 28-9, 118-19
Pigeon Bus 51
planning 115
police services 116
politics 105
pollution 106
postal services 119
Prince Naruhito 105
Promo Arte 44
public baths 35-6
pubs 82-5
puppet theatre 93, 109
puppets 63

R

radio 119
Raijin 12
rental 114
renting 99
restaurants, *see* Eating
    index (p125)
Rikugi-en 34
Rinnō-ji 50
Rokku 45
Rokuryū 36
Roppongi 6, 74-6
Roppongi Hills Development
    15, 27
Roppongi Oriental Studio 29
Ryōgoku Kokugikan 20
Ryokan 102

S

Saigō Takamori 18
sake 60
Sake Plaza 33
Sambutsu-dō 50
saunas 35-6
Sea of Trees 49
senior travellers 115
Sensō-ji 12-13
sentō 35
Shibuya 6, 26, 52, 76-7
Shin-kyō-bashi 50
Shinjuku 6, 52, 77-8
Shinjuku-gyōen 34-5
Shinobazu-ike 19
Shitamachi 45
Shitamachi History Museum 33
shopping 16, 52-63, *see also*
    Shopping index (p126)
Shōyō-en 50
shrines 9, 19, 38-9, 45, 48, 50, 81
silverware 62
soccer 95
solo travellers 87
Sony Building 81
special events 92
spider sculpture 15
Spiral Building 29
sports 20-1, 95
stationary 63
Statue of Liberty 46
Studio Alta building 43
subway travel 114
Sumida-gawa 22
Sumō Museum 20-1
sumō wrestling 20-1, 95
Sunrise Tours 51
Sunshine City Alpa 27
Sunshine International
    Aquarium 41
Sunshine Planetarium 41
swords 55

T

Taikokan 33
tanuki 45

Tatematsu, Masahiro 86
tattoos 24
taxes 52, 64
taxis 114
telephone services 119
temples 7, 12-13, 38-9, 45, 48, 50, 81
Tepco Electric Energy Museum 33
theatre 91, 93, 109
Three Buddha Hall 50
Thunder Gate 12
time 119-20
tipping 64, 120
toilets 120
Tōkei-ji 48
Tokugawa Edo 103
Tokugawa Iemitsu 103
Tokugawa Ieyasu 103
Tokugawa Shōgun Cemetery 8
Tokyo Big Sight 29
Tokyo Disneyland 41
Tokyo International Forum 27
Tokyo Joypolis 41-2
Tokyo Metropolitan Government Offices 27
Tokyo Metropolitan Museum of Art 33
Tokyo Metropolitan Museum of Photography 23
Tokyo National Museum 8

Tokyo station 6
Tokyo Stock Exchange 27-8
Tokyo Tower 28
Toranomon 65
Tōshō-gū 50
Tōshō-gū jinja 19
tourist information 120
tours 51
Tōyōkan 8
Toyota Amlux 29
Toy Museum 42
train travel 28, 112-13, 114
trams 51
Transportation Museum 42
travellers cheques 118
travel passes 114
Treasure Hall 50
trekking 49
Tsukiji 69-70
Tsukiji Produce & Fish Market 6, 10
Tsukishijō-gaishijō 10
Tsurugaoka Hachiman-gū shrine 48
TV 119

U
Ueno 6, 79
Ueno kōen 18-19
Ueno Zoo 42
Uyoku 105

V
vegetarian travellers 72
vending machines 62
Venus Fort 38
video 118-19
Vingt-et-un 51
visas 113
visual arts 110

W
walks 43-6
Watari Museum of Contemporary Art 33
weights 117
women travellers 120

Y
Yamanako-ko 49
Yasukuni-jinja 39
Yayoi Museum & Takehisa Yumeji Museum 33
Yebisu Garden Place 23
yoga 36, 116
Yoga Center 36
Yoyogi-kōen 35
Yūrakuchō 69-70

Z
zoos 42
Zōshigaya Cemetery 51

EATING

Akiyoshi 72
Arossa 76
Asterix 65
Aux Sept Bonheurs 71
Bengawan Solo 74
Bernd's Bar 74
Birdland 69
Botan 66
Café Artifagose 68
Caffé Michelangelo 68
Cam Chien Grippe 71
Chichibu Nishiki 69
Court Lodge 77
Daikokuya 77
Echikatsu 79
Edogin Sushi 69
Edokko 66
Fonda de la Madrugada 71
Fujimamas 71
Fukuzushi 74
Hanashibe 73
Hantei 79
Havana Cafe 74
Home 71
Humming Bird 74
Ibuki 77
Inakaya 75
Ippūdō 68

Izu-ei 79
Kanda Yabu Soba 66
Kantipur 76
Keika Kumamoto Rāmen 77-8
Khazana 73
Khroop Khrua 66
Kisso 75
Komagata Dojō 67
Kurumaya 78
Kyūbei 69
La Ranarita Azumabashi 67
Las Chicas 71
Le Bretagne 72
Lion Beer Hall 69
Matsuya 66
Maxim's de Paris 69
Mikuni's Café Marunouchi 69
Mominoki House 72
Monsoon Café 75
Moti 75
Mugyodon 65
Munakata 69-70
Muromachi Sunaba 70
Nair's 70
Natural Harmony Angolo 72
New Torigin 70
New York Grill 78
Olives 75

Owariya 67
Pho Garden 65
Positive Deli 73
Rakutei 65
Reikyō 76
Robata 70
Sabatini di Firenze 70
Saigon 72
Sakana-tei 76
Sasa-no-Yuki 79
Sasashu 72-3
Seryna 76
Shin-Hi-No-Moto 70
Shizenkan II 76-7
Shunsenbō 68
Sonoma 77
Spago 76
Sushi-sei 65
Taillevent-Robuchon 68
Ten-Ichi 70
Tofu-ya 65
Toh-Ka-Lin 65
Tokyo Bellini Trattoria 76
Tonerian 73
Trattoria Marumo 65
Tsukiji Sushikō 70
Ueno Yabu Soba 79
Vin Chou 67

ENTERTAINMENT

Abbey Road 82
Advocates Bar 94
Agave 82
Arty Farty 94
Bernd's Bar 82
Blue Note 89
Bodeguita 82
Bon's 83
BuL-Let's 86
Bunkamura Theatre
    Cocoon 91
Cine Amuse East &
    West 88
Cinema Rise 88
Club 328 86
Club Ace 94
Club Asia 86
Club Dragon 94
Club Quattro 89
Crocodile 89
Enjoy House 83
Gas Panic Bar 83
Gas Panic Club 86

Geronimo 83
Harlem 86
Highlander 83
Hobgoblin Tokyo 83
Insomnia Lounge 83-4
Intrigue Theatre 91
Kabuki-za 93
Kamiya 84
Kanze Nō-gakudō 93
Kinswomyn 94
Kokuritsu Geikijō (National
    Theatre) 93
Kokuritsu Nō-gakudō 93
La Jetée 84
La.mama 90
Las Chicas 84
Lexington Queen 86-7
Liquid Room 90
Loft 90
Maniac Love 87
Milk 90
Mix 84
Motown House 1 & 2 84

National Film Centre 88-9
New York Bar 85
Old Imperial Bar 85
Pink Cow 85
Roppongi Pit Inn 91
Salsa Sudada 87
Scruffy Murphy's 85
Session House 91
Shibuya O-East 91
Shibuya O-West 91
Smash Hits 85
STB 139 (Sweet Basil) 91
The Ruby Room 87
Trading Places 85
Vanilla 88
Velfarre 88
Virgin Toho Cinemas Roppongi
    Hills 89
What the Dickens 85
Womb 88
XYZ Bar 85
Yebisu Garden Cinema 89
Yellow 88

SLEEPING

Akasaka Prince Hotel 97
ANA Hotel Tokyo 97
Andon Ryokan 102
Four Seasons Hotel
    Chinzan-sō 97
Ginza Nikkō Hotel 98
Grand Hyatt Tokyo 97
Hotel Century Southern
    Tower 98
Hotel Ibis 98
Hotel New Ōtani 98
Hotel Ōkura 98
Hotel Parkside 99

Hotel Seiyo Ginza 97
Hotel Sun Lite Shinjuku 99
Hotel Sunroute Akasaka 99
Hotel Yaesu-Ryūmeikan 99
Imperial Hotel 97
Keiō Plaza Hotel 98
Kimi Ryokan 102
Kodomo no Shiro (Children's
    Castle) Hotel 99
Mitsui Urban Hotel Ginza 100
Park Hyatt Tokyo 97
Roppongi Prince Hotel 100
Ryokan Katsutarō Annex 102

Sakura House 99
Sawanoya Ryokan 102
Shibuya Excel Hotel Tōkyū 100
Shibuya Tōbu Hotel 100
Shinjuku New City Hotel 100
Shinjuku Park Hotel 101
Suigetsu Hotel Ōgaisō 101
Taito Ryokan 102
Tokyo Station Hotel 101
Trimm Harajuku 101
Villa Fontaine 101
Yaesu Terminal Hotel 101
Yama no Ue (Hilltop) Hotel 101

SHOPPING

Ameyoko Arcade 54
Atelier Magic Theater 62
Axis Building 61
Bic Camera 57
Comme des Garçons 58
Fuji-Torii 55
Fukumitsuya 60
Haibara 63
Hakuhinkan Toy Park 61
Hanae Mori 58
Hanazono-jinja Antique Market 54
Heiwajima Antique Festival 54
HMV 56
Hysteric Glamour 58-9
Illums 61
In The Room 61
Inachu Lacquerware 55
International Arcade 54
Isetan 53
Issey Miyake 59

Itoya 63
Japan Sword 55
Japan Traditional Crafts Center 55
Kiddyland 61
Kinokuniya 56
Laforet 59
Laox 57
Loft 61
Mac Store 58
Mandarake 61
Marui 53
Maruzen 56
Matsuya 53
Meidi-ya 60
Mikimoto Pearl 62
Mitsukoshi 53
Muji 60
National Azabu 60
Nogi-jinja flea market 54
Ohya Shōbō 55

On Sundays 55
Oriental Bazaar 56
Puppet House 63
Sakuraya Camera 58
Satomi Building 56
Sekaido Stationery 63
Sofmap 58
Sunshine City Alpa 53
T Zone Computers 58
Takashimaya 53
Tasaki Shinju 62
Tōgō-jinja flea market 54
Tōkyū Hands 53
Tolman Collection 56
Tower Records 56-7
Undercover 60
UNIQLO 60
Virgin Megastore 57
Yodobashi Camera 58
Yoshitoku 63

Sights Index

Sight	Page	Map Ref
23 Tiny Museums of Sumida-ku	37	(3, F3)
Akihabara	25	(13)
Asakusa Kannon Onsen	35	(11, B1)
Azabu-Jūban Onsen	35	(9, B3)
Bashō Museum	30	(3,F5)
Bunkamura Museum & Theatre Cocoon	30	(5, A2)
Beer Museum Yebisu	23	(7, C2)
Chiyoda Kuritsu Sogo Taiikukan	36	(3, E5)
Condomania	37	(6, A1)
Contax Gallery	28	(12, C4)
Criminology Museum of Meiji University	37	(3, D4)
Edo-Tokyo Museum	11	(3, F4)
Finlando Sauna	35	(4, B1)
Fukagawa Edo Museum	30	(3, F5)
Ghibli Museum	37	(3, A4)
Ginza	16	(12, C5)
Ginza Graphic Gallery	28	(12, C5)
Green Plaza Ladies Sauna	35-6	(4, B1)
Hakuhinkan Toy Park	40	(12, C5)
Hama Rikyū Onshi-Teien	34	(12, C6-D6)
Hanazono-jinja	39	(4, C1)
Hara Museum of Contemporary Art	30	(3, C9)
Harajuku	14	(6)
Hie-jinja	39	(8, B2)
Idemitsu Art Museum	30-1	(12, B4)
Imperial Palace East Garden	34	(12, A3)
John Lennon Museum	31	(1, B2)
Kabuki-za	17	(12, C5)
Kite Museum	31	(12, C2
Koishikawa Kōraku-en	34	(3, D3)
Kōraku-en Amusement Park	40	(3, D4)
Koshi-no-Yu Sentō	36	(9, B3)
Laforet Museum	28	(6, A1)
Mammy's Touch	29	(6, B2)
Mega Web	40	(3, E8)
Meguro Parasitological Museum	37	(7)
Meiji-jingū	9	(3, A5)
Metropolitan Museum of Contemporary Art Tokyo	31	(3, F5)
Mori Art Museum	15	(9, B3)
Museum of Maritime Science	40-1	(3, E9)
National Children's Castle	41	(5, C2)
National Museum of Emerging Science and Innovation	41	(3, E9)
National Museum of Modern Art	31-2	(12, C4)
National Museum of Western Art	32	(10, B2)
National Science Museum	32	(10, B2)
Nature Study Garden	34	(3, C8)
Nezu Institute of Fine Arts	32	(3, B6)
Nikon Salon	29	(12, C5)
Ōedo-onsen Monogatari	24	(3, E9)
Ōkura Shūkokan	32	(8, C3)
Omote-sandō	14	(6)
Ota Memorial Art Museum	32	(6, A1)
Parco Museum	29	(5, B2)
Rikugi-en	34	(3, C2)
Rokuryū	36	(10, A1)
Roppongi Hills Development	27	(9, B2)
Roppongi Oriental Studio	29	(9, C2)
Ryōgoku Kokugikan	20	(3, F4)
Sake Plaza	33	(12, B6)
Sensō-ji	12	(11, B1)
Shibuya	26	(5)
Shinjuku-gyōen	34-5	(3, B5)
Shitamachi History Museum	33	(10, B3)
Spiral Building	29	(6, B2)
Sumida-gawa Cruise	22	(11, C2)
Sumō Wrestling	20	(3, F4)
Sunshine City Alpa	27	(2, C2)
Sunshine International Aquarium	41	(2, C2)
Sunshine Planetarium	41	(2, C2)
Taikokan (Drum Museum)	33	(11, A2)
Telecom Center Building	27	(3, E9)
Tepco Electric Energy Museum	33	(5, B1)
Tokyo Big Sight	29	(3, F8)
Tokyo Disneyland	41	(1, B2)
Tokyo International Forum	27	(12, B4)
Tokyo Joypolis	41-2	(3, E8)
Tokyo Metropolitan Government Offices	27	(4, A2)
Tokyo Metropolitan Museum of Art	33	(10, B1)
Tokyo Metropolitan Museum of Photography	23	(7, C2)
Tokyo National Museum	8	(10, B1)
Tokyo Stock Exchange	27-8	(12, C2)
Tokyo Tower	28	(3, D6)
Toy Museum	42	(3, A4)
Toyota Amlux	29	(2, C2)
Transportation Museum	42	(13, E2)
Tsukiji Market	10	(12, D5)
Ueno Zoo	42	(10, B2)
Ueno-kōen	18-19	(10)
Venus Fort	38	(3, E8)
Watari Museum of Contemporary Art	33	(6, C1)
Yasukuni-jinja	39	(3, C4)
Yayoi Museum & Takehisa Yumeji Museum	33	(3, D3)
Yebisu Garden Place	23	(7, C2)
Yoga Center	35	(1, B2)
Yoyogi-kōen	35	(3, A6)

FEATURES

Reikyō	*Eating*
Cinema Rise	*Entertainment*
Mix	*Drinking*
Sapporo Brewerie	*Highlights*
Tōkyū Hands	*Shopping*
Parco Museum	*Sights/Activities*
Shibuya Tōbu Hotel	*Sleeping*

AREAS

Beach, Desert
Building
Land
Mall
Other Area
Park/Cemetery
Sports
Urban

HYDROGRAPHY

River, Creek
Intermittent River
Canal
Swamp
Water

BOUNDARIES

State, Provincial
Regional, Suburb
Ancient Wall

ROUTES

Tollway
Freeway
Primary Road
Secondary Road
Tertiary Road
Lane
Under Construction
One-Way Street
Unsealed Road
Mall/Steps
Tunnel
Walking Path
Walking Trail/Track
Pedestrian Overpass
Walking Tour

TRANSPORT

Airport, Airfield
Bus Route
Cycling, Bicycle Path
Ferry
General Transport
Metro/Subway
Monorail
Rail
Taxi Rank
Tram

SYMBOLS

Bank, ATM
Buddhist
Castle, Fortress
Christian
Diving, Snorkeling
Embassy, Consulate
Hospital, Clinic
Information
Internet Access
Islamic
Jewish
Lighthouse
Lookout
Monument
Mountain, Volcano
National Park
Parking Area
Petrol Station
Picnic Area
Point of Interest
Police Station
Post Office
Ruin
Telephone
Toilets
Zoo, Bird Sanctuary
Waterfall

24/7 travel advice
www.lonelyplanet.com